Amariah The Boy

Amariah The Boy

Amariah The Boy

Roland Amariah Gonzales

DEDICATION

I dedicate this, my first work, to those of you whose tales are unsung. For the downtrodden, beaten and bloodied. For those whose outlook on life is bleak at *best*. Know that fire and *immense* pressure are needed to forge diamonds. You, therefore, are not brittle. Know too that while things may not necessarily get better...they can always get worse.

TABLE OF CONTENTS

PREFACE

"A white cat sat next to the pond." To recall generalities in one's youth is a simple enough task. The act itself requires little effort and thus demands little of the individual. To recall specificities in memories, to re-live experiences, to call to life the painful specters of long dead and buried emotions, to identify pivotal moments in your life *as such* then re-live them again, to present them in vivid detail...requires a degree of introspection which is monumentally draining. It is the act whereby one creates something which is not the static rendering of an entity but rather a living, breathing, dynamic being.

"A white cat sat next to the pond on remnants of a weeping willow. The willow had stood proudly for 100 years, somehow spurning its natural lifespan until either Mother Nature or an indignant deity hurled a lightning bolt to correct the natural order. The willow enjoyed its earned repose for another two years until it was found by a man who repurposed it into a baby's crib for his newborn daughter.

The white cat knew neither the man nor his child, nor did it mind so much the ugly blackened scar that ran the length of its stump opposite the pond. The white cat was preoccupied with enjoying what was left of the afternoon as a lone ray of brilliance from the setting sun provided its white fur a fiery countenance. The white cat's tail twitched as its gaze followed a pair of dangerously close iridescent emerald dragonflies flitting above the reeds."

Some memories are, of course, much more potent than others. They're sharper, more vivid, able to be perceived with near-perfect clarity. The first taste of honeysuckle and wild berries freshly picked on a lazy Missouri morning under a cloudy sky.

Contemplating for a moment the colorful abstract masterpiece on the knees of your pants, earned from an afternoon well-spent tumbling and playing tag with friends.

The melodic chiming laugh of the little girl who was fond of wearing cotton-candy-pink cowgirl costumes.

The face of the little black boy in class as he wept upon his finger-painting rendition of *my happy home* being thrown into the trash by the angry woman teacher. The look of satisfaction on her face as the boy's parents drag their crying child out of the room, informing him there'll be no ice cream *this* day.

The time during recess when you accidentally cut yourself on pine needles (of all things!) while sliding them between your fingers and relishing the tactile sensation. The stinging that followed as you clenched your fist to push away the pain.

These memories can be re-played in moments of nostalgia, if one wills it. Over and over in your mind—and *if* you can concentrate hard enough—you might again hear laughter from your first love, savor the tastes of something long forgotten, or perhaps even remember the pleasant and comforting scent of a loved one long since passed.

Other memories are so distant that one cannot be certain if they ever happened in the first place. We squint across a chasm of uncertainty toward fires of the past, eager to bask in their warmth, to find reassurance in what was. Unable to make out the finer details, we labor in bridging a connection from our *now* to our *then*, an act of tossing handfuls of sand into that chasm. A bit of desperation and heavy dose of self-convincing later, a tentative bridge is formed, shaky and unstable.

We haphazardly race to that fire of what was, that roaring inferno perceived in the dark from a distance, to find only smoldering embers remain. So much time and effort were spent on forming the bridge that we failed to see the fire first dwindle, then sputter...and ultimately die out. These remaining embers we grasp tightly and clutch close to our heart, away from the inexorable march of time. Before they, too, are carried away.

HAPPIER TIMES

"Our foundations are set in place during childhood. Hard times make for hard foundations. Sturdy, solid. The edifice erected thereafter, its style, its shape...its flow and direction...are entirely up to the builder."

I've never known my blood father. Or, perhaps it is better to say that I have never known more than his *face*, thanks to a faded photograph I chanced upon. It shows my young parents, my mother still a teenager.

Roland Lombardo Gonzales was Spanish, Mexican and Jewish, or so I was told by his side of the family. I know nothing of his childhood, save that he wanted to join the army out of high school but was thwarted by his overprotective mother. Lacking the structure and discipline he yearned for, he was overcome by disappointment and turned to drugs. When I look at that photograph I see that I wear his face as my own. Dark eyes and hair, tanned skin, and a smiling face full of both kindness and mischief. His face was thinner than mine—somewhat gaunt even, thanks to his daily regimen of some narcotic or another.

I have never known his praising voice, his comforting scent, his laughter as I did something silly, or his strong arms as he proudly lifted me up and admired me, his first-born son.

Nor did I receive any form of guidance, thoughts, or care from him after my birth, wholly absent from my life as he was. My early life was spent with my mother, Kathleen Theresa Sullivan. She was the second youngest of the four daughters of Margaret Tolen. Grandma Margaret and her daughters only gave birth to girls, and I think Margaret's mother had done the same.

Roland Amariah Gonzales

Kathleen grew up a hellion, and while she did well in school academically, she had no time for rules and such. Everyone who knew her was *amazed* that my first word wasn't *fuck, shit* or some other expletive.

And everyone in the family, Grandma Margaret included, was equally amazed that I was a *boy*.

My mother was raised by several father figures over the years. Whenever a father died (a somewhat frequent occurrence, oddly enough), Grandma Margaret quickly sought another man to fit the bill and help with her troublesome girls. When Mom was two her blood father, Doug Sullivan, fell to his death from the top of a building under construction, piss drunk enough that he likely didn't feel a thing.

My mother was made of northern European stock. Mostly Irish, Scottish and a pinch of Norwegian. Her appearance reflected this readily enough, with light skin, and hair bordering between red and blonde... and of course those soft, smiling Irish eyes.

She became pregnant at the age of 16 and gave birth to me via caesarean at 17. With my father absent from her life, she sought a replacement as she had learned from *her* mother. Kathleen met him at an Alcoholics Anonymous (AA) meeting. She was 19.

Kenneth Edward Morgenthaler was two years my mom's junior. Kenney was of German stock, a towering mountain of a man.

They wed shortly after meeting and Kenney assumed the role of my father. We moved to Georgia when Kenney enlisted in the army, an effort to clean up his life and provide for his new family, which soon included my baby sister Gracie. I was around three then and have little recollection of these times. What I do recall: Standing in my crib and clutching the bars of my cage as I stared in wonder at passing headlights at night. They looked menacing and alien to my toddler's mind.

Swimming with my mother and Kenney at a hotel pool, and Kenney tossing me high into the air as I squealed in laughter and joy.

The day at Knott's Berry Farm, zooming along on Soap Box Racers and plummeting in screaming excitement on the Parachute Sky Jump.

Playing with a wooden flintlock toy gun that Kenney had bought for me from that same place.

For a time, as with all things, it was good.

Georgia was a far cry from what little happiness I had known in California. The dirt roads pocked with fist-sized holes and laden with

2

fire-ant mounds became my playground and are as well-worn into my mind as the mobile homes filled with irritable neighbors.

I remember the *heat*. That dusty, dirty, sticky heat that followed me from the open sun to the shade. Hard to be happy in that unrelenting heat.

Some of the mobile homes held children who played with me on occasion, though I can't recall any friendships... more association by circumstance.

Our home was similar to its cousins: stumpy misshapen legs of cinder blocks, faces of dirty gray clouds set against a blue sky. Patches of reddish-brown, courtesy of the nearby unpaved dirt road, marred their appearance, a collection of small girls who haphazardly apply their mother's discovered blush and eye shadow.

The days all bled together, each one indistinguishable from the next. Moments became hours became days became months, like listening to the same song on repeat for the thousandth time. Still, I'd known nothing different up to that point. For me, this was life.

Roland Amariah Gonzales

Mom hollers my name from the doorway. I look up from the patch of dirt I'm hunkering down on, my playground. It's *scorching* outside. A regular Georgian afternoon. I raise my hand to shield my eyes from the sun's blinding glare and peer through the gap between my small fingers.

I yell back yeah Mom, what is it?

Mom shouts to steer clear of the nearby tree line. She says there's snakes in the trees, snakes in the grass, snakes in the water. She turns around to go back inside then adds over her shoulder there's snakes everywhere not in your room. Wander around and you'll get bit!

Her advice is enough to terrify me away from the comforting shade and stick to the dirt road that spreads out under the burning sun. I choke and wipe my eyes as cars drive by and kick up dust. Sometimes I run into the house crying after a big chunk of something finds its way from the road into my eye, courtesy of a passing car too busy to slow down. I hate getting stuff in my eye and would rather play in the shade. But playing in the dirt is a whole lot better than getting eaten by a snake.

A weathered and frequently slammed screen door covers the entrance to our home. We don't have the thing that slows the screen door down, so it always shuts with a BANG! The front door is some cheap material made to look like oak but isn't. Inside, the floor is covered by brown carpeting, useful in both concealing *and* accumulating stains from the outside world...or last night's reheated spaghetti.

The kitchen seating area is a plastic table and two booths made up of the same stuff as the front door. Painfully bright yellow and white diamond-patterned linoleum covers the floor. Wallpaper featuring daisies and stained with untold hours of cigarette smoke lines the kitchen walls.

My bedroom is nothing special, with boring white walls. A small window provides a spectacular view of my neighbor's wall, just out of arm's reach. I've never known anything different, so I don't care too much. My bedroom is a place for sleeping, nothing more.

Every day is the same. After I wake up, I race into the sitting room and flip the channel to the daily reveille on our old turn-dial tube television. I hope to see Kenney, the only dad I've ever known, with all the other soldiers as they salute the flag and my country's patriotic music plays. I crawl on my belly to the TV, looking over my shoulder to make sure Mom's back is turned in the kitchen. I'm not supposed

4

to get too close to it. Mom chops an onion into little bits so she can mix it with ground beef for spaghetti. I hate onions, they burn my eyes something fierce, but Mom says they're good for my hair and nails. She says spaghetti can last a whole *week* if you make it into sandwiches. I believe her because we eat the stuff almost every night!

My nose is almost an inch away from the TV screen. I'm so close I can make out a hundred million tiny boxes of color that make up the image on the screen. I try to find Dad. Mom calls out from the kitchen while she's chopping away, Roland *Amariah* Gonzales, you get away from that TV! You'll burn your eyes right out of your head!

I look over my shoulder in surprise and gasp. The sounds of onions getting chopped hadn't stopped and I *know* she doesn't have eyes in the back of her head. I looked when she was asleep once, just to make sure. I move away from the TV but don't blink 'cause I'm sure the moment I do, Dad'll pop up and I'll miss him. Try as I might, I never see Dad on TV, though that doesn't lessen my effort or my hope. Dad is a soldier and I *know* when I grow up, I'll be just like him.

When Dad gets home from army training I race to the door. He gives me a proud smile and says *there's* my little soldier as he tousles my hair. I help him take off his worn and faded black leather boots, then set them by the door. He shouts out, *Atteeeen-SHUN* and I quickly put on his *shiny* boots which sit next to his worn and faded pair. I stand as tall and proud as a half-past-three-year-old can muster. I march around the room with a serious look on my face, arms swinging by my side as Dad calls out in cadence one, two, three, four! He smiles then laughs and says good job, soldier! About face! Now I want you to—

I look up and see his smile is gone because he realizes I'm clomping around in his shiny black leather boots instead of his worn boots! He yells ahhhh son! No, take 'em off, those are my spit-shines!

I like his shiny boots more and try to run away as fast as I can. Dad runs after me then lifts me high up into the air. I squeal with laughter as he pushes me up to the ceiling and slap my hands against it. He growls and says with all the seriousness in the world if I mess up his spit-shines he's gonna make me run a mile in the rain and mud and *then* shine 'em up after. He says it'll take me so long that I'll get out of college by the time I'm done!

I gasp in fright as he keeps his serious face, then start laughing hysterically after he mock-throws me against the ground and tickles me with one hand while taking back his shiny boots with his other. I love

5

my dad. I want to look *sharp*. I want to look like him. I want to *be* like him. My dad, the soldier.

The early days in Georgia are simple enough. Dad leaves for the day to train in the army, then comes back home at night. We eat, laugh, and enjoy life together. Mom puts me in preschool with a bunch of other kids. She's always real happy when she picks me up from school and hugs me, , but her breath sometimes smells bad. Sour, kind of like when Grace got sick and threw up everywhere. I ask Mom about the smell one time and her face goes from happy to angry as quick as you can blink! She says never you *mind* that! She says to mind my own business and if I act smart again, I'll get a whoopin'.

I don't know why she's so mad. I just wanted to know if she's sick.

She picks me up in her arms and dances to her favorite music when we get home from pre-school. My arms and legs flop all over as she spins around and it's so much fun, even if her breath has that *awful* sour smell. She's happy most of the time and does a lot for me...like making food and telling me stories.

She teaches me to read well ahead of the other kids and tells me how smart I am. She says not everyone can read from the age of two and then gives me a great big hug. I love my mom, and even though she gets angry at me sometimes, she's still my mom. I tell her when I grow up I wanna marry her 'cause she's the best Mom in the *whole* wide world.

Mom laughs and says well what about Daddy? I'm already married to him!

I frown and think for a moment then say well he can stay married to you too, because I love Dad too, okay?

Mom looks at me with a silly face for a moment then laughs and says, okay! She gives me a big kiss on my cheek and I laugh while she tickles me before I manage to wriggle free and run away.

Dad's training starts to go longer into the night and sometimes he's gone for days at a time. Dad says something *big* might be coming around the corner and when Mom watches the news and thinks no one is looking I see her cry.

The more Dad is gone, the meaner Mom gets. Mom gets more and more angry and more and *more* sad at the same time. The more upset she gets the more she hits me, and I try to be good but sometimes it doesn't matter *how* good I am and she hits me anyway. She sometimes hugs me after and says she's sorry and didn't mean to, but not always.

6

Amariah The Boy

Mom drops me off at preschool, same as always, but now when she picks me up the sour smell on her breath is gone. I'm glad, but I'm also sad there haven't been any smiles or hugs for a while. We don't dance anymore at home either. I mostly spend my time outside on our front dirt-patch, digging holes so I can connect them into tunnels and push the toy car through that Dad got me.

It's Friday and Dad leaves right when Mom and I get home from preschool. He says he's gonna be gone for the whole weekend doing training and he'll see us when he gets back. That's *bad*. Mom gets *real* mean when Dad is gone for so long. Mom takes me and Grace to the grocery store afterward and her driving is *scary*. She snarls at me that she *hates* wasting her free fucking time making sure I don't set the house on fire or something else stupid like she *knows* I would.

I look down at the car floor and say I'm sorry. I try to stay quiet and out of sight when Dad is gone so I don't make Mom mad.

When we get home Mom puts Grace in her room then says she's gotta piss like a rushin' racehorse and runs off to the bathroom. I tell Mom from the kitchen that I'm hungry and ask if I can eat. She calls out from the bathroom yeah, there's some leftovers in the fridge, toss 'em in the microwave!

I put some leftover meatloaf, mashed potatoes, and green beans on my blue plastic plate decorated with a cartoon frog from a TV show I watch. I put it in the microwave and watch the food spin around for a minute, then sit down at the kitchen table and eat my kind-of-warm food.

Mom growls from the bathroom hey kid, bring me some toilet paper, we're out!

I freeze mid-bite. I don't wanna go in the bathroom when Mom's in there. She does her number two with the door open when Dad isn't home! I know I won't be able to eat afterward if I go in there because it always smells bad. I try to wolf down my food as quick as I can and yell just a minute, Mom, I'm almost done eating!

She snaps at me I said come *here*! After a moment she screams *NOW!*

Did I forget to put more toilet paper in the bathroom? I thought I had. I don't know why she's so mad. I messed *something* up, or why else would she be so mad? I lower my fork and swallow my food and there must've been a big ol' lump of coal in my food because it feels like there's one in my throat right now. It slowly moves down to my belly and weighs me down like a sinking ship. I slowly walk toward the cupboard, my shoulders hanging low. I'm not standing tall and proud right now.

I sniff and use my shirt sleeve to wipe away the tears welling up in my eyes. I know what's coming. I grab the toilet paper from the cupboard and bring it to the open door of the bathroom. Mom is there, sitting on the toilet. I think to myself as I struggle not to cry that she doesn't do this when Dad is home, do her number two with the door wide open. It's gross and I *hate* it and I wonder if all the ladies do this. I hope not.

Mom extends a gnarled claw, her cruel talons facing the sky, and shouts give it here, boy!

Tears are flowing down my face now. I'm scared and *know* if I get close, she'll hit me and I don't wanna get hit no more and I wish Dad was home. I have a great big snot bubble and am a miserable sight. I cry out wait, Mommy! Can I have a hug? Please? I love you, Mom!

Mom shouts you can have a hug after your whoopin', now I said hand it over! The more you make me wait, the worse it's gonna be, you little shit! Come *here!* Now!

I thought she couldn't reach me at the door and I was safe, but I'm wrong. I freeze in terror when she lurches forward off the toilet seat. She grabs me by the wrist, then wrenches me over her lap as she falls backwards onto her throne. She claws my shorts off and I plead no Mom, no! Please! I love you, Mommy, I love you, please?

She tans my hide, and my cheeks go from a pleasant tanned white to an angry burgundy.

She shouts in-between smacks. When. I. Say. Come. You. Better. Run. Boy! Do. You. Hear. Me?

I scream in pain, yes, yes, I hear you! Please, Mom! I'm sorry, Mom, I'm sorry!

Overexerted, she lets out a loud fart and tells me go finish your fuckin' food and it *better* be *all* gone by the time she gets out. She hisses she better not see food in the trash, neither!

I run back to the kitchen sobbing and my ass is on fire. I try to wipe all the tears and snot from my face while pulling my shorts up, but it's too difficult and I fall over. Mom sees and laughs from the bathroom. I stand up, pull my shorts up and go to the table. I eat while I hiccup and sob. Mom bellows from the bathroom that I better knock off my *fucking* whining or she'll give me something to *really* cry about.

Amariah The Boy

I wish I didn't mess up so much and make Mom so mad at me. She always says she's doing all she can to raise me by herself, God knows, while Dad is off playing army. Mom says with Dad gone training all the time—well, *she's* basically my dad, *too*, so I better give her *twice* as much respect.

I finish eating my food and try not to throw up. I feel real sick when Mom is mad at me *and* makes me eat. I put my plate in the sink, rinse it off, and go to my bedroom. Mom walks off to her room to calm down Grace who's crying from being woken up. Before Mom slams her door she yells out that she's had a *long day* and she's tired of *all* this fucking *bullshit*.

I quietly close my door so she doesn't come back out and hit me for being too loud.

I sit on my bed, look out the window, and stare at the wall of my neighbor's house for a good long while. I need a nap because I think I've had a long day and I'm tired of all this fucking bullshit, too. I bury my face in my pillow so I can cry in secret because Mom gets *pissed* when she hears me cry.

I think to myself that Mom is a lot nicer when Dad is home and they're both playing with Gracie. I wish Dad was here. Mom always fawns over her beautiful baby girl. She says Gracie is the *proof* of her and Kenney's love, the bond that will keep them together forever. Mom laughs sometimes and jokes that she only has so much love to give and it all goes to Gracie, but that's okay because babies need more love.

I mess up so much *all* the time that Mom doesn't really give me hugs anymore, she only gives me the back of her hand. She says she's a firm believer in the Lord Jesus, and she says she'll *never* spare the rod lest I become spoiled.

Dad still hugs me. I'm still his little soldier. Sometimes he gives me presents from the army. Glowing sticks and army food and other neat things. When he's home he laughs and plays with me. I wish he was home more. I love my dad, but Mom gets upset when she sees him paying too much attention to me.

She's quick to bring Grace over and shove their precious baby into his arms when Mom sees Dad pick me up. She tells him don't forget about *your* daughter! Mom never lets me hold Grace and says to stay away from her, so to me Grace is just a screaming blob that I never see except when Mom carries her around.

Roland Amariah Gonzales

Dad always laughs and puts me down to pick up Grace as he smiles and says, c'mere, you!

Dad and Mom smile at Grace as she coos and gurgles. They laugh and kiss her on her forehead, then hug and kiss each other. I try to get in the middle so I can get a hug too, because I like hugs a whole bunch, but Mom looks down at me in irritation and says to go get her some water or something else.

I stop running to meet Dad when he gets home because all I ever do is get Mom water or something else that she needs right then and there.

Grace is okay I guess, as far as babies go. She laughs and cries and poops a lot and everyone loves her. When she gets big enough to walk, she also gets big enough to get in my way all the time, *and* she gets strong enough to pick up things. *My* things. Whatever I hold or am fond of she too must hold, whether it's my toys, a coloring book, or anything that she sees me touch. If I don't want to share something then she breaks it. Sometimes even things I *do* share are broken just so she can see the look on my face.

I decide I don't like babies very much. All they do is tear up your coloring books and break your crayons and poop, and I don't understand *why* Mom and Dad like this destructive pooping creature so much.

Mom lets Grace do *whatever* she wants when she's big enough to walk. Mom always says Grace is her darling little baby girl and oh, look at her Roland, isn't she so precious?

10

Amariah The Boy

Grace leaves the crib in Mom and Dad's room and invades my room when she's big enough. It's not that bad, because we share a bunkbed and she stopped pooping herself...for the most part. Since I'm older and bigger, I get the top bunk, though this only lasts a little while 'cause Grace wants the top bunk too, 'cause that's where I'm at. Mom says to let Grace sleep up on top. Mom says I'm lucky to even *have* a bed.

I protest, telling Mom that Grace rolls around a lot when she sleeps and sometimes falls off her bed onto the floor. Plus...the top bunk is *mine*! I'm older and bigger!

Mom yells at me from the sitting room to let Gracie take the top bunk.

Whatever Grace wants, Grace *gets*.

I refuse to let Grace climb the ladder and kick at her from the top. She angrily looks at me and then whines and cries and...oh shit, there's Mom with a wooden spoon eager to make my acquaintance. I cry out and try to scoot away. Mom isn't tall, but she's *tall enough* to grab my leg and yank me toward her.

I'm both cowed and in pain after several stinging hits to my arms and legs. I descend the ladder and angrily rub at my arm as Grace climbs past me to sit atop her throne. She looks at me with this smug fuckin' *evil* face full of satisfaction.

Later that night, Grace—in her roll-around sleeping manner—rolls right off the top bunk and slams onto our dirty, root beer-colored carpeting and starts screaming! Mom rushes into the room, first to hit me and *then* to ask what I did.

I angrily point at Grace and yell she fell Mom! She fell, just like I said she would!

I try to rub away the new pain.

Dad is home and roused from his well-earned sleep by the late-night shouting. He comes into the room and asks what the hell is going on?

I hurriedly explain: Gracie fell, Dad!

Dad is puzzled. He says from where? Up top? Why the hell was she up on top? She's *too little* to be up there!

He looks at Mom, as if it was the most obvious thing in the world and says Gracie falls off her tiny bed all the time! Why the *hell* would you put her up there, Kathleen!?

Mom angrily says she didn't *think* this would happen and Dad tells her that's the problem Kathleen, you *never* think.

11

Roland Amariah Gonzales

Mom sighs loudly and looks away.

I smile then look up at Dad and say *I* thought it would happen and even said so to Mom! He gives her an irritated look then high-fives me and says good job, son.

Mom shoots me a downright fuckin' *loathsome* look then stomps out of the room.

Dad watches her walk out then sighs and pats my head. He picks up Gracie and stands her up on her feet then tells her honey, you can't sleep up there, okay? You're gonna fall again and get hurt! You sleep down here and listen to your brother, alright?

Grace nods and Dad wipes her tears away, then he helps her climb back onto her little spot on the bottom bunk. He takes a knee then puts his hand on my shoulder and says you did good, son. You look after your sister while I'm gone, alright?

I say okay and he pulls me in for a hug. I feel my body go limp as all my stress and pain melts away. It disappears, gobbled up by a bunch of feel-good ants. I love my dad.

Amariah The Boy

Dad says he's going to be gone for a long time 'cause he has to go fight in a war. Mom starts to drink a *lot* from brown bottles and, oh hey, that's that same sour smell I knew from before. The more Dad is gone the more she's got the bottle in hand and is either real happy or *real* angry. I hide from her most of the time because her happy and angry change places far too quickly for my liking.

I have a pet goldfish that was a present from Dad and he gave it to me before Grace could walk. Dad won Mr. Fish for me at the county fair. I laugh every time I put my finger in Mr. Fish's bowl because he gives it little kisses! Mr. Fish can't do anything else, but he doesn't hit me or call me names, so I decide he's my best friend.

I'm half past four years old and Grace is a quarter past one when she picks up Mr. Fish's bowl to take him outside. If there are two things that Grace is *real* good at, it's falling off beds and dropping things...*all* the time. I yell *no*, Gracie, *stop*!

She whines unnnh in protest because she can't say much else yet.

I try to pull Mr. Fish's bowl out of her hands and she screams. I hear Mom's thunderous footsteps as she stomps out of her room toward my own. I try to wrestle the fishbowl away from Grace as I yell for her to give it to me. I whine that she's going to hurt Mr. Fish!

Mom storms into the room and slaps my face so hard that I go flying to the floor on my back. I see stars for a moment and my face is on fire. Mom screams you stop bullying your baby sister and you let her play with that fucking fish!

The sour smell from her stinking breath is so strong that I gag a bit. Mom's got this awful look on her face. She looks down at me while blinking slowly and swaying a bit.

I stand up and stare at her with anger in my heart as tears well up in my eyes. My hands clasp at that awful stinging pain in my face as I try to catch the sting-bee and toss it away. I think to myself I didn't do *anything* wrong. I was trying to save Mr. Fish!

I choke back tears as I try to voice my thoughts, but she smacks my other cheek *hard*. She always says she loves the Lord Jesus very much and says she *always* takes striking the other cheek to heart.

I don't know much about the Lord Jesus but he sounds like a real *prick* if all he does is go around hitting people all day.

Mom puts her face right up to mine and growls don't you *dare* talk back to your elders. You honor your father *and* your mother! She stabs two fingers painfully into my chest as she adds *and* you better wipe that look off your *fucking face* before I move it for you!

Mom stands there with her cruel fingernails prodding my chest as she watches my face sink from crying to indignant anger, then crying again. Finally, I look ahead, vacant and defeated.

Satisfied that her position and authority are respected, she returns to the other room and back to her bottle, laughing loudly at a show on the TV. She occasionally farts loudly and chuckles at that too.

Grace picks up Mr. Fish's home and takes two steps toward the TV room then trips and drops the bowl onto our carpeted bedroom floor. Even though the floor is soft, the bowl shatters. I cry out in shock as Mr. Fish flops around, knowing from the zoo books Dad bought me that fish need to be in water to live. I yell at Gracie not to move an *inch*, there's glass everywhere! I say *now* look at what you did—you're gonna cut your feet!

Grace offers an indignant unnnh!

I turn to get a cup of water from the kitchen. As I leave the room, she whines to get my attention. When I look back she steps on Mr. Fish, then looks at me. I howl in anguish, my tears cascade a waterfall down my face. Before I know what I'm doing I step through the glass barefooted and push her hard off Mr. Fish and into our dresser.

Grace cries out in pain and Mom comes running with her wooden spoon in hand. She doesn't even blink before setting on me with her favorite ass-whoopin' spoon. I try to protect my face as she beats my legs, arms, back, and ass for a good five minutes and bellows with a hideous snarl on her lips and the cruelest look in her eyes WHAT DID I JUST TELL YOU? WHAT DID I JUST SAY?!

I yelp in pain and terror then manage to get away, but running across the room only increases her fury. She hits me so hard that she breaks her favorite ass-whoopin spoon across the back of my legs. She shouts great! GREAT! SEE WHAT YOU MADE ME DO?

She then spanks me for another five minutes by hand while I try to cover my butt with *my* hands.

The sound of my sister crying against the dresser finally draws my mother's righteous wrath away from me and she comforts Grace. I sit across from them and curl into a ball, covered in aching welts. I alternate between angry sobs and screaming into my knees as my body shakes and I bury my face in my arms. I wish Dad was home. Mom is never this bad when Dad is home.

14

Amariah The Boy

Mom snaps her fingers at me to get my attention and demands I look at her. I refuse, as small an act of defiance as I can manage. Mom digs her fingernails into my cheeks then grabs my chin and yanks my head up. She says if I *ever* hit my sister again, she'll beat me so hard I won't be able to *walk*. She says Grace is just a baby, she doesn't know what she's doing!

I stare into her eyes with all the hate my tiny heart can hold and breathe heavily.

She slaps my face and then for good measure hits the other cheek again. For the Lord Jesus. He *loves* it when she hits both cheeks, as I understand.

I start crying again and yell that Grace killed Mr. Fish on *purpose*! I *saw* it! She stepped on— But I stop, because Mom raises her hand to hit me again. I shrink back in terror then wince and cover my face and whimper meekly. My head hurts. Everything fuckin' hurts, and I don't wanna get hit any more.

Mom says it's just a *stupid* fish. Calm down. We'll get another one. She breathes a heavy sigh and mutters fucking kid before she ungracefully throws Mr. Fish's body in the wastebasket. She picks up my whimpering sister and is about to leave me alone in the room when she notices shattered glass for the first time and, in surprise, yells there's *glass* everywhere! What if your sister steps on it!? Pick up this fuckin' glass, then go stand in the corner until your father gets home!

I think to myself Dad said he wouldn't get home for *two days*.

I carefully pick up the glass and put it in the wastebasket before I pause, then stop to scoop out Mr. Fish's flattened and broken body. He's not flopping around anymore. I stare at him with a mute expression. I quietly look toward the kitchen and see Mom opening a chocolate pudding cup for my sister to stop her crying. I creep toward the front door then quickly run outside. Mom bellows hey! HEY! as the screen door slams shut behind me.

I run toward the tree line filled with snakes. I don't care if they bite me anymore. I clutch Mr. Fish's body in my hands. I know Mom won't come here 'cause of the snakes so I'm safe...at least from her. I hide behind the trees as I see Mom come flying out of the house. She stumbles about as she searches for me. She trips over one of the many holes on our front dirt-patch that I had dug and tumbles to the ground, then screams out you gotta come home some time and when you do...your ass is *grass*!

15

Roland Amariah Gonzales

I breathe as quietly as I can so she can't hear me behind the trees, then wait some more in case she's trying to trick me then jump out and catch me.

After a short forever, I give one last glance toward the house then walk around in the trees until I find what I'm looking for: a place where I can bury Mr. Fish.

I look at Mr. Fish now that I'm away from danger, and tears start flowing down my face. I moan softly then hiccup and say I'm sorry, Mr. Fish, I'm so sorry. I didn't stop Gracie and now you're dead.

I dig a small hole in the soft earth with my hands to bury my friend. I pluck a few flowers and toss 'em on top of his grave, then sit and cry.

Mr. Fish can't give me fishy kisses anymore.

I look toward the house and know I can't go home yet. I have to wait until it gets dark. I have to wait here with the snakes until Mom calms down. I walk around the woods for a while. Maybe I'll find a snake to bite me...then I can go to the hospital and get away from Mom! ...or maybe I'll die. Maybe I can catch a snake and throw it at Grace and Mom! Then *they* would die and it would be just me and Dad! But Dad would be sad if Gracie dies...

I look around but can't find any snakes, so I go home empty-handed.

Mom is sleeping—she drinks herself to sleep every night—and I quietly make myself a peanut butter and jam sandwich (strawberry's my favorite), before brushing my teeth and going to sleep.

Mom remembers being mad at me the next day but can't remember why and lets it go. She says she needs to lie down all day with this pain in her head.

I'm in charge of Gracie whenever Mom is in bed all day after drinking *too* much the night before, so I'm in charge at *least* twice a week. The problem is, Gracie does the *opposite* of whatever I say. She particularly enjoys stomping on stuff when she walks around bare-footed, like she did to Mr. Fish.

Fire ant hills are all around our house and *I* know to stay away, but not Grace!

Knowing well the painful sting of a fire ant's bite, I walk with her outside until I bring her to one such hill. I point at it and say see those red ants, Gracie? Don't step on 'em! Those are my *favorite* ants!

Amariah The Boy

She looks at me with a lopsided grin then looks down and stomps her bare foot directly into the fire ant hill. I act shocked and yell out oh no, not my ants! Those are my favorite ants, Gracie!

She looks up at me with her smug evil face. Her expression becomes puzzled when she sees me smile and wait. Watching her. I want to remember this moment.

The fire-ants, angry as *hell* at the giant who smashed their home and killed a few of 'em, attack her in a *frenzy*. My smile becomes a grin and I burst out laughing when I hear her first screams of agony and terror. She hops up and down in a fit and tries to stomp them but they crawl up her legs and keep biting. I look toward the house and yell out Mom, Mom! Come quick! Help, Mom! Ants are biting Gracie!

I make a half-assed attempt at brushing them away as Mom emerges from the house to help her. I earn a few painful bites from the ants in the process of pretending to care about my absolute prick of a baby sister, but it's *well* worth it.

Mom rushes outside and yells what the *fuck*, Rol, why weren't you watching her!? Oh Jesus, oh no, my *baby*!

Mom beats away the ants with her kitchen towel. Grace continues to scream in pain and does her mad little dance on the anthill before Mom yanks her away. I think to myself I hope Mr. Fish is watching from fish heaven. I wonder if this'll send me to hell, because it seems like the kind of thing that would...then realize that I don't really care.

The Lord Jesus or perhaps Mr. Fish is on my side. Fire ants become the gift that keeps on giving as Grace repeatedly seeks revenge on them. She re-visits their homes, minus my presence, to introduce them to her bare feet. Each high-pitched shriek of pain I hear from Grace brings a smile to my face and I race to the TV room window to see her do the Fire Ant Shuffle every chance I get.

Sometimes Grace likes to look at me and start crying when we're alone in *my* bedroom (I don't care what Mom says, Grace doesn't belong here. It's mine). I hear Mom's thunderous hooves in the distance before she charges into the room and smacks me in the face with her new wooden spoon. It's a wonder I can *eat* anymore with the number of times that spoon has hit my mouth. Mom doesn't give me time to explain—she jumps into the room and smacks my face like she's holding a tennis racket and my face is the fuckin ball. I see Grace smile and laugh while I get my ass beat.

Roland Amariah Gonzales

I get *so* frustrated 'cause I don't lay a finger on Grace, yet she howls like I stepped on *her* fish! After getting my ass whooped for the 100th time, I have enough of it all. The next time Grace looks at me and starts crying for no reason, I *immediately* hit her right in her stupid ugly face. I know I've got a *world* of hurt coming in about 20 seconds but by the Lord Jesus, if I'm gonna get smacked around then so is she! If I spare the rod then Grace will get spoiled and she's already spoiled enough.

I come to learn that Mom's righteous ass-whoopin' is the same whether I lay a finger on Grace or not! Grace stops her fake tears after she decides that the hilarious show of Mom beating me isn't worth the admission price of getting punched in her stupid ugly face. No one *ever* disciplines Grace because she's *only a baby* and Mom says babies don't know what they're doing.

I sure as hell don't think Grace is ignorant of what she's doing and you know what? I don't trust babies anymore either because babies are *liars*. Regardless of how I feel though I never hit Grace for fun. I'm not Mom. I don't *like* hurting Grace. It makes me feel bad. I just want her to stop getting *me* in trouble...because I like Mom hurting *me* even less.

Amariah The Boy

Dad is a soldier. An infantryman to be exact, during the Gulf War. The Gulf War was a conflict between Iraq and Kuwait in the early 1990s that the USA got involved in for some reason. Dad says we're fighting 'cause it's important to do the right thing and we're the good guys and we're always right, so that's good...I guess.

Mom is miserable for the first few weeks when Dad leaves home to go fight in Iraq. Then she gets real happy all of a sudden. She leaves Grace and me at home and goes out most nights. I don't know where she goes but she always comes back with that awful sour smell on her breath and she's either singing and dancing...or *super* pissed off...so I stay away. She doesn't pick me up and dance with me anymore – she saves that for Grace. And Mom doesn't work or anything like that either. She says being a full-time Mom is work enough and she ain't got time for nothin' else.

The neighbors, an older couple who look like every other adult in the area, look after us whenever Mom says she has an appointment at the hospital or some other place. They don't have kids of their own, and I don't think they know how kids work because they tell Grace and me it's bedtime the *moment* Mom leaves!

I don't know why these think it's bedtime already. It's only two in the afternoon! They put us in a hot room with no fan and when I complain that it's so hot and I hate it they say close your eyes and you'll fall asleep faster. They warn me and Grace to keep our eyes closed and say they'll *know* if our eyes are open, so we better not even try! Then they go into the sitting room and turn up the TV.

The neighbors get upset and complain to Mom if I get up and walk around, or if Grace does the same, or if either of us have to use the bathroom too many times. They say look here, Kathleen. It's hard enough looking after ourselves without having to look after your kids and we don't know if we can do it anymore, we just don't know.

Mom apologizes a bunch of times and scolds me in front of them for being naughty. The more they complain the more she apologizes and eventually she gives them money. After she pays the neighbors we get home and Mom takes out her ass-whoopin' spoon. She says she's gonna get her money's worth before she hurts me. I don't try to run away anymore 'cause where am I gonna go? Dad isn't here. I scream in pain and try to cover the places where she's hitting me, but it just makes her hit me more.

Roland Amariah Gonzales

Mom gets tired of giving the neighbors money and they refuse to watch us now that they're not getting paid. Mom tells me they're tired of my bullshit and my misbehaving. She says she doesn't want to leave me and Grace home alone, even though I'm in kindergarten and I'm already four! So Mom gets some guy she knows from the place she goes to at night and he watches us.

The man is tall, but not as tall as Dad. He has a moustache and light skin, lighter than Mom's. He usually wears a red and black flannel shirt. And he *always* has the same sour smell on his breath as Mom, and he's *never* nice. Me and Grace hide from him after Mom leaves for her appointments, and he says he likes it this way, out of sight, out of mind.

One day the man drinks a *whole lot* from his bottle. Then he says he's pissed 'cause he has to watch two brats who won't shut the hell up for ten minutes. When Mom leaves the house she says she'll buy him a case of beer for all his fuckin bellyaching.

After she's gone he says we better not make a fuckin' *noise* or they'll be hell to pay. Me and Grace hide in our bedroom while he drinks in the TV room. Grace is scared of the man. She says she wants Dad then starts to cry.

I hear SHUT YOUR SISTER THE FUCK UP! from the other room. I whisper Gracie, please! and beg her to stop crying. I pick up one of her stuffed bears and dance it in the air before I hand it to her, 'cause she likes that.

Grace stops whimpering for a bit and I quietly close the door. After a couple of minutes she can't help herself and starts to sniffle a bit, then starts to hiccup and cry. I think oh, *shit!* Oh no oh no as I hear the man stomping toward our bedroom. I hear him yell out mother*fucker!* As he gets closer.

I tell Grace under the bed, *hurry!*

She's slow so I push her under our bed then scurry under there myself. The man bursts into our room and the door slams into the wall. He yells WHAT DID I SAY? Where the fuck *are* you, you little shits? Come here! Now!

He whips his belt against the bed and it's so *loud.* I squeeze my eyes shut and pray to Lord Jesus to save us both and promise I'll *never* be bad again and please, Lord Jesus, I love you please make this bad man go away!

There's only so many places to hide and I learn real fast that under the bed is not a very good place *at all.* The man's scary, snarling and

20

angry face suddenly appears under the bed. He shoots his arm under to grab hold of my sister. Grace reaches out to me and screams in terror. I grab her arm and try to hold on but he's so much bigger than me and I can't hold on. He yells come *here,* God dammit and Grace screams and cries in terror before he wrenches her out and holds her against the floor.

I'm paralyzed by fear as he holds her in place with one hand and uses his belt to whip her with the other. Grace shrieks in pain and cries out for Dad, but Dad isn't here, he's fighting in Iraq. Grace is on the floor sobbing, hiccupping, and screaming. She holds up her hands to protect herself as the man reaches back to hit her again.

I scramble out from under the bed and hit his legs with my fists and I kick him. I yell DON'T HIT MY BABY SISTER! and then kick him in his balls even though Dad told me *never* hit another boy there. The man coughs out oof! You little fucking shit! And shoves me backward hard.

My head slams against the wall so hard that I can't see for a moment. I blink a few times, stunned, before I'm slammed against the floor and he jumps on top of me. He whips my face and body repeatedly with his belt and shouts I'm gonna learn you *real* good, boy! You think you a man? You think you can stand up and be a man and hit me?! HUH!?

Agony and oh God oh Jesus in heaven, angels save me please, Daddy where are you. I try to cover my face but he holds my arms down with his knees. His belt finds my mouth, face, and ears. He strikes anywhere he can and I squeeze my eyes shut while he shouts but I can't understands words anymore.

He strikes me hard with his fist and my head jolts to the side. I see Grace. She's scurried to the corner of the room and stares at me in terror, her eyes wide as she pees herself. Her hands are over her mouth and she's not crying anymore.

The man hits me again and now I'm looking at the wall. I can't feel my face anymore and I can't see out of one eye.

The man is breathing heavily and says, this is what you get, you understand me? You should never raise yo' hand against yo' elders! This is what happens when boys are bad and God as my *witness* it will happen again if you *ever* try to hit me again, you fuckin' hear me boy?! Huh?

I hear a loud slap noise somewhere but can't feel anything.

Roland Amariah Gonzales

He growls I don't want to hear another fucking word out of *either* of you!

The red-and-black-flannelled man gets up and leaves the room, slamming the door shut.

I lay there and look at the wall, numb. Something shuffles against the floor and hugs my head. It's crying and smells like pee. The man returns to the sitting room and turns up the volume on the TV so he won't hear us anymore. I wish Dad was home. My Dad the soldier. He would kill this bad man. Dad would shoot the man in his fucking face. I wish I was big and strong like my dad. I wish I wasn't four years old. I wish I was big enough to kill this man.

I wish I'd never been born.

Time passes and I hear a phone ring. The TV stops making noise. I think it's Mom telling the man she's on her way back from the store. The man hangs up the phone and comes into the bedroom. Me and Grace are hiding in the corner behind the dresser. The man doesn't look for us, just says at the room clean yourself up in the bathroom, then leaves the door open. I find my body, struggle to stand then walk to the bathroom.

I see my face in the mirror and I get real scared. My lips are split open, bleeding. I have bright crimson welts all over my face and arms and chest. One eye is swollen shut. It's black and I can't see out of it. I don't know if I'll ever see out of it again. Everything hurts. I use wet toilet paper to clean my face and it stings.

I weep. Quietly.

Mom gets back home and the man tells her what happened. He hastily says the boy and Grace got into a fight and so I swung my belt to hit the boy but hit her by mistake, then separated the two and gave that boy a whoopin' he won't *never* forget! No one should *ever* hit their sister!

Mom is swaying a bit side to side and I can tell as I peek from behind the door that she's been drinking. A lot. She blearily nods, then looks at me and shakes her head, scowling. She's fresh from the bar where she made a quick stop, full of righteous wrath for her misbehaving son who frequently ruins her buzz with his miserable existence.

The man thanks her for the case of beer and walks up to me and crouches down. He puts a hand on my shoulder and says loudly sorry bud, but you messed up. He leans in close and whispers to me if I say one fucking word, he'll leave my body out in the woods for the dogs. He gets up and smiles at Mom, looks hard at me, then leaves.

As soon as the front door shuts, Mom growls come here, boy!

I run and scream no! in panic and fear. She bolts after me and tackles me to the ground. She pulls down my pants and reaches for something to hit me with and finding nothing, unplugs the telephone cord and starts whipping my ass...the one place I *hadn't* been hit. The fresh new pain brings fresh new cries for mercy that are unheard.

That man doesn't come to babysit anymore and Mom says if I wasn't such an absolute *bastard,* she'd be able to enjoy her life more and maybe babysitters wouldn't want to avoid me. Mom never says anything like this to Gracie. She's still sweet with my baby sister.

She doesn't like me because I'm bad and Grace is good.

Roland Amariah Gonzales

When I'm alone in my bedroom I cry into my pillow and think how life would be so much better if Grace had never been born. People wouldn't hit me and Mom wouldn't go out and drink all the time...maybe. Life would be *good*. Maybe. I hate my sister. I hate my mother. I hate myself and I hate life.

I wish I'd never been born.

Dad returns from war and he's real happy, 'cause he says we won. I don't know what we won, but I'm happy that he's happy. Mom is thrilled that he's back in one piece and for a few weeks treats me kindly in his presence. She gives thanks to the Lord Jesus at the dinner table for bringing Dad home alive and insists that I say something when it's my turn to give thanks.

I say the words when it's time to pray but don't believe them anymore.

Where was the Lord Jesus when the red-and-black-flannelled man beat me and Grace? No angels came to save us. Nothing happened. No one cared.

Mom doesn't go out at night anymore. Now she's home all day and night. I don't say a thing to Dad how she drank and was gone all the time. Everyone is happy now and I don't want to screw that up...like I screw up everything.

Mom stops hitting me now that Dad is back and instead gives me time-outs, which I prefer even though they last *forever*.

Grace watches and mimics Mom and is less of a prick too, now that Dad is home. Dad tells me what war stories can be told to an overeager boy just over the age of half-past four. He tells me about the deserts and oil fires and explosions and airplanes flying overhead. My dad is a war hero and I wanna be just like him.

Me and Dad toss a football around in front of the house every now and then. I like spending time with my old man but I *hate* that football. It always hurts when it hits my hands or my body and I don't understand why people like doing stuff that hurts.

I look angrily at the football laying in the dirt and yell out the ball hurts, Dad! I try to shake the pain out of my hand, having stubbed my finger for the 100th time. I tell him I don't like this very much, can we go play something else?

He sighs and walks up to me then crouches by my side and says son, pain is part of being a man. You want to be strong like me, right? You still want to be a soldier?

Amariah The Boy

I nod my head with certainty and say I *absolutely* want to be like him.

Dad smiles and says well I'm glad you haven't changed your mind!

I grin back. He raises his hand to high-five me. I cry out in terror then cower and cover my face before bursting into tears and sobbing please, no!

Dad's eyes are wide as he looks at me and slowly says son...it's just a high-five.

I look at him and wince, then see that his outstretched hand isn't going to hit me. I wipe my face and quickly smack my hand against his own and try not to sob.

Dad takes me back inside and tells me to go play with Gracie in our room. He tells us not to come outside and shuts the door. He calls Mom into the sitting room and turns the TV up loud.

Muffled noises grow in intensity and become shouting. Grace and I look apprehensively at each other, then at the door. I carefully open it a bit and I hear Dad yell why the *hell* did you leave Roland and Grace at home alone with some guy you met at a bar? Are you fucking *stupid?* What the *fuck* happened while I was gone? What the fuck were you *doing?*!

Mom screams back at him that she doesn't want to be stuck inside all day with two kids while Dad is out having fun and that she wants a life too, and she fucking *deserves* to go out and enjoy herself!

I peek and see Dad standing in absolute disbelief as he angrily mutters fun? I was at *war* Kathleen! Fighting every *day* to stay alive. Earning money to feed you and the kids, pay the bills, keep a roof over our heads! What the fuck is *wrong* with you? How can you be *that* dumb?

This was all my fault. I hadn't high-fived Dad. I leave the bedroom while holding Grace's hand and shout at them to stop fighting. Seeing me and Grace crying eases their fire somewhat and they set aside the shouting for another day.

Dad is great at providing life lessons, a real pro. It's the weekend and with the war being over he's home for once, not needing to go out and train. I convince him to put down the football and play "the American and the Iraqi" instead. He's got a great big smile because nothing makes him happier than seeing his son want to be a soldier like him. He says from across the sitting room alright, boy, go and get your gun! I'll be the Iraqi, you be the American!

Roland Amariah Gonzales

I smile and walk to my room then freeze. Oh shit. I don't *have* my gun. A boy who lives down the road stole it from me while my old man was fighting in Iraq!

The gun was nothing special, really. It was a piece of wood fashioned in the shape of a 17th century flintlock pistol with *Knott's Berry Farm* etched onto the side. It was a memento from a simpler time, a happier time in California. Back before all the trouble. All the pain.

Billy was the boy's name, and stealing from me was his game. Weeks before, I had seen the wooden flintlock gun in his toy box and thought for a moment oh neat, I've got one of those! I wonder where he got his, he's never been to California? Later, a thorough search around my room and the house yielded nothing, so I asked Billy where he had gotten the toy gun. He lied through his ugly teeth and said his mom had bought it for him at the store.

I let him keep it though. If I made trouble, Mom would've hit me.

So, I turn to Dad and say uh I want to play football instead!

Dad *knows* I hate football. He looks at me quizzically and says what? No, come on, let's play the other game.

Me and my big mouth.

I bite my lip and struggle to think of something and finally say, um, my friend Billy has it and he's playing with it right now, okay?

Dad laughs and says well, go get it back then, son! It doesn't belong to your friend, it's *yours*. I didn't buy it for your buddy!

I sheepishly look at the ground and search for an answer then murmur um, it's okay. He can play with it for now. I'll, uh...I'll get it back later.

Dad stops for a moment and studies me carefully then says alright kiddo, what say we go and get it together? Lead the way!

I say hopefully huh? Oh, okay. Yeah, sure! I open the front door and race down the steps and hear the screen door slam behind me. Dad doesn't normally slam the screen door because he doesn't like loud noises, he *hates* that. When I reach the bottom of the stairs I turn to find my old man still on the other side of the door, *in* the house.

I run up the stairs and try to open the screen door, but Dad's locked me out! I pull on the door handle and he looks at me sternly and says listen to me son, you go and get what is *yours* and you *never* let anyone take *anything* from you ever again, do you understand me?

I beg him to let me back inside and say I'm sorry, Dad! I'm sorry, please let me in!

Amariah The Boy

He calmly shakes his head no until I kick the door, at which point he snaps hey! You kick the door again and I'll give you something to cry about. Save that for the other kid and go get your gun back! I'll be right here watching. March!

I pull one last time on the door handle and look at him, but he's not budging. I look over my shoulder at my neighbor's house. It looks like it's on the other side of the world but was only about three houses down, easily within earshot.

I pace around the front yard for five minutes clenching and un-clenching my hands into fists. I think for a moment then look back at the house and call out hey Dad, I need to go to the bathroom!

Dad fires back nope! Nice try, son! If you need to go that bad you can walk into the trees and wipe your butt with leaves!

I say ew!

Well, that didn't work. I look at my neighbor's house, the ugly twin of our own, and grit my teeth before walking toward it. I knock on the door as lightly as I can, hoping that no one will hear me. I look back at my house and offer a shoulder-shrug to Dad who's standing in the doorway sipping what looks like ice-cold sweet tea from a glass. He angrily shakes his head, then makes a motion of banging on the door with his fist, followed by pointing menacingly at me. His enthusiasm spills some of his sweet tea onto the carpet.

I hear from our house oh shit! babe! Paper towel!

I wish *I* had some sweet tea. My throat is dry and a passing breeze kicks up dust onto my face. I look overhead as the Georgian sun rains fire down on everything. It's *so* damn hot. It's *always* hot here. I hear the cicadas buzzing loudly. Why the hell did I suggest coming out here to Dad? Should've stayed inside and watched a movie.

I bang on the door as hard as I can and hear a woman's voice respond just a minute! I'm coming!

Billy's mom. Oh geez. She answers the door and searches overhead before I startle her with a hello. She looks down and surprised, says oh, hello there, can I help you?

I try to keep calm and ask can Billy come out and play? Billy's mom looks at me for a moment, as I guess I don't come around enough for her to remember my face. Weird, 'cause I live pretty close.

She calls out Billy come to the door, you've got a friend here!

Billy yells out okay, Mom! and runs up to the door. When he sees me he says unexcitedly oh, it's you.

Roland Amariah Gonzales

I ask awkwardly if he wants to come outside and play for a while.

It's hot as *hell* out here and I would've told him *no* if he'd asked me. I'm hoping he says no right this *minute* so I can go home.

Billy says sure! and starts to open the door.

I hastily tell him to bring that toy gun so we can play cowboys and Indians. He pauses for a moment, as if he's thinking about it.

He realizes what I'm talking about and says oh yeah, alright! Then he runs back to get his (my) toy gun and joins me outside.

I hear his mom call out don't stay out too late! We're having chicken-fried steak for dinner!

He answers okay mom, I love you! and runs down the steps.

I think man, I love chicken-fried steak! I wonder if his mom would let me eat over at their place and–oh, right—I look at my dad in the distance, still standing in the doorway, now without the glass of sweet tea. He looks at me and punches his right fist into his left palm. I lurch forward down the dusty dirt road, eyes wide with what I have to do.

I lead Billy toward the middle of the street, steaming in that Georgia heat, then abruptly stop and turn to face him. He looks at me in confusion before I say sorry, Billy! And then I wildly swing my arm behind my head, and then fling it toward him as *hard* as I can. My fist glides through the air and lands directly in the middle of his face. Billy cries out and grabs his nose, at the same time dropping my toy gun onto the dirt.

He presses his hand to his nose as blood erupts from it then howls in shock and pain, crying loudly, and holds his bloody fingers up for the both of us to see. I too begin to cry. Billy looks at me in fear then runs home screaming for his mother. I grab my toy gun, see Billy's blood on it, and frantically wipe it off on my shirt. I learned from the TV that you should clean blood off your gun, or it leaves evidence!

I run home screaming and crying loudly for my dad.

Dad has been watching the entire scene unfold.

I'm bawling as I approach the screen door. There was *so much blood!* I'm *positive* Billy's going to die and I'm going to prison for *murder!* Dad is going to be so mad at me for killing Billy! I glance up and then quickly look away from his face. For a moment I think I saw him smiling behind his hand.

He struggles to keep in barely contained laughter and chokes out a good job son, ya did real good! You're a hero! He tries to clear his throat. Maybe he missed what happened or saw something funny on TV?

I run to my room.

I can't sleep that night 'cause I'm *sure* the police are gonna come take me away.

Mom calls me into the TV room the next day and tells me I can't play with Billy anymore. She says if I go near Billy's house I'll go to *prison*. I think to myself I fuckin' *knew* it. I wait until Dad is gone for the day, training in the army, and take both the toy flintlock gun *and* my shirt with the bloodstains and bury them out in the tree line, just like I saw on TV.

One day, me and Grace are playing with Dad in the grass near that snake-filled treeline, chasing each other around and the like. Falling together into a laughing pile, I giddily say hey, Dad! Have you met Mom's new boyfriend?

Dad laughs and gives me a funny look and says yeah, son! His name is *Daddy*.

I laugh and correct him. *No*, his name is *Randy*! Dad's grin dies in an instant and he brings back a much smaller smile.

He says is that so? Well, that sounds silly! and he tickles Grace and me much to our laughter and delight.

Mom had been enjoying another man's company while Dad was at war. She had met him when she went out at night and brought him home several times. She'd tell me and Grace to go play in the other room and then she'd turn on the TV. Sometimes, she'd go out and meet Randy somewhere and leave us in the care of a babysitter, like the red-and-black-flannelled man.

I wake up to the sounds of an angry hushed conversation later that night. Frantic low noises and sudden angry shouts, then quiet again followed by crying from Mom. Grace is too young to understand what's happening, but some part of me knows I'm not going to see Dad again. I can't sleep that night. I apologize to Mom and Dad repeatedly the next day and tell Dad I was just joking, but it makes no difference. Mom is oddly calm and quiet and they both tell me not to worry and nothing's wrong.

The divorce is so quick I don't even know it happened. One day, I come home from kindergarten to see that all our things are in boxes. Mom tells me we're moving to a new house but Dad and Grace aren't coming with us. She says she and her new boyfriend Randy are gonna move elsewhere in Georgia for the time being, and they're gonna drag me along too.

I don't *want* to go with them. My mom hates me and beats me and she leaves me with strangers who beat me! I want to be with my dad! I run to Dad with tears in my eyes and hug him tight then beg him can I please just go with you? I'll be real good and I won't do anything to make you mad ever again. I promise, Dad! Please!

Dad looks at me with tears in *his* eyes and hugs me then says he can't take me with him. He says he loves me very much. He says to be strong for my mom. He says to be tough, to be his little soldier.

I moan and sob no, *please, Dad!* I don't *want* to go with Mom! *Please!* I want to be with you and Grace! I'll be good Daddy, *please* don't make me go with Mom!

Tears are streaming down my cheeks and soak his shirt. He hugs me and says shh. His voice cracks as he says I love you, son. Be good, okay? I'm sorry, boy. Maybe you can visit us sometime, okay?

Mom and Randy come out of the house and stand near the car.

Dad lets me go and then gets into his car with Grace sitting in her baby seat in the back. I try to open the door, but Mom yanks me back and holds me in place as he and Grace drive away.

After they drive out of sight she whispers just out of Randy's hearing this is *all* your fault.

I break into tears and cry out no!

Randy looks down at me then rolls his eyes and heads into the house, his jaw clenched.

Mom snarls at me and tells me you couldn't keep your god-damn mouth shut and now we'll all *never* be together again.

I wail. Sorrow envelops me as the dirt claims me.

Mom leaves me lying in the dirt and dust long enough for my tears to form a small pool of mud about the size of my face.

I spend the next few months crying into my pillow damn near every night until I fall asleep, exhausted and with terrible headaches. The days are filled with Mom looking out the window and drinking while Randy is off at whatever job. I miss Dad *terribly.*

After some time, I cautiously approach Mom in the sitting room of our ratty little rented house. I quietly ask her if I can go visit Dad and Grace. I tell her I've been real good and haven't gotten in trouble or *anything* in a long time.

Amariah The Boy

She puts down her bottle of beer and grabs me hard by the shoulder. Her breath is sour, reeking from a day spent drinking, and I gag a bit when she says he's *not* your dad and he ain't here no more. He's in California with your sister.

Roland Amariah Gonzales

NEW FAMILY

Time passes and the crying lessens. I've just started first grade and I haven't made any friends. We're still in Georgia, in a new place, and I lost the only kind-of-friend I had after Dad made me punch him in the nose. There's a girl down the road who I really like, a girl who wears cotton-candy-pink cowgirl costumes, but she moves away shortly after we become friends.

Mom says she's sending me out to my family in California because she needs a fuckin' break. She says if I'm good I *might* even see Dad while I'm out there!

She packs a few handfuls of clothes into my backpack, tosses me in the car with it, then tows me to the airport. I'm not saying goodbye to much that's here, other than Randy...and I like Dad more.

Mom says I'm going on a grand adventure and I should be very grateful for the opportunity. She says during the drive that I need to be good for anyone and everyone, but *especially* my aunt and uncle. She says they'll throw me out on the streets in a heartbeat and that's where the red-and-black-flannelled man is waiting to get me.

I'm terrified. I know that my dad is somewhere in California and I hope I can see him 'cause maybe he'll change his mind and take me to live with him. Then I won't have to live with Mom anymore.

I hate wearing shoes because they really hurt my feet, even when we're sitting in the car. I complain to Mom that my feet hurt and without looking she says yeah, tell your aunt and uncle about it, then turns up the radio. We arrive at the airport and I walk on the sides of my feet so they'll hurt less, but I can't walk so fast this way. Mom yells to hurry up or I'll get a whoopin'.

She motivates me with a swat to my rear-end and growls you'll miss your fuckin' flight. My bottom lip juts out but I hold back my tears and try to walk normally to speed up my steps, but it *really* hurts. I'm about to cry, so I dig my fingernails into the palms of my hands so I don't think about my feet so much.

Amariah The Boy

Mom drags me through the security gate and all the way to the boarding gate.

Once we're surrounded by people, Mom is much nicer and she makes sure that everyone around her sees how much she loves me. She lavishes me with kisses on my cheeks and forehead and hugs me for what feels like forever...I hate it. Other moms see us and they start to hug their kids the same. When Mom hugs me I feel like someone put a fat wet slug on my forehead and my neck stiffens.

One of the passengers who's waiting for our plane to arrive, some huge lady with a tomato face, asks Mom if I'm flying alone. Tomato-face asks shouldn't you be flying with your son? You know, it's not safe for him to fly alone!

Mom tells tomato-face how I've been talking about visiting my aunt and uncle for *months,* and how I'm just *crazy* about them and how could she possibly keep him from his family! She says she has a new job and can't make the trip with me and that I'll be gone for a year but she'll miss me *so much*! She says hey, the *worst* thing that could happen is the plane goes down and if that happens well, what could *she* gonna do about it?

Mom and the tomato-face lady laugh together and the woman says to me aww, well, aren't you a very brave little man, flying all by yourself!

I smile at her and don't say a thing because I don't have a *clue* who my aunt and uncle are. I can't recall their *names,* let alone their faces, or where they live or *anything* other than what Mom told me on the drive to the airport.

The plane opens up and Mom hands me off to some airline employee who walks me onto the plane and I hear Mom yell out Mommy loves you, Rol!

I turn around and wave with a smile and she smiles back and blows me kisses.

A pretty airline lady in a red dress walks me to my seat, and I see she's wearing these nice black see-through sock-things under her dress that pretty ladies wear. They look soft, so I squeeze her leg and it feels kind of like a ball, but it's real warm and nice. I look up at her and ask what is this?

She looks down and smiles at me, gives me a little laugh, and says they're called stockings.

Then she helps me get into my seat and buckle my seatbelt.

Roland Amariah Gonzales

I look around at the families flying together, the moms and dads with their boys and girls. Parents help their kids buckle seatbelts and I feel very alone and cold. I don't want Mom there but I do want...well...I don't know what I want. I don't want to be alone.

I was little more than an infant when we flew from California to Georgia, so the memory of it is gone. This feels like my first flight.

The pretty airline lady and her friends do some kind of dance thing with a bunch of airplane stuff after the captain talks for a while, then most of them sit down. The pretty airline lady checks on me again, then goes to her seat as well.

A moment later the roar of the engines burns away any thoughts I have. As we leave the ground, I grip the armrests, squeeze my eyes closed, hold my breath, and clench my jaw. I discover that I'm *terrified* of heights and flying alone is *hard*, and I shake like I'm real cold for some reason. Some of the kids near me are crying, and I don't wanna be a crybaby, so I keep my jaw clenched and take short breaths until it's over.

Once we're in the air I summon all my courage to lift the window shade. As I look out across the clouds, I feel something between fear and wonder. I gaze out across this sky-world and feel something like...home. I wonder if my aunt and uncle will be nice to me, like the people seated around me seem to be with their kids. I wonder if the people around me are like my mom, and they only love their children when they're around strangers who are watching.

The pretty airline lady brings me little bags of honey-roasted peanuts and as much juice as I want. She helps me open the bags. When she leans over to open them, her hair goes in front of my face and it smells nice, like flowers. Mom doesn't smell like flowers at all. Mom smells like the bathroom.

The plane lands in California and the pretty airline lady takes me by the hand and walks me to the baggage area and stays with me. She asks if I know my uncle or what he looks like and I just shake my head no and say nuh-uh.

A man approaches. I don't recognize him, but he seems to know me and calls out my name, then he shows both the airline lady and myself an old photo of me as a baby.

In the photograph I see a little tanned blob-creature held in the arms of a grinning man standing next to my smiling teenage mother. The pretty airline lady checks the man's ID. After he'ss cleared she squeezes my hand, lets me go, smiles at me, and tells me goodbye.

My uncle crouches down, sits on his heels and puts his hands on my shoulders, then squeezes them reassuringly. He says let's get a good look at you, then he studies my eyes before looking me over. He says hm...boy, are you *short!* Are you *sure* you're five?

I look down at the ground and he laughs then smiles at me and says c'mere RJ, I'm just kidding! and pulls me in for a hug. The hug from the man feels...different from hugs that Mom gives me. She only hugs me around other people and loudly says how important I am to her, or how much she loves me. Mom smiles when people look at us kindly but there's no smile in her eyes, only her mouth, and she always looks in my eyes like we're sharing some kind of secret joke. People are walking all around us in the baggage area and there's a lot of noise, but he doesn't loudly tell me how great I am or anything like Mom does. He's just hugging me because...he wants to? I don't get it. Why?

I start to cry and I don't know why I'm crying because no one hit me this time and I didn't do anything wrong, but I'm still crying for some reason. My uncle pats my back then pauses and laughs and says *hey*, hey RJ, you're all right. Was it a long flight? Are you tired?

I nod and he takes my hand in his, picks up my little backpack, and says let's get you home then.

We walk back to his car, then he's driving and I'm going to a new home...again. The drive takes a long time because there are *so many* people here in California! Everything is so much bigger, and the buildings are huge!

There's *way* less trees and I can't see the woods anywhere. I wonder if they chopped it all down because maybe there were too many snakes. We eventually get to the house and my uncle helps me with my bag. I'm real nervous because, well, what if my aunt is like my mom? What if she drinks from the bottle and hits me and yells at me?

Roland Amariah Gonzales

My uncle introduces me to my aunt and I'm amazed because she doesn't smell like a bathroom at all. She's nothing like Mom! She says hello and introduces herself as Aunt Tami then gives me a hug, but it doesn't feel like my uncle's hug. My uncle's hug was long and he squeezed me like a gummy bear. Aunt Tami's hug is quick and dry and feels like an old cracker. She says to my uncle hey, does RJ know *your* name?

My uncle pauses to think for a moment then laughs and says no, no I don't think I told him. He says his name is Alex, but I can call him *Uncle* Alex.

I say while I nod in certainty okay I'll do just that, and they both laugh.

Uncle Alex is the sort of man who always has a joke to tell. He's got short, thin dark hair and he *towers* over me, though he's not actually that tall at all. I'm just real small. He has kind eyes, a small moustache that hides under his nose, and he's always got a smile on his face 'cause he's either about to say something funny or has already said it.

He's a happy person and I like to be around him as much as I can.

My aunt is *very* beautiful, with long black hair that goes all the way past her waist and her skin is the color of a warm sandy beach. She has pretty, light-brown eyes and big cheeks like a chipmunk. She likes to wear silver and turquoise jewelry when we go out and she adorns herself with as many rings, necklaces, and earrings as her fingers, neck, and ears will allow.

They're both dressed in comfortable clothes most of the time, though my aunt is certainly the more fashionable of the two. They see to it that I am as well dressed as a five-year-old boy can be.

Uncle Alex works on cars and usually comes home wearing a blue flannel shirt and jeans, both stained with oil and grease. Aunt Tami says she works with circuit boards on an assembly line. She says she doesn't want to get all dirty like Uncle Alex, so she prefers the kind of work that lets her stay clean.

We eat dinner and my uncle says I'm lucky it's the weekend because I've got a *lot* of work to do and I need to get enrolled in school come Monday. Before that, though, we're going to visit all my other family members. I didn't even know I *had* other family members except for Grace and Kenney and I say as much.

Alex smiles and nods but doesn't say anything further.

Amariah The Boy

They help me settle into my bedroom after dinner, make sure I shower and brush my teeth, then tell me good night. When I lay my head on my clean pillow I feel all the new sheets and blankets against my skin. I think to myself that this place is *so nice* and there are so many things compared to what I'd known in Georgia. It's all so *clean* and *pretty*. And quiet.

I feel dirty. Like I don't belong.

After they close my bedroom door, I hear Aunt Tami loudly whisper to Uncle Alex that she can't *believe* Kathleen sent me here with *two* pairs of underwear and some *socks*. She says *that woman* must not care about him at all! And did you *see* how he was walking? It looks like he's still wearing baby shoes! She hisses does Kathy expect us to buy new *everything* for him? He's not our kid and that stuff is *expensive*!

I feel bad, because I *know* I don't have good shoes and my clothes aren't so good either. I'm already making trouble for my aunt and uncle and I *just* got here.

Alex tells Tami hush, not here, let's go to the kitchen.

They walk to the kitchen and talk, but I can still hear Tami's upset voice. I fall asleep worried they're gonna decide I'm too much trouble and they're gonna kick me out on the streets, just like Mom said they would.

Roland Amariah Gonzales

The next day, Uncle Alex takes me to meet all *his* siblings, my aunts and uncles, as well as *their* kids, my cousins, for the first time.

Mary, the first cousin I see, is *rich,* or at least way wealthier than I'll ever be. I marvel at how big and beautiful her family's home is compared to what I knew back in Georgia. It's two stories tall and has more rooms than I can count and a *huge* pool *and* hot tub in the backyard! They've got a scary dog too, a big black one that barks at me a lot, so I stay away unless he's locked up.

Mary is older than me by at *least* a couple of years and she's dressed in a pretty pink dress and has matching bows in her hair. Her mother, my aunt Diane, married an Italian guy who doesn't speak to me, though I don't know why. Aunt Diane has a bird-like nose, long hair that lays down like a sad dog, and big ol' brown eyes.

She seems very stern but mixes her sternness with a sense of humor. I don't really understand her jokes and they seem more for Uncle Alex and the other adults. I can tell that she's like Alex because she likes to laugh, but she seems to have a lot on her mind. She strikes me as getting frustrated and irritable easily, but I don't know why.

Mary has two older brothers and they seem *way* older than her, maybe ten years or so! I don't know if they're her half-brothers or step-brothers. They're like their dad and don't talk to me or look at me either.

I'm there a short time before I realize that Mary doesn't like to play with me and she especially hates sharing *anything* with me. She snatches things out of my hands if I pick them up, then yells *that's mine,* you can't touch it! She scratches me with her fingernails when she snatches things away from me. Mary tells me *nobody* wants me around, and that I'm a burden to my aunt and uncle.

It's the first time I've heard the word *burden,* so I ask what it means.

Mary says it means no one *wants* you and you make them *sad* just by being *alive.* She says your mother is trash and so are you!

I angrily tell her that's not *true* she's trash, not me!

Mary gets angry, hits me, then runs to tattle on me for calling her trash. After that first time, whenever I'm forced to visit she usually provokes me, hits me, then runs to tattle on me before I can explain. I do my best to avoid her when Uncle Alex makes me go to her home. I decide that maybe a big rich house isn't so nice after all if the people in it are mean.

Amariah The Boy

Alex takes me to visit his youngest sister, Aunt Minerva, who is really pretty and has tan skin like me, and dark hair too. She wears glasses and looks like Mary's mother, Aunt Diane, only softer. More kind. She seems a little strict, but nothing like Aunt Tami.

Aunt Minerva married Pat, a German-looking guy who reminds me of my dad Kenney, only with less hair...and he's wearing a hat. He's *tall* though, just like Dad. They have a daughter, Cousin Camille, around my age, and she's nice and plays with me.

The last relative we visit is Aunt Yolanda, the oldest of Uncle Alex's siblings. Yolanda has a nose like Diane and huge poofy curly hair that looks like it's been dyed blonde. She wears so much perfume that it makes me cough when I'm close to her and she wears a business suit, not a dress or jeans. She's got two kids, a boy and a girl, who are at least ten years older than me.

Yolanda's daughter, Ohlanda, is *real* pretty and looks different from everyone else. She has light skin, whiter than my mom, and if Aunt Diane's eyes are big and round then Ohlanda's are the opposite. I ask her why 'cause she doesn't look at all like her mom. She looks at me then squints so her eyes are even *smaller* then grins and says *what*, you don't think they're cute?

I giggle and quickly look away. My heart starts to beat really fast and I can't talk to her without stuttering. She *is* very pretty and I don't know what to say so I just smile.

Yolanda's son Juan doesn't look at *all* like his sister and I scratch my head in confusion and start to say something until I remember that me and Grace don't look similar either.

He has a shiny red car and its roof comes down. When he sees me looking at it with my mouth agape in wonder he offers to take me for a drive. I ask my uncle if it's alright and he laughs then tells Juan sure but don't crash 'cause I don't know how to put RJ back together!

We go along the Pacific Coast Highway. It's late afternoon, the top is down, and the wind whips through the interior. I love the feeling of the wind rushing through my hair, and how the sun looks over the ocean. The water looks like gold.

Juan talks a lot, but I can't hear a thing he's saying 'cause of the wind. I respond to everything he asks or says with *what?* And I think he can't hear a thing I'm saying too because he laughs and says yeah.

He turns up the music and we listen to that instead of my yelling *what?*

Roland Amariah Gonzales

During this visit I learn that Uncle Alex's mom, my grandma Maria, shuffles between all of my aunts' homes, though she spends the most time with Aunt Minerva. Grandma Maria lives in a trailer parked in the driveway and doesn't go in the house all that often, unless someone makes food. She doesn't speak a lick of English and I can't speak *any* Spanish, so we don't talk.

When we sit down together, she forgets that I don't know Spanish. She drinks from a glass bottle and I don't understand a word she says. She gets angry and shakes me when I don't respond, then screams more stuff in Spanish. She doesn't do this when everyone else is around, only those few minutes when we're alone.

As the days and weeks go by, I learn to hate whenever Alex drops me off with Grandma Maria 'cause it's just a day of her shaking me, yelling at me in Spanish, and making me watch TV shows in Spanish. I keep telling her I don't *know* Spanish Grandma Maria, stop shaking me! Uncle Alex and everyone else laugh and tell me well, I need to *learn* Spanish! That's fine, but no one takes the time to teach me or put me in classes, so I never *do* learn, and Grandma Maria just keeps yelling at me.

Amariah The Boy

I frequently get in some kind of trouble, though thankfully trouble on this side of the country isn't met by a large spoon or the end of a telephone cord. I'm usually either sent to my room or told to stand in the corner, though I occasionally do earn an ass-whoopin' or two...but nothing serious. Thing is, I'm *always* in trouble around Aunt Tami, and to such an extent that I start to hide from her and avoid her when we're alone. This suits her just fine. And me, too.

My aunt and uncle have a single-story home with a mortgage that I hear them talking about. I'm not sure what that is, but it must not be good 'cause they always sound worried.

The whole house, except the kitchen, is covered in beige or cream-colored carpeting, and there are no stains whatsoever, in contrast to my filthy carpet back in Wherever, Georgia. (I swear it was that dirty when we moved in.) Most of the interior of this house is similar to a museum, in that everything has a strict no-touch policy.

My uncle doesn't care so much about artwork, so Aunt Tami decorates near every wall with the works of someone named Patrick Nagel. The ladies are pretty to look at, though I can only look for so long before I want to touch, too. And sometimes...I do. This earns me no small amount of trouble! Tami returning from work and then angrily asking whether I touched something is as common as standing in the corner afterward, regardless of my answer.

There's a small swimming pool in their backyard and I'm a little excited because I remember swimming with Dad when I was around two. My aunt's dogs are back there too, but I'm not allowed to play with them. She has two great big Chow Chow dogs that look like giant teddy bears. I want to wrap my arms around them and squeeze them 'cause they're so fluffy.

Aunt Tami speaks in a squeaky baby voice with them, so I think they're friendly. I ask if I can touch them and she says sure, go ahead. When I get close and try to pet them they growl and snap at me. I run terrified and screaming into the sitting room, closing the sliding glass door behind me.

Aunt Tami strokes their fur, then looks at me through the door with this cold smile, the same one Mom gives me sometimes. She says in that same squeaky baby voice to her dogs aw, my babies don't like him at *all*, do you my wittle-bitty babies?

Roland Amariah Gonzales

The dogs happily lick her hands and face as she buries her face in their fur and hugs them. I keep away from the pool unless someone puts those dogs behind the fence. They *clearly* want to eat me.

I like watching movies a whole lot. Alex and Tami have a large collection of VHS cassettes. I watch one in particular over and over—it's my *favorite*, the Michael Jackson movie *Moonwalker*. I really like the songs and dancing, and the part where Michael turns into a giant robot and then a spaceship to stop all the bad guys is *awesome*.

My aunt and uncle get tired of watching *Moonwalker* after maybe the 20th time and hide it from me and I don't understand why. It's *really* good and maybe if they saw it another 20 times they'd like it as much as I do.

They've got a bunch of Disney movies too and I love the sing-alongs. I like to sing, and songs are the best part of any movie we watch.

On the weekends he's not busy with work, Uncle Alex teaches me how to swim. It's scary because he doesn't let me put floaties on my arms and tells me this builds character. He takes me into the pool and puts me flat on the water with my belly down, then holds my outstretched arms and tells me to kick my legs *real* hard and *real* fast.

He walks backward away from me and lets go of my hands. I panic and cry out for him to catch me and he steps back *just* far enough to make sure I can't get his hands, but holds them out to me. He smiles at me but it's not like Mom or Aunt Tami's smile. It's different. It's not a mean smile that hurts. We do this a bunch of times until he doesn't need to help me anymore.

Aunt Tami helps me learn to swim in her *own* very special way. She walks by me when we stand near the pool then pushes me into the deep end. She laughs and says come on RJ, sink or swim! then keeps walking. She does this *every time* I stand next to the pool, so I learn to jump in before she pushes me. That way, I don't get water up my nose from being caught off-guard.

Sometimes my aunt and uncle throw pool parties, and if I'm not on the lookout she walks by and shoves me in. She smiles down at me like my mom as she watches me thrash around, choking and coughing in the deep end after having been pushed in for the hundredth time. Everyone else either ignores us both or laughs when they see me fall in again and again.

She follows me to the edge and when I try to climb out she shoves me right back in. She does this so many times that my arms are on fire from swimming so much. I sink to the bottom and use my legs to kick off the bottom and take a gasp of air, then hop to the shallow end. When she follows me then sees me crying she says oh my god, don't be such a baby!

It isn't until Uncle Alex gives her a look that she rolls her eyes then lets me climb out of the pool. I run inside to dry off and change my clothes, then get warm and hide away from her.

Aunt Tami has a niece and nephew by her older sister and they're older than me by a couple of years. I can tell she loves them very much because she's always hugging them and laughing with them. She never does anything like that with me unless she's trying to drown me. I wonder what they do that makes them so great and if they can show me too so she's not so mean to me all the time. They come and spend the day with us every now and then.

On one such occasion they get real excited and tell me they want to throw eggs at passing cars. I didn't know that was something people do... it sounds dumb *and* dangerous. I want to be more like them though because Aunt Tami likes them *way* more than me, so I go with them.

They tell Tami they're taking me to the park and that they're taking a backpack filled with bottled water and snacks. She tells them to keep an eye on me and make sure I don't do anything stupid.

They laugh and say no worries, we'll watch out for him!

When we leave the house and walk for a bit, I get cold feet and tell them I think it's a bad idea. I don't wanna get in trouble or get hurt by anyone. They call me chicken and start bawking like a chicken and my face gets real red and I'm about to cry, so I go along.

We walk up the road and turn the corner then walk a bit more until we're far away from the house. They pull a couple of eggs from an egg carton hidden in their backpack. They go to hand me one but I don't want it. They tell me I'm lame and roll their eyes.

They don't hide behind a bush or *anything* like that, and instead stand out on the sidewalk as cars go zooming by. They huck their eggs at a lightning-fast looking shiny red car...it looks like Juan's car, the one he drove next to the ocean.

In slow-motion, I see the eggshell explode as clear and yellow yolk splatters in every direction.

Roland Amariah Gonzales

The driver slams on his brakes and the smell of burning rubber soon fills the air as the tires squeal on the pavement and the car reverses toward us.

My cousins look about as scared as I imagine *I* did when the red-and-black-flannelled man was storming toward my room. They tell me to keep my head down and I'm about to have as big a heart attack as a five-year-old can. I don't think my cousins are having fun anymore. We rush back toward the house as quick as we can when a thin man with sand-colored hair and expensive-looking shiny sunglasses suddenly steps out of his car. He slams the door shut and screams HEY!

He runs up to us and, oh man, he's *real* mad. He's screaming and my cousins try to say they didn't do anything but he yells BULLSHIT! Show me what's in your fuckin' bag, now!

My cousins try to tell him that they don't *have* to show him what's in the bag and they don't *have* to do what he tells them, but he's having none of it and threatens to call the police. He says this is *vandalism* and we're all going to go to fuckin' jail. My cousins open the backpack and he sees the carton of eggs minus the two they just threw and he nods in anger.

He says you little shits are *so* fucked now!

I burst into tears and beg him not to run me over with his car! I'm *really* sorry and I didn't even throw anything! I whine I didn't even want to come out here!

He looks at me in confusion, then my cousins, and demands that we show him where we all live so he can tell our parents.

He slowly drives behind us as we shuffle on the sidewalk and one of my cousins whispers that we should all run in different directions when we turn the corner.

I cry out no!

My legs are the shortest and even though I got new shoes my feet still hurt a little bit. I *know* he'll run me over because we hurt his car, and I'm almost *certain* he gets to do that if he wants to.

When we get close to the house my cousins quickly run back inside with me in tow and close the door. They try to hide from the man as he parks his car in front and starts honking the horn. I quickly walk to my room but don't run 'cause I don't want Aunt Tami to yell at me for running inside.

I hear Aunt Tami say to my cousins oh? that was fast. Back from the park already?

44

Amariah The Boy

I hear loud banging against the front door. She says what on earth, who *is* that? then walks to the door and opens it to see the sandy-haired man.

I hide in my room and hear the man erupt in rage. Something about cars and eggs and do you know how much money that will cost. I'm *so* dead. Aunt Tami loudly calls all of us to the front door.

We trudge to the entrance and she painfully grabs a fistful of my hair and shakes me a bit then says great, what did *he* do?

I yell out ow! OW! and start crying.

Tami hisses through her teeth wait until your uncle hears about this, and she sounds like she's almost *happy*.

She's gonna tell Uncle Alex they should kick me out on the streets! Just like Mom *said* they would! I collapse onto the ground and try to hug her leg, sobbing and apologizing, but she kicks me away.

The man looks down at me in alarm and tells her no, no – the little dude didn't do anything, it was those two older kids! Those little *bastards* chucked those *fucking* eggs at my car. Who's gonna pay for that? If they fucked up the paint then that's a five-thousand-dollar paint job!

Tami stands in disbelief, still holding me by my hair, shocked either by the price tag or by the revelation that her perfect niece and nephew have done something wrong. She asks the man if he's *sure* it wasn't me and the man says no, it wasn't fucking *him,* I'm not fucking *blind!* Are you listening to a word I'm saying?

Tami lets go of my hair and promises to discipline my older cousins and apologizes profusely. She then offers to have them wash the man's car, but he says he doesn't want them to go anywhere *near* his car, so Tami goes outside and cleans it.

When the eggs are wiped off, the man huffs off, satisfied apparently that someone's ass is going to get whipped.

My aunt comes back in then closes the door. She calls her niece and nephew into the sitting room and asks them what in the hell is wrong with them and if they're crazy. I peek from around the corner and expect to see them get smacked but instead she shares a laugh with them and says that man was a *real* asshole! She says my cousins are lucky their mom isn't there and promises to keep it a secret because they're all such *good* buddies.

I stand there with my jaw agape in absolute shock. I can't *believe* my cousins just got away with something that *serious*! Aunt Tami would've drowned me in the fucking pool if that was my fault! She almost does it for fun anyway! As I enter the room Aunt Tami looks my way and doesn't apologize to me for blaming me or shaking me by my hair or *anything*.

It's my first experience with double standards and oh, I *hate* it. I hate my aunt and I'm jealous of my cousins' immunity to punishment.

Aunt Tami looks at me with disdain and can see that I'm pissed. She says if you're gonna have an attitude, you can take it right into your room.

I'm put in timeout for a couple of hours so she doesn't have to see my frowning face anymore. When my uncle comes home and wants to know *why* I'm in timeout, she says I decided to get an attitude but doesn't elaborate.

A few days later, Aunt Tami takes me to visit her older sister's house and I'm excited at first because one of my cousins has video games. He shows me for about ten minutes before Aunt Tami pops in and says wanna see something *really* cool?

I don't have time to respond before she drags me to the front yard and points out a bunch of random plants all over the ground. She says see all those weeds? You're going to pull them out! It's just like a video game, but real life!

This becomes my new and *only* activity any time I visit in the future. My cousins rarely help, unless they pissed off their mom. I pull weeds out of the ground but I never seem to get it right. I know this 'cause they keep growing back like, well...weeds.

Tami comes out to check my progress with a scowl on her face and loudly tells me that I'm doing it *wrong*. She says to pull them out by the roots and that I need to dig deeper.

I complain that we don't even *live* here and it's *hot*!

She informs me that if I don't do what I'm told then I'll be in big trouble when we get home.

I stare at the ground and mutter okay Aunt Tami, I'll do my best.

I then complain to her that the rocks on top of the dirt hurt my fingers and she asks me if I need gloves. I tell her I don't know because this is my first time doing this.

She enters the house and retrieves some yardwork gloves, then tosses them at my feet and says there you go, now get busy. She waits for a moment then says she's not staying out here in *this* heat and goes back inside.

Amariah The Boy

I put them on and feel something wriggling around inside and oh sweet *Jesus*, what *is* that!?

I emit a high-pitched shriek, flail my hands in the air and tear the gloves off. They go flying and hit the ground. Out comes a black widow spider.

Aunt Tami comes back out the front door and asks what all the noise is about and says to keep it down 'cause they're inside watching a movie and *no* I can't come watch, don't even ask.

I cry in panic and say a spider almost bit me and she says well, kill it!

It runs away before I can squish it and I really don't even want to get *near* it 'cause what if it jumps on me?

She says well, it's gone now and hopefully it doesn't come back to bite you. She laughs and says to watch out for all the other spiders in the plants, then goes back inside.

Aunt Tami comes out of the house after I spend *forever* in the burning-hot California sun. She raises her voice and trumpets my *goodness* what are you doing out here RJ, you need to go inside and drink water, silly!

She sounds like my mom when Mom announces to everyone how special and great I am and how much she loves me. I don't even know why she's saying this because if I *do* go in to get water or use the bathroom, Tami yells at me and says she didn't *say* I could come in...and of course now she's got to tell my uncle that I'm misbehaving.

When she tells Uncle Alex I'm bad, I get a whoopin', no questions asked. He believes Tami more than me 'cause hell, I'm just a dumb kid. I don't want my uncle to think I'm bad. I know he loves me, and you can't love people that are bad.

And I *definitely* don't wanna die alone on the streets after they kick me out because I'm a bad kid, so I just bake outside like a potato in the oven.

Roland Amariah Gonzales

I'm at a big family dinner and all my aunts, uncles, cousins and everyone are there. I remember Mom saying that Dad lives here in California, so I ask if I can go see him.

Aunt Yolanda says with a mouthful of food what? No, you can't go see your dad, he's not here!

I'm confused and say no, Mom said he's *here* in California, with Gracie!

Everyone gets real quiet until Aunt Diane informs me that Kenney is *not* my real father and I need to *stop* referring to him as such. Then she adds that Grace is my *half*-sister.

I pause for a moment as I remember mom drinking beer and saying something about Dad not being my *real* dad.

I say well, where *is* my real father? but no one tells me. Everyone eats in silence.

Aunt Yolanda clears her throat and says okay, that's enough little boy talk, and then she says to eat my food. Someone explains in Spanish what I said to Grandma Maria and she responds in kind. When she finishes talking everyone laughs, but no one will tell me what's so funny. They just say oh, *she* said to eat your food.

I don't believe that, and my face is red with shame. Everyone continues to speak Spanish and look at me then laugh. I don't like these people.

A few weeks later, Aunt Yolanda gets in touch with Kenney and tells him to bring Grace over to Aunt Diane's house so we can see each other. When Dad gets there I'm *super* excited. I run up and hug his legs then cry into his knees because I miss him so much. I wanna go with him and all these people are so mean.

He hugs me back then tells me to play with Gracie while he talks to my aunts.

I go into the other room but Gracie and I don't talk much. She can't really say a whole lot yet, but it's nice to see her...I guess. It's even better getting to play with all of my cousin Mary's stuff: for some reason, no one else is here, just my aunts and my dad.

I hear angry shouts from one of my aunts and sneak around the corner to see what's happening. They're all in the kitchen and my aunts are yelling at my dad and getting in his face. They tell him he needs to tell me that he's *not* my father. My aunts are real scary when they get in *my* face, but Dad is so tough that he doesn't budge an inch!

Amariah The Boy

He gets *real* mad and says *no way in hell*. Then he asks is *this* the only reason you asked me to come here with Grace? He says he's the only Dad I've *got* and he sure as hell is better than their deadbeat brother, Roland. Then he says speaking of Roland, where the hell *is* he? Has he *once* tried to be in RJ's life? Sent a birthday card? *Anything?*

Aunt Yolanda says something about Roland being in Mexico, not that it's any of *your* business, and he's not coming back any time soon.

I sneak back into the bedroom with Grace and we play for about a minute before my aunts call me into the kitchen and say it's time for *Kenney* and Grace to go home. They tell me to say goodbye, so I hug Gracie and Dad and ask when I'll see both again.

Dad says I don't know but hopefully soon, son.

They both leave and I'm real sad. Life is so much better with Dad, and I don't want to stay with these people. Aunt Yolanda offers to take me for ice cream, probably 'cause she can see how sad I am. I happily agree but instead of going to get ice cream she spends the whole drive lecturing me about how Kenney isn't my *real* dad and by the time we get there I don't want ice cream anymore.

Uncle Alex and his siblings never talk about my blood-father Roland.

Eventually I learn that I have an older sister by six years, *and* she lives in the area, *and* Roland is her blood-father too! But she has a different mom, so she's only my half-sister. Her name is Diane but everyone calls her Little Diane, on account of Aunt Diane having the same name first.

Little Diane comes to Alex and Tami's house and swims with me in their pool. She doesn't push me in or try to push me under the water or anything like Tami does. Little Diane is *really* pretty, so I stare at her a lot. She catches me staring once and teases me about it, and I say I can't help it 'cause she's so beautiful.

She grins at me then laughs and holds me way up in the air. And then she kisses me on my cheeks and looks into my eyes with a smile on her face.

I giggle and laugh before she tosses me into the pool.

Uncle Alex takes me to her home a few days later.

Little Diane and I spend the day together in her room and she asks if I want to watch a movie and I say okay. She grins then shows me the movie *Cujo*. It doesn't help my fear of dogs at *all*. She has another younger brother who isn't related to me, but he's only a baby, so we don't talk to each other 'cause babies can't talk. They only eat and poop.

Little Diane and I eat some snacks and I really like being in her room...it's very pink and fluffy and smells real nice, like flowers.

After Uncle Alex comes to get me, I never see her again, though I don't know why.

Uncle Alex takes me to see his oldest brother, my uncle Gilbert. Uncle Gilbert lives in a tiny house with his family and it reminds me of my home in Georgia, but it's even *smaller* and *dirtier*! There's an awful smell outside like the bathroom after Mom gets out. I don't like it.

Uncle Gilbert and his wife have a baby, and his wife doesn't speak a word of English, only Spanish. At first, I'm worried she's gonna shake the hell out of me when no one's looking. That's what people who only speak Spanish do from what I understand, but she doesn't and I'm surprised.

It gets so hot and they don't have an air conditioner! They put me in a small plastic kiddie pool with my baby cousin. I *hate* the kiddie pool 'cause my baby cousin wears his diaper then pees and poops when he's in the water. It's *gross*...and if I thought the front yard smelled like a bathroom then this kiddie pool is *definitely* the toilet!

I complain over and over to Uncle Alex that I wanna go home and tell him this place smells like a toilet.

He looks down and chastises me and says hey RJ, that's rude! You apologize right now.

I didn't know Uncle Gilbert heard me so I apologize, but don't know why. I'm not the one who makes it smell like a bathroom here, they do! They should apologize to me!

Amariah The Boy

Alex and Tami hold a pool party one bright and burning-hot summer afternoon. Tami's Chow Chow dogs are behind their chain link fence, away from the guests, though this doesn't stop their barking at everyone. The only thing that quiets them is a handful of french fries or scraps of burger meat.

Aunt Tami gives me a hamburger on a paper plate. As I walk away she yells at me to not feed her dogs *any* of *my* food. Everyone else is tossing food to the dogs so when she's not looking I throw the *whole* hamburger over the fence—I ate a bunch of french fries and I'm not hungry anyway.

The brown Chow Chow wolfs down the *whole thing* before the other one can get to it. He barks at me in thanks and even licks my hand when I hold it out, which makes me laugh. Tami yells at me and asks if I ate my burger and says how'd you eat it so fast? She says you didn't give it to the dogs, did you?

I lie and say it was great and Tami gives me a weird look and says oh yeah? Did you like it? then goes back to cooking.

The brown Chow Chow gets *really* sick and after going to the hospital ends up dying. I'm terrified that it's my fault 'cause Aunt Tami *told* me not to give her dogs any of *my* food but I did anyway. She's in the kitchen when, through tears, she tells Uncle Alex the doctor said the dog died of food poisoning. She sees me peeking around the corner and asks if I gave her dogs *anything*, then says *remember* that God is *watching*.

I look at the ground and say no...um...well...I gave it that hamburger you gave me, but everyone else was giving it burgers too!

Tami flies into a *fury* and she screams at me you fucking *horrible* little *shit*, god*damn* you! She wails and swipes at me with her claws before Uncle Alex pulls her into the other room and slams the door. And then from behind the closed door he shouts for me to go to my room. She shrieks at him and he bellows back and I can't hear anything but muffled angry noises and the sounds of things breaking, so I run to my room crying.

I sit in the corner of my closet, hiding behind toys that were never mine in the first place, my arms wrapped around my knees. I messed up *again,* and now Aunt Tami's dog is *dead* and it's all my fault! I should've just eaten that hamburger like she told me to! I hate myself because I'm so *stupid!* I ball my hand into a fist and hit myself on the head because no one is there to hit me and I was bad.

Roland Amariah Gonzales

I hear Tami shriek some more and thunder around the house, just like Mom. The front door of the house opens then slams shut and a car peels out of the driveway. I sit in the closet and my mind turns back to a time in Georgia, to another moment when I accidentally killed.

Other boys liked to go step on ants or torture bugs and watch them die. I got into trouble a *lot* in kindergarten for pushing other kids over whenever they tried to step on a snail or grasshopper for fun. I'd get put in the timeout chair by my teacher and told that it's not okay to use violence to solve my problems. No one really cared about the little snails and the grasshoppers.

Mom, Randy and I had moved to Somewhere, Georgia after Mom and Dad got divorced. Giant trees with sticky flowing sap towered overhead in our backyard, their flesh a writhing blanket of tiny green caterpillars. I watched a small brown bird fly down from its nest and snatch one up and gobble it in an instant! I gasped in shock, then took it upon myself to collect as many of the green caterpillars as possible to protect them from the birds. I walked from tree to tree in my quest and plucked the caterpillars with my right hand to store them in the clutch of my left.

The green caterpillars kept trying to wriggle free from my hot and sweaty grasp, so I squeezed harder because I was trying to protect them from a grisly end. I was so sure of my doing the right thing. I must have collected around 20 before I noticed they had all stopped squirming. I thought they had gone to sleep but then saw that they weren't moving at all. My firm and over-protective grasp, meant only to save them from the birds, had resulted in their death.

I dug a small hole, like I'd done for Mr. Fish, and placed the caterpillars inside before covering them with dirt. My mind returns to the present and I rock back and forth while hugging my knees.

I'm still sitting in the corner of the closet, hiccupping and sobbing. I think of those caterpillars and then I think of Mr. Fish. I remember how I felt *then* when he died and I can *feel* Aunt Tami's pain now. I can feel how angry she and Uncle Alex both are and their fighting reminds me of being with Mom and now I'm terrified and shaking, because I know that they're going to kick me out on the streets and I'm gonna die alone when the red-and-black-flannelled man finds me.

Uncle Alex finds me crying in the closet and helps me clean up then hugs me and tells me I didn't do anything wrong. I'm bawling and ask if they're going to send me back to my mom, and I sob that I don't

52

Amariah The Boy

wanna go back to my mom, and he says no, you don't have to go back, but I don't want you to be here alone with Aunt Tami for a while.

Roland Amariah Gonzales

Uncle Alex's side of the family are practitioners of Jews for Jesus and they drag me to their church place at least twice a week. My belief in Jesus, God, and all the angels wasn't very strong after the red-and-black-flannelled man beat the hell out of me and Grace. If God loves all his little children, where was he when that man whipped us both? Why didn't he send an angel down to stop the man?

Or...maybe God doesn't love me and Grace. Or maybe there is no god. Maybe god's not real. That makes more sense, 'cause if I was God, I wouldn't let little kids get beaten by bad people.

I don't say anything about getting beaten to Uncle Alex and instead tell him I'm not so sure if I really want to go to the *santacog*.

He says it's pronounced sin-nuh-gog and to put on my nice clothes and hurry up.

We go together a bunch of times until one Saturday morning when Uncle Alex and Aunt Tami are busy. Aunt Diane takes me with her kids to *her* synagogue and tells me since it's my first time, I need to lie about my age.

I say what? In church? Why?

She says it's so you can get into the younger bible-study class. She says if you get into the younger class then you can get a free bible! The three-year-olds get free bibles!

I'm as excited about lying about my age to get a *free bible* as I am having Grandma Maria offer to shake me for a good five minutes. I don't know if God is real or if he's watching, but I *do* know I feel bad telling lies in a church.

I don't know how many times everyone has told me that lying is bad and not to tell stories, but it's been a *bunch* up to now. When I get separated to the kids' section I tell the truth about my age and they put me with the older bible-study class. Well, the five to ten-year-old class anyway.

No free bible for me!

Aunt Diane is *real* upset when she finds out I didn't do what she said. She drives home and says to everyone in the car you know what? Since all of you know how to listen and RJ doesn't, how about everyone *but* him gets ice cream?

My cousins all cheer. Now I'm sad. I *love* ice cream and I should've fucking lied in church. My older cousin Mary makes all kinds of mmm-good noises when she's eating her ice cream and I tell her to shut her stupid mouth...and she tattles on me.

Amariah The Boy

When Aunt Diane hands me off to Uncle Alex she tells him that I won't stop misbehaving and saying naughty things. He just shakes his head at me and I feel bad.

I go to a different church with Uncle Alex sometimes and it's nothing special. They don't have a room for kids, so it's a lot of the man up front reading from his giant bible while everyone reads along. They all say stuff together and sometimes the man up front says a bunch of stuff and then everyone says amen.

I try not to fall asleep but it's *so* boring. When I do Uncle Alex gives me a small poke in the ribs, looks at me with a stern face, then points to the talking man...like I just missed something important.

Any time I have to go to the synagogue with Aunt Diane, she makes sure to ask all the kids if they have their bible and they all say yes. She asks me if I have mine then stops and says oh wait! You didn't get a bible RJ, because you can't follow instructions!

I start to say that I didn't feel right about lying, but she cuts me off and says nope! You can't follow instructions and that's why you don't have a bible!

No one ever gets me a bible so I have to share with one of the other kids in my bible study class. I don't think it's a big deal but whatever kid I share the bible with gives a great big sigh like he's trying to move the whole world.

No one talks to me when we get our cookies and juice...maybe 'cause I'm the only one without a bible...and now I feel ashamed for not lying to get my free fucking bible.

I *hate* going to church, and whether I'm in church or in school, I can't stop disappointing Uncle Alex. I hate myself for failing all the time.

Roland Amariah Gonzales

Most of the time, Alex and Tami and I eat breakfast together before I go to school, though sometimes either Alex or Tami is in a great big hurry and don't eat anything at all. I usually have a bowl of cereal or oatmeal, and sometimes Alex buys me oatmeal that has gummy fruits. That's my favorite.

When we eat together Alex likes eggs and toast, or maybe a bowl of cereal, and Tami the same. He usually stares off at nothing and sits there with his spoon or fork in the air above his food. He kinda chews his food but not really, and it makes me laugh. I wave at him and he blinks a couple of times then looks at me and smiles.

Uncle Alex and I don't talk a whole lot in the morning 'because we don't have a whole lot to say to one another, especially when it's so early. Sometimes I tell him about my dreams if they're really crazy and he nods and says uh-huh while he kinda chews. He usually asks me if I'm doing okay in school, and did I do my homework, and did I study for my tests, but I don't like these questions...the answer is usually *no,* or I have to lie, and I *hate* lying.

If I don't try to talk to him then breakfast is relatively conversation-free and I don't get asked any hard questions, which is just fine by me.

I can tell that Aunt Tami doesn't like to be around me but when we're with other family she acts like she loves me – just like Mom did. When friends or family tell her how great she is for looking after her nephew, who isn't even *related* to her by blood, she smiles and says that's what *any* good Christian would do! I smile when she tousles my hair and then hug her because it's best to stay on her good side. But the truth is, I don't like her at *all*...she reminds me so much of Mom.

Breakfast is followed by a ritualistic ass-beating before I set off for school. Uncle Alex laughs when I say no and try to cover my rear with my hands. He says it's for all the trouble I *know* you'll get into today!

He doesn't hit me hard like Mom did. He only uses his hand, a couple of solid swats to my ass to encourage me toward being good.

I rub away the pain with an angry frown on my face. What's the point of being good if I'm going to get spanked anyway?

Aunt Tami is just like Mom and spanks me more and more as our time together grows, though she never uses a phone cord or anything like that, just her hand and she says it hurts her more than it does me. I don't believe that for an instant because it hurts like hell for me and I don't see *her* walking away and rubbing the pain from her butt. She never does this in the morning before school though, just when she's mad at me for touching her things or making too much noise or not remembering something.

When Uncle Alex drives me to school he turns on the radio. When we arrive he tells me to do real good and not make any problems. He says he loves me and have a good day and I tell him I love him too.

When Aunt Tami drives me to school she plays the radio and says have a good day. A lot of times she doesn't even look at me. She doesn't say she loves me and that's fine.

Uncle Alex picks me up most of the time after school and he brings me to the car repair shop, because he says he's always got a lot of work to do. I skim over the parking lot on the flat wooden thing with wheels that he uses to slide under cars. I like to lay down on it and pretend I can fly, 'cause there's nothing else to do.

Sometimes when there's no one else around I have the whole parking lot to myself! As long as I don't get in his way he doesn't care so much what I do. He uses a blue kerchief to wipe away grease or oil from his face. He keeps it in his back pocket.

I never go to my aunt's workplace. She says it's not for kids and they're not allowed.

First grade is *so* boring. I just *did* all the things we're learning about back in Georgia, mostly on my own! The other kids are learning to read and I already know how. I complain to the teacher that I already know all of this, and she says hey that's great, that means you'll do that much better on exams!

I give a great big sigh.

I can't pay attention at *all* in class and I think this is *worse* than church. The things the teacher says are *most* important are raising your hand to speak and waiting until you're called on, following the yellow line on the ground running from the class to the bathroom, and standing outside in the sun after lunch so she can take us back to the classroom. I'm terrible at *all* the important stuff and *always* get in trouble because of it.

The teacher uses a card system for how good we are for that day. There's a green card for good...I think black cards mean someone died, since no one ever gets a black card. Blue is the worst I ever see, and only when *I* get it. She puts her little judgement cards in these little pockets on the wall next to the chalkboard. The pockets have each student's name on them so the *whole class* can see them and that's supposed to make us think about our bad-color *all* day. I rarely go home with a green card, and instead end up with at *least* a yellow. The teacher tells me I'm *so* smart, but I need to learn to follow the *important* rules, not just do well on my exams and classwork.

I hate sitting and staring at the wall while everyone else finishes their classwork or their exams. The teacher tells us that when we're done we should put our heads down on our desks, but that's boring *and* dumb. Instead, I play a game where I pretend to look at someone else's paper when I'm done and my paper is already flipped over.

I keep the teacher's face in the corner of my eye and quickly look away or put my head on my desk when she looks at me. She *hates* this game because she thinks I'm cheating and walks up the first couple of times to take my test away so I can't finish, but I'm already done! I laugh and say I'm already done, but she's not laughing.

She's pissed.

I get a bad card for doing this but it's more fun than closing my eyes or staring at my stupid desk. Sometimes I talk to people too when I finish my work. That gets me in trouble as well.

I don't play my games or talk to anyone when I already have a yellow card unless I *can't help it,* and then that means I get an orange card... and orange cards equal a good ass-whoopin' for misbehaving when I get home.

I learn...again...that telling lies *is* better than telling the truth. After I tell Aunt Tami that I got an orange card, she spanks me until my ass is cherry-red. I hate it.

A bit later I get *another* orange card! When Alex asks at dinner how I did for the day I lie and say I only got a yellow card. I figure the worst that could happen is they talk to the teacher and she says nuh-uh! He got an orange card!

But they never *do* have that talk! Now I'm *sure* it's better to lie and probably not get caught than to tell the truth and definitely get punished. Why *ever* be honest, if all that does is get my ass beat?

I love the science projects in class, but sometimes they're gross. We learn about the life-cycle of peanuts by putting them in bottles of water and then watch as the peanut grows a long green stem from its shell, but soon enough the entire room smells like the boys' bathroom! I ask the teacher why and she says the smell is part of the growth cycle. I wonder if there are peanuts growing in the bathroom too.

We also learn that celery is the thirstiest plant. When we put red food coloring in a water bottle with celery it makes the celery change reddish too. I do really good when we're doing something with science or math or drawing or reading. What I don't do so good is sitting there and doing nothing!

I decide I'm not going to get in trouble anymore in school for talking to other kids, so I bring a spinning top from one of my cereal boxes. I'm thinking I'll play with it when I'm done with my worksheets or exams. The teacher takes away toys if we play with them in class instead of doing classwork, but I think I'll be okay since I won't play with the top until *after* I'm done.

I finish my worksheet then bring out my blue and yellow spinning top and start rolling it around the desk and to be honest it's not that much fun...but it's better than looking at the inside of my eyelids.

I hear the teacher's chair quickly scrape the floor and in a moment she stands over my desk and says oh, look at that! Is that a new toy for my collection? She holds out her hand and says thaaaaaaaaank you, hand it over!

I complain to her that I didn't play with it until *after* I was done with my work, so I didn't do anything wrong!

She takes it anyway and puts it in her desk drawer. I'm really worried, since she gives away the captured toys to anyone *she* decides is good and she says I'm *never* good. I can't let her give away my toy! I come up with a plan.

I talk to another boy who had his toy taken away a few days earlier and tell him that the next time the teacher gets called out of the room I'll run up, go into her desk, and get *both* of our toys. All he needs to do is run to the doorway and tell me when she's coming back! It's a great plan and I *know* it'll work!

A few days later another teacher calls her out of the room. She tells us all to stay at our desks and she'll be back in a few minutes.

Me and the boy look at each other. When she gets to the door I whisper *now!* to the boy and we bolt to our respective spots. The class gasps and a few kids say umm, I don't think you should be doing that. I ignore them since they're all dumb as hell and *just* learning how to read.

I open *all* her drawers and find the one with our stolen toys. There's so many. Too many! I don't have time to sort through them so I dump them onto the floor and find my spinning top, which I pocket, then grab the boy's green-and red-striped ball and pocket that too. The boy loudly whispers *HEY!* and runs back to his seat. I shove all the toys back into the drawer and run back to my seat too.

The teacher walks back into the room not ten seconds later and I try to look at the clock like I'm bored, but I'm breathing kind of heavy. This is the most fun I've had in a while and the teacher asks me why I'm breathing so heavy and I tell her I saw a bee.

Lucky for me some of the other kids grin, nod and say oh yeah, *big* bee, it just flew out!

Because they want to get their stuff back, too.

It's almost lunch time and we're about to go eat but one girl raises her hand and tattles on me! She says to the teacher, Teacher, RJ stole from the desk even though he *knows* he's not *supposed* to do that because it's *against* the rules!

Before I can think, I chuck a pencil eraser at her head and hit her square on her forehead. She cries out in pain then grabs her head and starts to weep like she's at her cat's funeral.

Taking a page from my mother I then yell out you bitch!

The class gasps. The teacher is *furious,* and the girl gets a gold star on her green card, the meaning of which is completely lost on me since I've never gotten one. Probably because I've never told on anyone before. I get a blue card. My eyes are wide as I loudly say fuck me! The class gasps again and the teacher either doesn't hear me or pretends not to.

The teacher tells me to go stand outside since I am in *serious* trouble.

I stand outside for a full ten minutes before I see Aunt Tami's oldest nephew, the one who threw eggs at the shiny red car. We go to the same school, but he's in a grade higher. He's going to the bathroom and sees me standing outside. I quickly tell him I didn't raise my hand too many times before I answered a question, and he says oh, okay and keeps walking.

Our class lines up for lunch and the teacher tells me to get at the back of the line. My shoulders are hanging real low right now and I'm not standing tall or proud at all.

When we get back from lunch, she sees my look of suicidal abandon and sternly tells me that if I'm good all day, *really* good, and if I raise my hand and follow *all* the rules and *everything,* I can get my blue card replaced with an orange card.

Amariah The Boy

I feel a glimmer of hope and my shoulders pick up. My blue card *does* get reduced to an orange card because I follow all the stupid rules even though I feel like a soda bottle that's been shaken hard for three hours. The teacher decides not to call home and I think I'm in the clear.

This is confirmed when Uncle Alex doesn't say anything other than his usual mechanical how was school today? What did you learn? Did you do good?

Aunt Tami is sitting there calmly but something about her feels weird.

I nod and say yeah, school was school, I got a yellow card 'cause I talked before I raised my hand.

Alex says uh-huh, that's good.

Aunt Tami stands up then races around the table, pulls me out of my chair, and screams at me for lying. She says that liars are bad which means *I'm* bad! She shrieks how many times have I lied so far!? She adds when are you NOT lying? She beats my ass so hard that I can't sit for the rest of the day.

I protest in tears afterward that I only got an *orange* card, but she says that her nephew *told her* he saw a blue card on my name. She starts hitting me again and she's pouring all the hate and fury of the world right onto my ass courtesy of her now very-red hand. I hate her stupid weasel-faced nephew and that's what he is.

Uncle Alex's eyes are wide—he didn't expect this at *all* coming home from work and I think it's the first time he's heard anything about it. I yell it isn't fair 'cause Aunt Diane told me to lie and get a free bible. What's the difference one way or another if I'm lying to get a bible or lying about a stupid card! So what if I can't walk on a line to the bathroom? I finish my work before everyone and it's all stupid anyway!

I say I hate this place and I hate them and I wanna go home.

Uncle Alex looks angry and hurt. He sends me to my room and I feel terrible. I think about home back in Georgia. Memories of Mom aren't *good*...but maybe she's changed and is nice now? I hope so.

Roland Amariah Gonzales

First grade comes to an end. The summer of 1992 starts and nothing special happens. Uncle Alex and I patch things up between us as he seems to understand me better and I, him. Aunt Tami and I keep our distance from one another though we maintain some semblance of tolerance. Everything seems like it's gotten back to what passes for normal. That is, until Mom calls the house to tell Alex and Tami that she wants me back.

I partially hear Uncle Alex in the kitchen as he tells Mom in an irate voice that he's already signed me up for second grade. He says getting a plane ticket for RJ so *soon* is going to cost a *lot* of money!

Mom's tiny voice barks through the phone, saying she doesn't care and wants her boy back.

Uncle Alex and Aunt Tami drive me to the airport a couple of weeks later. He's got tears in his eyes and says he's going to miss me. He jokes that I can look forward to not getting spanked every day, now that I'm leaving them. Aunt Tami laughs in agreement and I can tell she's the happiest she's been in a *long* while. Alex gives me a big hug at the boarding gate and I hug him back, because I love him a whole lot.

He says again he's gonna miss me and I tell him I'll miss him as well. Tami gives me a cursory hug and grins like today is Christmas. She says oh *yeah*, I'll miss you too!

I prefer to remember Uncle Alex as being fond of me. I think that, perhaps, he loved me as the son he never had. He disciplined me when I acted up, but never really got into it like Mom did, beating me until she was out of breath. I got the feeling that he *wanted* me to be there. He was honestly happy just to see me grow.

Aunt Tami? She was always different. Behind the thin veneer of her plastic smile and pretty face I felt something cold, menacing, and not at *all* kind. From Day One she made it clear that she held no love for me and resented my living with them.

I'm at the boarding gate and hope I'll see that same pretty airline lady in the red dress, but I don't. It's just some guy in a dark blue suit. I wave goodbye to my uncle and the airline man takes me by the hand then leads me toward the plane.

When I look over my shoulder I see Uncle Alex pull out his dirty blue work kerchief and wipe away his tears, a sad smile on his face as he waves goodbye.

Time to fly back to Mom in Georgia.

CLINTON

I wake up to the pilot's announcement that we're touching down in *Missouri*. I'm half-asleep as I slowly realize in a panic that I'm landing in the wrong place! I try to tell the dark- blue-suit flight guy, but he's busy.

I sit with the other passengers while we're landing, full of worry.

After the plane lands, the dark-blue-suit airline guy helps me grab my backpack and leads me off the plane toward Baggage Claim. I nervously say to him hey mister, I think I'm in the wrong place, I'm supposed to be in Georgia.

His eyes go wide for a moment before he double-checks my ticket, then tells me it reads Missouri.

He stays with me for a couple of minutes until Mom recognizes me from the crowd, calls out my name, then walks toward me with a smile. The man hands me over to Mom and waves goodbye.

Mom hugs me real hard, so I hug her back. She's hugging me and there's no one around, so I know it's just for me, but I don't feel anything like I did when Uncle Alex hugged me. I wonder why.

She sees my backpack and says is this it? Is this *all* they sent you back with?

I can see she's getting angry.

I say no Mom, Uncle Alex and Aunt Tami bought me a suitcase, but it's not here yet. Maybe it's still in the plane's belly.

She says oh, good.

Summer break is about halfway-over and I've got California-summer clothes and California-winter clothes. Mom's real happy that I have so many clothes. I wait with her until the suitcase arrives, then we're off to the car.

The drive from the airport is long and there's nowhere *near* as many buildings from Kansas City to my new home in Clinton. While we drive, she tells me she's still with Randy and they're happy.

I think to myself oh, the guy you cheated on Dad with.

Roland Amariah Gonzales

Mom drives to a small mobile home similar to what we lived in, back in Georgia. It's tan and ugly-yellow in color, like an infection. We live next to train tracks and our only neighbors are an elderly Black couple, Harold and his wife Winifred. Mom introduces me to them and I'm polite and respectful but don't know them so well, so I keep my distance.

Mom works at a fast-food place and when she gets home she smells like french fries and hamburgers, which is great. Every now and then, Randy takes me to see Mom and to get a hamburger. Sometimes, Mom has to dress up like a clown if it's someone's birthday. On one such occasion, I see a boy stomp on her giant clown shoes and laugh at her. Mom smiles her not-smile and tells him not to do that.

The boy looks at her indignantly and does it again! I push the boy over and he starts crying and now *his* mom is yelling at *me*.

Randy drags me out of the place and now I'm not allowed to go there when Mom's working. When Mom sees me at home she hugs me and says her little man was just looking out for her! She says how *much* she loves me.

I don't know why I pushed the boy over...I smile when she hugs me, but I don't feel anything again, and again I don't know why.

Amariah The Boy

Mom puts me in a summer school program. I ride the school bus in the morning and that same bus home in the early afternoon. There are some Black kids, all from the same family, who live nearby and they ride the bus with me. I don't talk to them or anyone, because no one seems nice, so I just try to look out the window and be invisible the whole ride.

One day, I'm riding the bus back home and a little girl from that family says to me hey you. Hey!

I ignore her and look out the window, counting the streets before I get home. Only five to go. I'm so close. A paper ball hits me in the eye and I look up, angry. The girl says hey, how come you look so *dumb*, and her siblings laugh like she's the funniest person in the *whole world*. I reply well, it takes dumb to *know* dumb!

A couple of other kids on the bus laugh at her. The girl doesn't like that one bit and now she's *real* mad and throwing *more* things at me! I think to myself, only two more stops to go.

A heavy eraser bounces off my forehead *hard* and it hurts. I don't know why they're being so mean! I tell her with angry tears in my eyes that her momma is gonna spank her for acting so bad.

I must've flipped some kind of *crazy* switch 'cause now she and her two brothers are wild-eyed, like Aunt Tami's angry dogs. Spit is flying from their mouths as they scream at me and call me all *kinds* of bad names. We get to our bus stop and the bus driver yells for everyone to calm down and more importantly get the *hell* off his bus!

I don't move 'cause they're *still* screaming at me, telling me how they're going to beat me up and to get off the bus first so they can kick me down the stairs and beat me up.

The bus driver makes them get off the bus first and they just stand outside, waiting for me. He honks the horn and yells, go on, now! You better git or you can walk yoself to school and tell yo momma *why* you gotta walk!

The girl and her brothers shout some nasty words at the bus driver, then at me. They say they're gonna beat my ass and tell me to hurry up so they can kick the shit out of me.

One of them hurls rocks at the bus! The driver roars YOU *LITTLE* SONOFABITCH! and starts to get out of the bus, but they scream and run off, *still* yelling nasty things.

He watches them until they're down at the next road then shakes his head and says to me in a tired voice alright boy, you go on now and run on home too, I can't stay here forever.

I get out and as *soon* as he drives away those kids all run back with rocks and start hurling them at me! I'm scared and my heart is pounding as I run as fast as I can to my house. The door is locked and Mom isn't home! I damn near have a heart attack. I hear the girl and her brothers scream that they're gonna beat me until I'm dead and throw me in a ditch. Just then, my neighbor Harold yells from inside his house what in the hell is going on out there?

I run to his door. He sees me, grabs me, then shoves me behind him and yells at the three kids you go on and git now! He tells them he's known their momma since she was a little girl and they can bet their *backsides* that she's gonna whoop 'em all *real* good if they don't git right now.

They leave after swearing some more at me and Harold takes me inside. Harold's wife Winifred asks what in Jesus name is all this fuss about?

Harold tells her that the Johnson kids are acting up again, she gives a great big sigh, shakes her head, and says lord have mercy. She says to me now you jus' go right ahead and sit yoself right here on this sofa, honey chile. She brings me some sweet tea and a plate of shortbread cookies filled with strawberry jam. If I was confused why those kids were so mean before then I'm doubly so for why Winifred is so *nice*. Is she going to make me pull her weeds?

I sniffle a bit, still pretty shaken up, when Harold sits next to me. He puts his hand on my knee and softly says now boy, don't you go wastin' them tears on those kids or nothin' else, ya hear me? Lookit me when I'm talkin' to you now, it's bad manners not to look at folk when they're talkin' to you.

I look up expecting to see him angry and am surprised to see he's more concerned than anything. He says now listen son, tears ain't gonna make no one *like* you and they sure as hell ain't gonna make bad people good, ya hear me? You gotta be a man, ya undahstand? Where's yo daddy at? Is he here?

I shake my head no and choke a bit on the sweet tea, coughing before I tell Harold that my dad's in California.

Amariah The Boy

Winifred sits herself right next to us and says hush now Harold, he jus' a baby, don't you go tellin' him he needs to be a man jus' yet. Then she turns to me and says how old are you, baby?

I say with a mouthful of cookies that I'm almost seven.

She gapes at me in disbelief and says you're six now? Baby, you don' look no more than three! *Maybe* four! Now hey, don't talk with your mouth full, it's impolite, ya hear?

I start to say sorry but my mouth is full, so I stop and nod instead. She turns to Harold and says, see hun, he's just *six,* then she looks at me again and repeats *really* now? Are you sure?

I look at her, raise my eyebrows. Of course, I'm sure! I know how old I am, I'm not dumb. I nod again, keeping my mouth shut, then I swallow and inform her that I'm *almost* seven.

Winifred shakes her head and repeats, Lord have mercy, but you're small! then drinks some tea.

Harold gets a frown on his face and starts nodding a little faster while rocking his body back and forth. He mutters to himself...ain't got no daddy or *nothin'.* Then looks me square in the eyes and says boy, I can *promise* you that if you don' go and toughen up *real* quick, you gonna have a harder time than most folk, *'specially* 'round here.

A frown is on my face now and I ask well, what am I supposed to do? They were throwing things and saying all kinds of awful things to me and I didn't even do nothin'! All I said was their momma was gonna give 'em a whoopin' for acting so mean to me!

Harold says ain't *no one* whooped those kids in a good *long* while. Hell, that's they problem! No sir, if you gotta be 'round them then you bes' off makin' friends with one of 'em when they all alone. Now, they don't like you 'cause you different and that's *sad,* but that's the *truth.* And don't talk 'bout their momma at all! Mos' folks don't take kindly to that, unless you know 'em and are askin' if their momma's okay.

I nod my head and they both get up and mill about their home. I must have fallen asleep before I feel Winifred gently shake my leg. She says about an hour's gone by and that Mom's home now, and I can go on, if I like.

I hug them both goodbye and go home. From that day on, Harold and Winifred are the grandpa and grandma that I've been sorely missing.

I don't see the crazy girl or her brothers on the bus after they get in trouble with the school for throwing rocks *at* the bus. I do, however, encounter the youngest brother, Jimmy, when I'm walking on the road near my house, right after school starts in September.

I like to go on walks and look at all the trees as they quietly shed their red, gold, and purple leaves, each one a schoolgirl playing he loves me, he loves me not.

I see Jimmy walking along the road opposite me and call out hey Jimmy! Hey!

He looks up at me before his eyes get real wide, and now he's running away from me. I run after him and yell hey, Jimmy I just want to talk! Hey, will you stop, please? and I catch up to him.

He looks terrified and starts to cry not to hurt him and quickly says he didn't do *nuthin'* and his sister's the one who's so mean, not him!

I don't know *how* he got the idea that I'm gonna hurt *him,* since they were the ones chasing *me,* not the other way around! I say Jimmy, I just want to play kickball with someone and ask if he can play with me. He wipes his tears away before his face breaks into a wide grin. For a second I can feel that he doesn't have any friends either and is real lonely too.

We kick a ball back and forth in the dirt field which separates my house from Harold and Winifred's. Winifred sees us playing and comes sit outside to watch us with a smile on her face and gives us some sweet tea when we're thirsty. A couple of hours go by until late afternoon when I wave goodbye to Jimmy 'cause he hears his mom calling.

Jimmy and I play together a few more times and I ask if he can show me his house, since he knows where I live. He's hesitant at first but then he takes me along the railroad tracks. As we walk together we pick up rocks then toss 'em into the stream that runs quietly nearby.

There's some honeysuckle blooming nearby and we both delight in plucking the flowers and savoring the sweet taste. We even find some wild berries growing along the way! When we get close to his house I hear shouting and angry sounds from adults. Jimmy looks at me real quick and says in a hushed tone that he can't play no more today and he's gotta go home. I'm sad but say okay and go home.

I go back to Jimmy's the next morning to see if he can play. As I get close to the house I hear more yelling so I drop down real low and move quietly behind the bushes and plants, careful not to make any noise. I'm a soldier now, sneaking behind enemy lines! I grab a stick like it's a gun and rub some dirt under my eyes like I saw on TV.

Amariah The Boy

I find a nice spot behind a tree where I can spy on everything that's going on. There are so many people living in this house! I can't say for sure, but I'm guessing that I can see Jimmy's mom, grandma, some other adults, of course Jimmy's mean older sister and brother from the bus, and I think his much-older brother, but no Jimmy.

Jimmy's much-older brother is pacing back and forth like a panther I saw one time at a zoo. He looks *real* mad, and when people get in his way he shoves them hard. Jimmy's mom is trying to say something to the much-older brother and grabs him by the arm, but he doesn't like that one bit so he pushes her *hard* and she falls over. The men shout at him, but no one tries to stop him and he just keeps walking back and forth. Sometimes he even punches himself in the head!

Now Jimmy's grandma is yelling something at the much-older brother, but he doesn't care about that either. Jimmy's mean older sister is yelling something too, and she's throwing her arms up and down and crying. The much-older brother screams something at all of them, but I can't tell what he's saying 'cause it doesn't make any sense. He walks over to a window and punches it, and now there's blood *pouring* out of his arm!

Jimmy's momma, grandma, and sister are screaming and my eyes go wide. I finally notice Jimmy sitting against a tree. He's just staring at the ground. I quietly turn around, stay low, get to the railroad tracks, then run on back home.

I don't see Jimmy or his siblings after that...I think they moved. I never go back to that house again.

Roland Amariah Gonzales

I'm in second grade now and Mom calls Grandma Margaret to get money for school clothes. The ones that Uncle Alex and Aunt Tami sent with me don't fit anymore and Mom says it's gonna get too cold for California clothes anyway.

I talk to Grandma and tell her I love and miss her, then she sends money to Mom.

Mom takes me to some place called Second-hand. We look around for clothes and she lets me pick out what I want. After that, we go to the dollar store to get school supplies. I get pencils, a neat eraser shaped like a dragon, and a small box of crayons.

Winter in Missouri is a whole lot colder than winter in Georgia. The sudden shock of freezing weather and stinging cold nips at my nose, ears, and fingers! I bundle up in whatever jackets or coats we have. At first, I use Randy's extra coat, since Mom forgot to get me one at Second-hand. When I ask her, she says she used the rest of Grandma's money to buy us food.

Some of the kids in my class ask why my coat is so big. I just shrug and say I dunno.

Second grade in Missouri is *much* easier than California's first grade. In Mrs. Cook's room there are no color cards *or* calling home if you mess up too much. We even have nap time with snacks which I enjoy the most, 'cause eating and sleeping are two things that I'm *really* good at.

The school in Missouri is not just easier but also different. All the classrooms are connected with hallways in *one big building* and we only go outside for recess. In California all the classrooms were separate from the cafeteria, the gym, the bathroom or the auditorium and you had to go outside to go from one to the other.

I'm finally being challenged for the first time when mathematics gets more complicated, with the inclusion of long addition and subtraction. I have trouble with long subtraction and have to stay inside to finish my worksheet while everyone else plays outside during recess. Mrs. Cook says I shouldn't have been goofing off in class!

I look down at the worksheet and stare at all the numbers to try and make sense of them. Recess is almost over and I haven't gotten to play *at all.* I say to the teacher look, can you just tell me if this is long subtraction or short subtraction, because I need to know which one it is so I can do this.

Amariah The Boy

She says do the problem the way I showed you in class and you'll find out. But none of the numbers make sense and I swear the way she showed us is different from how we did it in California...and I just don't get it. If I look at the numbers for too long I start to think of anything else and it makes me upset because I want to go outside and play.

Recess is over and all the kids are back in the classroom. One of them asks me why I didn't go outside and another says oh, RJ had to stay inside 'cause he's dumb! and a lot of the kids laugh.

I hate being stuck inside. I hate feeling trapped in one place. It feels awful! I love going outside and I enjoy the swings most of all. It's the wind, the feeling of it rushing through my hair and over my face. Sometimes, I swing *so high* that I almost fly over the top before I come crashing down. The recess teacher doesn't like it though and blows her whistle. She warns me to stop, or I'll get hurt!

...but I don't care. I want to go higher and higher into the sky, and I get a little closer every time.

Most of the playground is set on old cracked and faded-gray asphalt, though there's the occasional patch of grass here and some trees there. There's a jungle gym but it's old and looks dirty as hell, so I don't go near it too often. We have a seesaw as well but all the boys like to jump off when the other side is high up in the air and the girls won't ride it with me.

One time, a kid bit his tongue when his friend jumped off! He was screaming and hollering and blood was *pouring* out of his mouth! So I stay away from the seesaws and stick to the swings.

I get into a fight with another kid who steals my turn on the swings. This is after I have to get out of line when the recess teacher calls me over to ask where I got my coat and why it's so big. When I get back to the swings the boy tells me with a smug look on his face finders-keepers!

I say nuh-uh! and tell him I had to go talk to the recess teacher and it's *my* turn! Then I order him to get off the swing!

He tells me *nope,* and now he's swinging and saying how great swinging is.

I try to grab the swing to force him off and he tries to kick me in the head.

I get real mad because he *stole* my swing, so I walk over to where there's some tiny gravel, like you find in a fish-tank, grab a handful and throw it at him.

Roland Amariah Gonzales

He jumps off the swing and now we're throwing fistfuls of rocks at each other and the recess lady is blowing her whistle, but we're not stopping.

She's red in the face from blowing her whistle so much! She reminds me of the tomato face lady my mom talked to that one time at the airport as she runs up to us. She pulls us apart, because we've already run out of rocks and now we're smacking the hell out of each other. She says lord in heaven, what is *wrong* with you two and yanks us apart by our coats while we're *still* swinging at each other.

She takes us to the guidance counselor and I try to explain that the boy *stole* my swing and I can't let *anyone* steal from me, but she doesn't care! The punishment is *super* unfair. She says we can't go back to recess *ever again* until we each write "I will not throw rocks" one hundred times. I have enough trouble writing *five* sentences, let alone a hundred!

Eager to do anything *but* those sentences, I make the most of the art teacher's open-door creative-process policy. She tells the class if you feel that your work isn't your *very best*, please feel free to come in and work on it so you can fully express yourself.

I spend the next school week of recess time hiding in the art room and working on my clay-spider-family project to avoid punishment, much to the annoyance of the art teacher. After four days she says come on kid, you're cutting into my smoke break. And then she complains that I'm there *every day* and asks how many spiders do you need to make?

I tell her that I've made a sister for the brother but now I need the mommy to have a boyfriend...*plus* daddy...and they all have to be *perfect.* I keep adding new spiders to the family for as long as I can keep this up and, oh hey, this one looks kind of good.

I ask the art teacher if I can get some paint to color one of the spiders pink with green polka dots. She sighs and shakes her head then mumbles something as she goes to the supply cupboard. She doesn't seem happy.

I feel bad about taking her smoke break away, but not so bad that I want to write those stupid sentences. It wasn't even my fault, I didn't steal anything, *he* did! He should have to write *I will not steal swings like the stupid jerk-face I am* a hundred times! *Plus* another hundred for throwing rocks!

Amariah The Boy

At the end of the week the guidance counselor comes to the art room and says I finally *found* you, little mister! She asks why I haven't turned in my sentences yet. The art teacher raises her eyebrows and says *oh,* so *that's* why you're here.

The guidance counselor is annoyed and tells me that the other kid turned his sentences in the *next day* after he was told to write them! She asks why I'm taking so long.

I tell her I need to work on my art project and it's *super* important. She looks at the art teacher who shakes her head *nope* and then the guidance counselor shakes her head and walks out.

The next day, the art teacher says ok RJ, you've made enough spiders...what do you have now, eight?

I object and say no, ma'am, I've only got six. I made a spiderdog, too.

She doesn't care and sends me to the guidance counselor's office where I sit with a furled brow and write those sentences.

Roland Amariah Gonzales

I'm excited to turn in the sentences and go back outside for recess, so I can be around the girl I like. Her name is Stephanie and she's the *prettiest* girl in second grade. She's fair-skinned, with narrow brown eyes that squint and get smaller if she smiles real wide. She's got freckles on her soft round face, and shoulder-length brunette hair. Sometimes she wears a little bow clipped to her hair.

I follow her around as often as I can, much to her dismay, because she doesn't like me back. She tells me I'm gross and that's all she says to me.

Her birthday comes around and her mom helps her bake chocolate brownies for the class. She passes out a square to every kid in class and gives one to Mrs. Cook too. She then says with a great big smile that two of the brownies have chocolate chips in them for people she *really* likes. When she smiles this time her eyes are the squintiest I've ever seen and I sigh 'cause I think I'm in love.

I quickly take a bite and say hey Stephanie, I got your chocolate chip!

She looks at me like I just tried to kiss her dog right on its butt then leans close to me and says quietly, but matter-of-factly, no you did not. I did not give you one because I do not like you, RJ. I think you're disgusting.

I'm stunned and sad and I think that's the most she's ever said to me other than ew, go away.

I laugh quietly with both a broken smile and broken heart, then look down at my desk and let the rest of the brownie sit there. When we all clear our desks for a math test, I quietly throw it away with the napkin. I don't know *why* she doesn't like me. I never did *nothin'* to her and I'm nice around her all the time.

I don't try to follow her around during recess anymore. I just stay by the swings.

Puppy love is the *worst* kind of love and I fall victim to it *constantly*. The first girl I knew was the love of my life wore a pink cowgirl outfit to class every day during kindergarten. That was in Georgia, around 1991. Mom and Dad had just divorced so Mom, Randy and I moved to some other house. I didn't have any friends nearby until I found out that my classmate lived down the road. I was allowed to walk there by myself because it was only three minutes away and Mom said she didn't give a shit where I went or what I did, and she said I can go and get hit by a car for all she cared.

Amariah The Boy

This girl often invited me over to play a fun game where both of us laid down in the middle of the road and then waited for a truck to come get us. She said she'd seen this in a scary movie called *Pet Sematary* and that we'd live forever after the truck came, 'cause that's what she saw in the movie.

I wasn't sure about her game and I never heard of the movie. I was just happy to be around her because I thought she was real pretty, and she said she liked me.

When no trucks came or when she got bored, she'd look kind of sad and say well, maybe tomorrow, then she'd give me a great big hug and that was my favorite part! The hug from her felt like eating cotton candy but all over.

She had a little sister around the same age as Gracie, two years old or so. This girl loved watching how fire danced at the end of a lighter and played with lighters any time she could get ahold of them. She loved to burn cardboard or paper or even clothes. If her parents saw her playing with fire they'd smack the lighter out of her hand and yell at her and she'd cry, but a lighter somehow *always* found its way back into the clutch of her little fist.

My friend didn't play with fire but she didn't stop her sister from doing it either. I was confused how her sister could even *use* the lighter because when I tried at home with Mom's, I couldn't at all. My friend told me that *her* mom took the lock-thing off because she was tired of the hassle.

I left home to go play at my friend's house one day, but there was no house. All that was left were black and smoky ruins. I didn't say anything to Mom, since she was busy drinking from her brown bottle and only screamed at me when I interrupted her.

The next day, I asked my teacher where the girl in the pink-cowgirl outfit had gone and the teacher told me the girl wouldn't be coming to class anymore because her family had moved somewhere very far away.

I was sad. I thought the girl really liked me, but she didn't say goodbye or *anything* and now I had no one to play with or lay down in the road with.

I never laid down in the road again after that. I didn't really understand how the game worked and didn't want to mess up doing it by myself.

75

Roland Amariah Gonzales

With Jimmy and his family gone, I've got no one to play with. None of the other kids like being around me in school and I never get invited to play at anyone's house. Mom speaks to some girl's mom at a parent-teacher conference, and the other mom has her daughter invite me to her birthday party. The girl lets me know when I arrive that the *only* reason I'm there is 'cause her mom *made* her invite me.

I bring her a Little Foot toy dinosaur from the movie *The Land Before Time*, a really good movie that was real sad too. I cried a whole bunch, but I really liked it. I get the dinosaur at a toy store and I give it to her. She unwraps it and says thanks, then tosses it in with all the wrapping paper trash. I sit off in the corner and wait for Mom to pick me up. I don't go to any birthday parties after that.

Spring arrives and all the snow melts away. Lacking any kids to play with, I spend my time in both nature and my imagination. The train tracks near my home are a fun place, though there are never any trains. I like to pretend that a circus train comes to town and I run away and join it. I leave town with a bunch of really exciting new friends, and they all like me and show me how to walk the tightrope and tame lions, too.

When it gets hot I like to collect tar from the lumber under the train track's metal rails. The tar semi-melts under the scorching heat of the Missouri sun, making it sticky and painful to touch. But if I'm careful, I can use a stick, a rock, or a rusty piece of rebar to gather up a bunch and then I've got myself a big glob of tar!

I gather tar balls and place them on rocks or throw them. Sometimes they *splat* and stick to things. I like how they feel sticky and squishy once they cool down a bit. They've got a nice smell too, like gasoline.

Branching away from the train tracks are trails that lead to the great unknown.

I explore as many as I can before nightfall. I'm seven now and Mom says I can explore outside by myself until the sun goes down. I find more honeysuckles and wild berries which I eat straight from the vine. I think of Jimmy and I'm sad that I haven't seen him in a long time and wonder where he went to.

A creek runs the full length of my favorite trail, and it's home to crawdads. I play with them by trying to pick them up without getting pinched and then toss them back into the creek as I make airplane noises. I wonder if they appreciate sailing through the air like I did when Dad threw me up and into the pool.

Amariah The Boy

I leave the house in the morning and come back when I need to use the bathroom or want some water or food. I never see *any* other kids around and I wonder if I'm the only one out here. There's nobody to play with...where *is* everyone?

I watch a really neat show on TV where a guy on a bike goes real fast and zooms up a ramp and over a bunch of stuff and I decide that I can probably do it too. So I ride my bike around the area and search for a spot that kind of looks like a ramp, then spend the next five minutes getting motivated. I ride up to it and probably stop a dozen times before I say to myself okay, I can do this.

I build up as much speed as I can, starting from some lady's front yard and head toward a steep drainage ditch, about fifteen feet (5m). My plan is to fly over the road and the ditch, but instead I hit the far side of the ditch and the bike's handlebars slam into my throat. I crumple onto the ground. I wheeze and gasp for air as my body rolls into the ditch.

I lie face-down in the ditch and struggle to breathe...and I can't. I'm afraid to touch my throat. What if it's crushed? Am I about to die? I spend a moment thinking how lucky I am that the ditch is empty of water.

I start to breathe, but shakily, then I roll onto my back. My throat hurts real bad. With trembling hands I feel my throat and neck, then I slowly draw my hand away to see if there's any blood. I can't look for a moment, and then I squint and see nothing red.

I start to move the rest of my body, my arms and legs, to see if anything is broken, then I stand up and kick my bike for hurting me.

I sob through the pain as I walk my bike home. When cars pass by I look away so they can't see my face... it's red with shame and tears of pain. I'm an idiot.

When I get home, Mom isn't home...like usual.

No one's here.

Roland Amariah Gonzales

Grandma Margaret's husband was named Flavian, though everyone called him Irish. He's not my mom's blood father, though he very much filled the role of being her dad. Grandpa Irish was a charitable and compassionate old man who spent his time on skid row in Los Angeles, doing what he could to help the homeless, the drug-addicted, and the lost.

He eventually took a knife to his side from a crazed drug addict as thanks for his efforts, though that didn't end him.

Grandpa Irish had these little chocolate-wafer sweets that he kept hidden way up in the cupboard where no one but him could reach, 'cause he was so tall. Grandma Margaret gifted me with a little green and yellow dragon costume. She told me to put it on then go scare Grandpa. Irish would act real scared, then give me a chocolate treat so I didn't roar more or breathe fire.

Mom, Dad, and I live in a rough part of Artesia, which at the time was known as the 190s. There are shootings, stabbings, drive-bys, and lots of other crime there and Mom says don't go outside or someone will snatch you up. It turns out that danger isn't only outside when a man high on PCP kicks down our front door.

I *immediately* jump into action.

I hear Mom scream and I look up to see a crazy-looking scary man, so I immediately bolt for my room and frantically put on my dragon costume. I run back out and roar at the man with my wing arms outstretched.

I cannot fathom what the man saw in his drug-addled state of mind as a two-year-old dragon child suddenly appeared and roared at him. This crazy man stares at me in bewilderment, shock, and confusion. Dad comes into the kitchen from the garage, sees what's happening, and retrieves his home-defense door guard, a 2 x 4 plank of wood. He swings it directly at the man's face, and so hard that it breaks the wood! The man blinks twice, mumbles something about airports and jellybeans, then leaves.

Just before we move to Georgia, Grandpa Irish dies of throat cancer. The man loved his cigars.

Grandma Margaret gives me a small jewelry box with Grandpa Irish's gentleman accessories. She says I'm the only man in the family and it's important for a man to look proper, Irish would want me to have it. Grandma Margaret says Irish loved me very much and he's always watching over me. I cry and cry because Grandpa Irish is gone.

Amariah The Boy

After the headache from too many tears goes away, I hold the box close and keep it in my room. Grandma says I'd better protect it and keep it out of sight so people can't steal it.

After a week of hiding it in my room, I open up the treasure box and see that it contains cufflinks, button cuffs, and other assorted fine wear for an upstanding gentleman. I put on a button-down shirt from both Grandpa Irish's funeral and my Mom and Dad's wedding, then I add all of my grandpa's nice shiny stuff and look in the mirror.

I wonder if I'll be big like him someday. He could reach *every* cupboard. I think of Grandpa Irish and cry some more. I look at the shiny things one last time and am *extra* careful when I put them back in the box, because that's what Grandpa Irish would have wanted.

I return home from school one day in mid-April, five years later, and think of Grandpa Irish. We had a writing assignment in Mrs. Cook's class about describing our grandpas and grandmas. As I walk home from the bus stop I think of taking out the box. I used to talk it like it was a telephone to heaven. I haven't seen the box since before Mom sent me to live with Uncle Alex and Aunt Tami.

I search my room carefully then *ransack* it as I desperately search for Grandpa's jewelry box. It's important for a man to look proper and I can't look proper without it! Where is it? Grandpa Irish wanted me to have it and I can't find it! I didn't lose it. I couldn't have!

Mom hears all the noise and calls out from another room, Rol what are you *doing* in there; you sound like a tornado! Then she laughs at her observation.

I pause for a moment. I think of how to say this and whether I might get in trouble. There's no way around it so I say hey, Mom have you seen Grandpa Irish's box? The one that Grandma gave me.

Mom is at first quiet, then I hear her walk to my bedroom. I freeze for a moment in fear, since I think she's coming to hit me. But instead, she slowly approaches the door and she's real quiet. She sheepishly says she lost it when she moved all our things from Georgia here to Missouri.

I'm stunned. I can't believe it. I can barely get any words out before I start crying and yelling no!

Mom hugs me, and now I'm babbling and sobbing. How could she lose it? I say Grandpa Irish is *dead* and he's gone *forever* and now I've got *nothin'* to remember his face!

79

Roland Amariah Gonzales

Mom rubs my back and holds me close and tells me how sorry she is and how sometimes things just go missing.

I think to myself wait a second. Mom is *never* this nice.

I don't believe her and so I press her and ask her *how could she lose it,* Grandpa was like her *dad,* she said so!

She changes her attitude like a light switch, gets angry and says fine, you know what? You want to pout and give me attitude? You can pout here in your room! Then she closes the door with me in there. I hear the TV volume go up.

I weep and scream in anger and kick the trash can in my room. I throw things around 'cause I'm *sure* she lost it on purpose just to make me sad.

Mom comes back into my room and smacks my face for misbehaving and I get grounded to my room for a week.

Amariah The Boy

Second grade comes to an end in the summer of 1993 and we move to a small apartment complex that's got four neighbors. I'm sad that I have to say goodbye to Harold and Winifred, but they say we'll still be in the same town and I can stop by whenever I like.

Mom says that won't be a problem.

The new home is okay. All the neighbors are nice though no one has the same feeling as Harold and Winifred.

A small creek runs near our building and I walk to it often to see if there's anything interesting floating around. There are no kids my age, so I spend my free time throwing rocks into the creek or playing in a small patch of river birch trees nearby. Gone are the warnings of snakes everywhere in the grass, trees, and water, since they're not too common out here, though Mom says to be careful all the same.

I branch out and explore a wider area of surroundings, though I can't go too far because Mom says I'm still too little, even though I'm seven going on eight. If I beg hard enough, she takes me to the park and helps me fly the kite she got for me from the dollar store. I watch it soar in the air and remember when I flew from California to here, when I lived in the clouds. I lose myself as I imagine drifting along with the breeze, free and high up in the sky.

It's hard to get Mom to take me to the park 'cause when she and Randy aren't at work they say they're going out to a place called the Newsroom. I don't know what the Newsroom is but they come back drunk every time, so most of the time I'm by myself. When they don't go out and drink they stay home and smoke some stuff that Mom calls weed and it smells awful. Sometimes Mom forgets where she puts her weed and she yells at me for hiding it, but I never do! I don't wanna touch it 'cause it stinks worse than their cigarettes.

Whenever Mom says she's not taking me to the park, I go outside and find a quiet tree to climb or lay under and listen to the nearby stream as it gently moves over the rocks. When the day is windy and the clouds are sailing overhead, I close my eyes and feel the wind rush through my hair. It feels like I don't weigh anything, and I could even float away if I wanted to.

The summer passes by quickly, a blur of poking around the trees and creek next to the house, walking or riding my small bike as far away from the house as I dare, and begging Mom or Randy to take me to the park or go on a long drive with them on back-country roads.

Roland Amariah Gonzales

As the chill of autumn approaches, Mom decides that she wants a dog. She tells me that even though it's *her* dog, he's *my* responsibility and I have to clean up all of his poops.

I don't like that idea very much.

The dog is a fantastic Labrador with soft white fur and he's my very best friend. He's my only friend. I name him Rock since, when I throw a ball, he chases it and then brings me back a rock instead.

Rock and I run around the area as far as I can go and we eventually meet a kid who lives far down the road.

It's especially cold now in late September. The creek has frozen over and the boy teaches me a game called Let's Jump on the Ice Covering This Creek and See if it Breaks. We stick to the ice near the bank of the creek, so when we smash it we don't fall in.

I play the game by myself as the weather gets colder and no one is there to play with me.

It's an arctic night, the night before, and I excitedly put on all of my winter clothes and rush out to the creek with Rock in the early morning. I jump up and down on the ice near the bank but it won't break 'cause it's so thick, so I go a little further out, then a bit more, until suddenly I'm standing in the middle of the creek...but don't realize it.

Rock barks at me a few times but he doesn't budge from the bank.

I look down and see water moving under the ice. I mutter oh no, it looks real deep here. I say to Rock on second thought, Rock, you stay right there, 'cause I don't wanna fall in.

I take a couple of steps back toward Rock and the bank then hear a crack. I stop moving. My eyes go wide as I look at Rock. He stopped barking and whines a little. The ice breaks under my feet and I yell in surprise.

I fall through the ice and there's a flash of burning pain... it's so cold I can't think straight, and Rock is barking at me while I hold onto the ice and I say oh no, oh no! over and over.

I'm in the icy water so long that I can't feel my legs, and the water is pulling me under the ice, so I hold on as best as I can. I look around for help but no one's there and I'm all alone and it's so cold.

Rock jumps back and forth on the bank and he's barking like mad. He barks a bit more then rushes toward me and I think he's trying to bite me so I move my arm away, but he keeps trying and bites down on my arm and I cry out in pain.

Amariah The Boy

Rock tugs me out of the creek toward the bank, then he licks my face and I'm so cold.

I say oh no, Rock my legs don't work, I can't walk, boy.

I start crying 'cause I'm scared they'll have to chop off my legs, since they don't work anymore. I mumble over and over oh no, Rock, my legs won't work.

It's hard to think.

I try to crawl to the house by pulling myself forward with my hands across frozen grass, but there's too much snow on top. I still can't feel my legs.

I'm going to be in so much trouble if Mom sees me like this.

Rock nuzzles my face and barks and pulls me by my jacket toward the house. Together, both of us shivering with cold, we make our way back home. I'm breathing really hard and shaking about as much, but I manage to get my hand around the doorknob and get inside.

My hands and my whole body are shivering so much that it's almost impossible to take off my soaked clothes. I somehow manage and then put them on the radiator. Rock sits next to it so he can get warm too.

I crawl toward the bathroom and fill the bathtub.

I remember a class we took on cold safety and how you can't go from ice-cold weather to hot water or you might hurt yourself, so I make the water warm and not hot and just sit in the bathtub for a long time. I can feel my legs pretty quickly and now they're burning and red and they *hurt so much* that I miss when I couldn't feel anything at all! After forever, the pain finally goes away.

Mom and Randy are out at the Newsroom. Mom says I'm old enough to be on my own now 'cause I'm seven. If she finds out I did something stupid then I'll get a whoopin' *and* she might get a mean babysitter again! I carefully get out of the bathtub and am happy to see that I can walk. No one's going to chop off my legs yet!

I throw all my wet clothes into the washing machine and use a towel to dry off Rock as best as I can, then wash that towel too. I hold Rock close and we both shiver under a blanket next to the radiator. He licks my face and I make him promise not to tell anyone.

Mom and Randy get home from the bar. I'm already dry and changed into fresh clothes and they don't know anything about me falling into the creek and Rock doesn't say anything either because he's a good boy.

Roland Amariah Gonzales

A week later, Mom notices a tear in my jacket from when Rock pulled me out of the water and she asks what happened to it. I glance over to her and her brown booze bottle then quickly look back at the TV so she won't get mad at me for looking at her drink. Mom gets real mean when she drinks. I tell a little white lie and say, um, Rock and me were playing outside and he accidentally tore it.

Mom is pissed because Rock *just* got in trouble the day before for chewing on her shoes. I forgot. She calls Rock into the room, holds the jacket up to his face, then yells no!

Before he can get away, she hits him on the nose with a rolled-up newspaper. Rock yelps and tries to run, but she holds onto his collar.

I feel awful. It's my fault for jumping on the ice in the first place. I yell to Mom it was just an *accident* and Rock didn't mean to! He's sorry!

Mom keeps on whacking Rock and she's got that *mean* look in her eyes, like Rock did all the evil in the world to her. I try to leave and she says no Rol, you need to watch this, you need to *beat* this *fucking dog* when he's bad, capiche? Otherwise he'll *never* learn!

I'm horrified as she whacks him more and more and Rock yelps in pain.

Mom lets go of Rock and he runs to my room with his tail between his legs, yelping all the way. I go after him and hear Mom mutter she ain't got time for all this shit before she turns up the TV.

When I get to my room, Rock is hiding in my closet. He flinches then whimpers when I hug him around the neck. I tell him it's all my fault and how sorry I am. I bury my face in his soft fur and tell him he's *such a good boy.* He's such a good boy and I love him so much and I'm sorry. He licks my face and I start crying again, but I don't know why.

STAYING WITH DAD

Third grade is just *barely* underway in the small town of Clinton in 1993. After the first week, Mom asks if I want to go visit my dad out in California. I'm surprised 'cause I never thought in a million years I'd hear her ask me that. I say yeah, sure. Of course! - you mean next summer? What about Rock? Who'll watch him?

She looks through me and doesn't respond for a while, nodding to herself while holding a bottle in one hand and a cigarette in the other. She absentmindedly says yeah, that'll work.

But she wasn't talking about *next* summer. Mom drives me to Kansas City the following Monday to board a plane back to California. She says that I'm going to Redondo Beach where Kenney lives with his new wife and my sister Gracie. Mom never tells me why she's sending me out to Dad, and I don't ask. I wanna see him real bad, and that's enough for me.

I'm sad about leaving Rock with Mom and hope he doesn't get into trouble while I'm gone. Mom says she'll take *good* care of him and not to worry. When she tells me not to worry, it usually means I should worry!

I fly with the same airline company from before, and since I've flown by myself already, it's less of a hassle for everyone. Mom gives me a quick hug at the gate and hands me over to the airline lady who walks me to my seat.

This time the airline lady is old. She's not as pretty as the airline lady a year ago, but still, she's nice. She brings me a bag of honey-roasted peanuts and says if I need anything to let her know.

I'm only a little scared when I fly this time. I can't wait to see Dad! I don't even mind that I have to see Gracie, too.

The flight is easy, and I marvel at the night lights of Los Angeles as we make our approach. I'd flown here before, but only during the day.

After we land, the nice old airline lady tells me to stay put and she'll walk me to my Dad in the baggage area. As soon as I see him, I yell out Dad! and run straight to him.

Roland Amariah Gonzales

He lifts me up *high* into the air and he's laughing and I'm laughing, too. He puts me down and Gracie is jumping up and down from the excitement and giggling. I even hug her too, 'cause I'm so happy to be there.

Dad drives us to Redondo Beach and asks if I'm okay. I say yeah, Dad I'm great! and he smiles and says that's good to hear, son.

When we get to the house he asks me about life in Missouri. He wants to know about school, what friends I have, if there are any cute girls I like, and my life with Mom and Randy.

I tell him about the things I've seen and done since he and Mom divorced and he frowns a bit as I talk. When I finish he hugs me close and tells me he's sorry.

Dad shows me around his house and it's huge! It's built on a steep hill and it's only one floor tall, but also *kind of* two. It has a *giant* lower room that Dad says is a den. It's always nice and cool down there. Dad has neat toys and stuff that he got for me and Grace to play with but because we're so little we can't go down without permission, since he says we might fall down the stairs.

I say to Dad I've walked down stairs a *whole* bunch, maybe even a *thousand* times! Why can't I go down these by myself?

Dad's new wife appears briefly from the bathroom door to say stairs are *dangerous.* She says she doesn't want us going through her and Dad's bedroom all the time either, and that's the only way to get to the stairs. There's also an outside door, but we can't go outside without their permission 'cause that's dangerous, too.

I blink as I process all those words then say uh...okay.

Dad shows me the room that I'll be sharing with Grace then tells me to take a shower and change into my pajamas. He says it's late and time for bed. He starts to leave the room as I get undressed, then says hold up a minute. He has me show him my arms and legs and tells me to take off my shirt so he can check something.

I laugh 'cause I don't understand why, but I take off my shirt, then spin around like a helicopter 'cause I'm so excited to be here. When I stop spinning, I see that Dad is carefully studying my front. He tells me to let him get a good look at my back, too.

I say huh? What for? Okay Dad, then I turn around.

He puts a finger somewhere on my back and asks what's this, son? Did you fall?

I say I dunno, maybe.

Amariah The Boy

Dad says there's a mark on my back then asks if it hurts when he presses his finger on it.

I say nope and he tells me alright, go hop in the shower, son. Brush your teeth too and get ready for bed!

When I get back to the bedroom Grace is already in her bed. Dad comes and tells us he loves us both very much. We give him a hug then he turns off the light and leaves.

The next morning, Dad properly introduces me to his new wife Renee, and I learn that he met her at the same place he met Mom, an AA meeting. Having learned his lesson with Mom, he made sure that his *new* wife was a devout, churchgoing, Christian woman.

A *good* woman, he says to me with a warm smile.

Renee loves Jesus and she *loves* smoking weed. When she's not going on about one, she's sitting back in thick clouds of the other.

She's a pretty woman with long, strawberry-blonde hair, fair skin, and long legs. She dresses in comfortable clothing around the house, lots of sweatshirts and sweatpants, and she doesn't go out much.

Dad doesn't smoke weed and he doesn't drink alcohol, but he does smoke cigarettes and so does Renee. Their cigarettes smell *nasty*.

Gracie is bigger now, nearly four!

Dad is still a huge guy, but he doesn't have short hair anymore 'cause he's not in the army. Now, his hair is *super-long* and it looks like a lion's mane.

He says he works with troubled youth and kids who are doing drugs and need help in recovery.

I look at him as I piece together what he just said, then say do you hold out a drug in one hand and a cookie in the other, then smack people with the cookie when they try and grab the drug?

Dad laughs and says yeah son, something like that.

Renee used to make sandwiches at a store but now she's taking pills for her back problems. She says work is *hard*. She's either home, going to her chiropractor, the grocery store, or church.

Roland Amariah Gonzales

Grace doesn't do much other than play with dolls, but she *is* old enough to go to pre-school, so Renee takes her there in the morning. Dad enrolls me in public school and drops me off sometimes in the morning, but he's usually already at work, so Renee takes me instead. The sun is usually shining, even if it's a little cold in the morning, so it's not that bad.

All the school buildings are separated again 'cause I'm not in Clinton, Missouri anymore. There are *so many* kids in my class and in the school!

School isn't *that* hard out here. There are no stupid color cards or yellow lines that we have to follow, and it's actually a lot of fun! The math and English parts are boring, but science is *always* a blast. We learn about plants and the teacher brings some from home with *real* worms in her flowerpots! She has us make *our* own flowerpots using plastic cups with crumbled cookies for dirt, and gummy worms instead of real worms. They're awesome.

We learn about whales and how their blubber keeps them warm in the arctic. Our teacher brings in a bag filled with *fat* and puts it in the classroom sink, then fills the sink with *lots* of ice and water. She then has us put one hand in the ice water first and the other in the bag of fat. It feels *disgusting* but it's not so cold. Now I know to put my hand or my body in a whale if I ever fall in the ocean, so I don't freeze to death.

During recess we play on the jungle gym, or we play handball or four-square. I make school friends, unlike back in Clinton, so I've *always* got someone to play with!

Dad and Renee teach me to make my own lunch. I usually opt for a peanut butter, banana, and honey sandwich with some carrots and milk on the side, 'cause these are my favorite.

Sometimes I can't wait all the way for lunch-time and eat everything during recess. I'm always hungry for some reason! I tell Dad about it and complain that my knees and legs always hurt too, and he says that's a good thing, son, it means you're growing!

When school is over, I wait for Dad or Renee to pick me up. Some other kids wait for their parents too, so we play tag on the jungle gym. I race up onto a bunch of platforms connected by monkey bars and sliding rails, then leap out to grab onto whatever I can. Sometimes I hurl my body toward the hard concrete floor so I don't get tagged. I always land on my feet so I never get hurt or anything.

Amariah The Boy

Some kids play soccer on a field nearby and I join in until another kid swings his leg at the ball, misses, and kicks a small chunk of skin off of my shin. It hurts *real* bad, stinging and aching, so I decide to stick to jumping off the jungle gym instead...that's safer! The ground doesn't *try* to hurt me on purpose, only when I'm dumb.

I also go to the school library when it's too cold or too hot, or if I just don't feel like playing with the others. The librarian is a *very* pretty woman in her early forties with fair skin, dark curly hair that she adorns with vibrant orange, yellow, and purple Hawaiian hibiscus flowers, and kind eyes. I look for a nice quiet spot on a beanbag chair, then read *Choose Your Own Adventure* books while I wait for Dad or Renee to pick me up.

When I read, I'm no longer a seven-year-old boy tasked with cleaning my bedroom, sweeping the floor, or washing dishes. Now, I'm on a quest to help Odin recover Idun's golden apples of immortality, or help villagers defeat an evil fire wizard, or fight ninjas, or journey to the bottom of the ocean with Captain Nemo, or some other fantastic adventure!

Occasionally, I take a break from reading and enjoy the *I Spy* books, so I can look at all the things inside. Dad's happy that I like to read so much and buys me books for home. He tells me that he wants me to play baseball or some other sport when I grow a bit bigger, but he doesn't limit my reading at all!

He gets me classical books re-printed for kids, like *Great Illustrated Classics*. Each page has a picture opposite the printed page, and I find myself skipping the text to gaze at all the pictures, then try to piece the story together with my imagination. Then, I go back and read the text to see how close the story is to what I thought it was.

I blaze a trail through *Treasure Island, Robinson Crusoe, The Last of the Mohicans, The Time Machine,* and several others. Dad even gifts me the works of C.S. Lewis, though I'm only seven and don't understand a lot of it. I make it to the third book of the Narnia series before I lose interest.

I speed read through most books in a day or two, though I have trouble retaining what happened if the story wasn't particularly interesting or it was above my understanding. I get in trouble with Renee when she picks a random page in a book I'd finished then asks me what happened and I'm unable to answer.

Roland Amariah Gonzales

Renee's voice is nasally and irritated as she says I'm *wasting* Dad's money on books and I'm not even reading them! She makes me write out "I will read my books and not waste my father's money" one hundred times as punishment.

Renee is *very* strict when Dad is gone at work. She's not like Mom, in the sense that she doesn't run around beating us all day for the hell of it. Instead, she makes us stand in the corner and stare at the wall for ages or write out sentences. I have a lot of trouble remembering things because my mind is *always* racing from one thing to another. Sometimes, it feels like there's a *million* thoughts flying around my mind all at once and it feels so *loud* that I can't think. I hate it. Renee gets angry when I tell her that I forgot something that she told me to do, but it's the *truth*!

Renee says I'm a *liar* and that *no one* forgets that much! It feels like she makes me write "I will not forget..." sentences at *least* ten thousand times! I end up having to spend my recess writing sentences instead of playing with friends. If I don't get 'em done at school, I'll have to work on them at home.

Amariah The Boy

Renee's grandma watches me and Grace after school when Renee goes to the chiropractor or says she needs a break from us. We sit in her living room on the couch or on the floor and watch TV, same as when Renee looks after us at our house.

Renee's grandma shuffles about her little house and brings us carrot sticks, cheese sticks and the like. She takes a cheese stick away from me when I chomp off the end. She says it's called *string cheese* because I'm supposed to peel it into strings and says I'm doing it wrong. She hands it back to me and watches me do it correctly. Satisfied, she shuffles off into another room.

Renee tells her grandma to not let me watch anything *bad*, so her grandma flips the channel to Nickelodeon and leaves me and Grace there. I like game shows like Double Dare, Legends of the Hidden Temple, and GUTS. I imagine competing on these shows and winning all the great prizes, like vacation trips to Disney World or other fantastic stuff that I never even *knew* I wanted to do until the TV told me so.

Sometimes, Renee's grandma puts on the USA channel and I watch American Gladiator, and that must be where you go after you win on GUTS or Double Dare, because I only see adults. I crawl close to the TV and peer at a pretty lady trying to win on the show. I *think* I saw her in a movie I watched when I was four...that I wasn't supposed to watch.

Renee has an older, overweight and balding brother in his late twenties. The man is a *huge* fan of Star Trek, which he watches in his room. He says I'm not allowed to watch, since Renee says it doesn't glorify Jesus, and he says he doesn't like me in his room anyway. When he leaves his bedroom door open, I peek in and see all *kinds* of neat-looking spaceships on his bookshelves! Some hang from the ceiling too, and I wonder if they light up. I also sneak a peek at his Star Trek show and not much happens, and there's barely any spaceships at all! Just people in different-colored pajamas who talk a lot.

After weeks of living in Redondo Beach, I learn that Renee has two states of mind— high and happy, and sober and *bitchy*. She never smokes weed in front of me and Grace, and instead goes to her room and smokes in private. She comes out of her and Dad's room bleary-eyed and says, RJ why don't you take Gracie and go play outside or in your room.

It's not a suggestion, though, it's a command.

Dad works a couple of different jobs that take him out on the road for long periods of time, sometimes *days*, or even a week or two! Dad

91

says he does something with oil now and that's why he's gone for so long. This leaves Renee often watching us by herself. Renee *hates* watching us, and I get the feeling that she wants to go out and party like Mom does.

When Renee's *not* high, my sister and I avoid her as best we can. Renee is *real* good at finding a reason to be pissed, and says she has OCD, too. Whether it's me and Grace singing, a sock not folded correctly, a floor not swept *perfectly,* or something else, she gets mad. She often tells me and Grace to do something, *just* so she can find a mistake then punish us. She screams at me and Grace, puts us in the corner for twenty minutes, then retreats to her room to get high and I hear her say Praise Jesus! A bunch of times.

She often says she just can't *deal* with us and needs something to calm her nerves. She says she's gonna tell Dad how bad we are and that we don't listen to her, but usually forgets 'cause she smokes so much weed. If she *remembers* her threats after smoking weed all day, she makes good on 'em.

If Dad comes home and hears we were disobedient, he spanks us, but it's usually just me getting spanked. It's not that Dad's a vengeful prick but more that he's doing things the right way this time. The *Christian* way. He says, similar to Mom, that he can't spare the rod or we'll get spoiled. Thankfully, he doesn't use an actual rod or a phone cord or beat the hell out of me like Mom does.

Dad places absolute faith in Renee to run the home as a good Christian wife should, and he works hard to provide for us all.

When Dad is gone, me and Grace are *severely* limited in what we're allowed to watch on TV, even more than when we're at Renee's grandmother's house. It happens that TV is Renee's preferred method of child rearing. She's fond of Christian broadcasting networks, or shows that promote Christian values. She informs me that these are the ones we can watch. These shows include Davey and Goliath, Care Bears, Gumby, and other similar programs.

Renee says ghosts, skeletons, monsters, demons, magic, or anything of that nature—let alone anything that doesn't glorify Jesus—is the devil's work. She protects us from that which she deems evil, then when she feels real good about herself, she retreats to her room to smoke her weed.

Renee is *so* committed in her righteous missionary-at-home work that when Halloween comes around, just after my uneventful eighth birthday, she convinces Dad to abandon Halloween *entirely* in favor of a local church-led Christian Harvest Festival. Grace and I aren't allowed to dress up in *any* costume that Renee thinks is evil. I wanted to be Batman, after hearing other boys in school talk about how cool Batman is. Instead, I'm some guy called Raggedy Andy and Grace is a pumpkin.

I complain loudly that I don't wanna *be* Raggedy Andy, and I don't even know what a Raggedy Andy *is!* Renee threatens me with sentence writing then makes me watch some cartoon movie about two rag-doll people who save Christmas from a talking wolf. I don't like it.

The Christian Harvest Festival is outside on a parking lot. We walk from stall to stall and observe all the Christian crafts made by followers of that faith. I am *terribly* bored and don't get excited at *all* about little figurines of Jesus with sheep, paintings of Jesus with sheep, or passages from the bible that talk about Jesus with sheep! Everyone here is talking about Jesus and his sheep and there's *not even* a stupid petting zoo with sheep in it! I just want to go trick-or-treating and get some candy!

Renee drags us from stall to stall, looks at everything and says oh, isn't this beautiful? She looks at me to make sure that I'm looking too, and that I agree with how pretty it all is.

I whine to Dad how bored I am. I think to myself how I *know* I'm getting screwed out of candy, and this is the one night of the year when you can get *all* the candy you want!

Renee says if I keep up the attitude, we can all go home and I can stand in the corner for the rest of the night, and how would I like that?

I look at the ground, grit my teeth, and say I'm sorry and then I say that I like being here and I love Jesus.

Renee gives me a smug smile and nods approvingly.

Dad sees how miserable I am and says hey, why don't we all go to the hay circle? He gives me a little nudge and a wink and says maybe we can get some *candy* there, eh? Eh?

I'm grinning from ear to ear now, jumping up and down in excitement.

Renee looks like someone slipped a frog in her underwear, then turns away and says she wants to look at crafts some more. Dad leaves Grace with her and we go to the hay circle together. After we sit down, some guy dressed like a farmer reads a passage from the bible about how you can't drink with demons and drink with the lord at the same time, then asks us all what the passage means.

Roland Amariah Gonzales

I jump up and quickly blurt out Jesus loves us and died for our sins and if we give our heart to him then we get to go to heaven!

I want candy. A lot.

The farmer guy says that this isn't *quite* the point of the passage, but that's not a *wrong* answer either. He says here ya go, and tosses me a small pouch of candy.

I excitedly jump up and shout yes! As I catch the pouch, then open it to see that it's got two smaller bags of *candy corn* inside. I *hate* candy corn. I scowl and *think* I say *Goddamit!* In my head, but accidentally say it out loud! All the kids gasp and stare at me with their mouths agape and now Dad is dragging me away from the hay circle saying he's sorry over and over...to everyone.

While I'm being dragged away I point accusingly at the guy dressed as a farmer and shout what?! They're only giving out *candy corn*! I *hate* candy corn. No one likes candy corn! I angrily throw a bag of candy corn back at the hay circle before Dad swats my hand and yells at me then apologizes again.

When we get away from the crowd and are out of sight I think I'm in a *lot* of trouble, but Dad just looks tired as he says son, I *know* you'd rather be trick-or-treating, but just give this a try, okay? We'll go trick-or-treating for a little bit when we get home, alright? And don't take the Lord's name in vain, that's bad. Then he says hey, they've got a stall where they're bobbing for apples, you wanna try that?

I nod and then look down at the ground. I feel bad. I hate making my dad sad even more than I hate candy corn, and I *really* hate candy corn. I say okay, but do you want the other bag of candy corn?

Dad says hell no, I hate that stuff!

I toss the remaining bag into a stall filled with statues of sad Jesuses, thinking maybe the people inside like this crap, then me and Dad walk to the bobbing-for-apples-place.

There's a group of people shoving their faces into a barrel filled with apples floating on the water. Their hands are behind their back as they try to bite and pull out the apples using only their mouths. I see a couple of kids get great big mouthfuls of water then cough and spit 'em up back into the barrel and say Ew! As I look on in disgust. I say to Dad uh, I don't think I really wanna do this. Dad just looks at me and shakes his head, so I try it once *just* to make Dad happy.

When it's my turn I lower my face into the barrel before seeing some kid's coughed-up french-fry! I gag and fight down a wave of

94

nausea, then make a half-hearted motion of trying to get an apple before bringing my head up. Dad is disappointed that I didn't get an apple but he doesn't push it. Trying to forget the french-fry and not to look *too* disgusted, I say I think I'd rather go sing songs about Jesus, so we go to another spot and do that instead.

We return home and Dad tells Renee he's gonna do a quick trick-or-treat around the block with me and Gracie. Renee is *pissed* and says oh my God, I don't *believe* you! Before going to their bedroom and slamming the door.

Dad tries to calm her down through the door but then we hear her spark a lighter and start coughing. In-between coughing, she shouts that *now* she has a headache and she needs to calm down and we should just *go already*, because we *obviously* don't care about the *Lord!*

Dad stares at the door with a concerned look on his face then turns to me and says come on Rol, take your sister's hand. Then he takes us outside.

We get *some* candy but it seems that everyone's either out of town, asleep, or a dentist, 'cause me and Grace end up with more dental floss and toothpaste than anything else.

When we get back home Renee pokes her head out to see our meager stash of goodies and says it serves us *right,* and we should be focusing on giving glory to the *Lord* and *not* ourselves. Then she slams their bedroom door again.

Dad loves Jesus too but he's different about it. He's more about a nice Jesus and less about a you're-all-going-to-hell Jesus.

Roland Amariah Gonzales

We go to this *huge* church in the evening, sometimes two times a week, and then early Sunday morning. The building is a far cry from the tiny synagogue I went to with Aunt Diane, back when she wanted me to lie to get a free bible. This place can fit hundreds, maybe even a *thousand* people or more. A guy on stage in a very nice suit runs back and forth and yells at the crowd, asking if everyone loves Jesus. Everyone cheers and screams Yes, we sure do!

People around me clap their hands and shout how they're not worthy. Some shout Praise Him and hold their hands up to the ceiling, and some are crying while others are laughing. There's too many different emotions. The people here are making me feel dizzy.

The nice-suit guy tells everyone to look into their hearts and give whatever they can so the church can help needy people. I see lots of blue-colored plastic baskets, like the ones I see in burger restaurants, being passed down the rows. My jaw drops when I see *huge* amounts of money in the basket! Maybe even a million dollars!

When the basket comes to me I reach in and grab a fist full of money. I've never *seen* this much money in my life! Renee takes a moment from loudly telling everyone how worthy she *isn't* to smack my hand and yell don't even think about it!

Renee stops me when I do something wrong, but sometimes she's real mean bout it.

Grace has some Barbie dolls that she likes to play with and I like their long legs, so I play with them too. I think they're real pretty, so I put them in sex positions when I'm alone and mimic bedroom noises. I have *some* idea how it all works from a movie I saw once that I wasn't supposed to see. I call Grace and ask if she wants to see something *really* cool then show her how to play with dolls in a way that she'd never even considered before!

Grace immediately tells Renee and Renee takes a painful grip on my arm then throws me into my bedroom. She says to stay in there until Dad gets home, and that I'm gonna get it now.

I'm in *so* much trouble and am scared but don't know why.

When Dad gets home I hear him talking in the hallway with Renee. I press my ear to the door and hear Renee say how screwed up I am. She says if Dad keeps me here I'm going to *ruin* Gracie with all my bullshit problems. She says I'm *not* their responsibility.

Dad says if not theirs, then whose? He says he'll have a word with me which makes Renee sigh then stomp off to the sitting room.

Amariah The Boy

I'm terrified and think I'm in a *world* of trouble as I scramble to stand against the wall on the bed. Dad opens the door then closes it behind him and looks real serious...and a little sad. He tells me to have a seat on the bed then says listen, son. What you did was wrong. You should *never* do those things in front of your sister. And then he says you shouldn't do those things at *all*, but *especially* not around your sister, okay?

I'm almost sick now, feeling guilty and ashamed. They're both real upset but I still don't know *why*. I quietly say okay Dad, then pause and ask, but *why* is it a bad thing?

Dad frowns, looks at me, then the wall, then me again, and says look, son, just don't do it again or you're gonna get in *big* trouble, got it?

I ask if I'm gonna get spanked now and he says no...but stay in your room for the night.

I mumble okay then turn toward the wall, lay on my side, and hug my pillow after he leaves.

I learn about sex around the age of four in Georgia. It's raining outside and I'm not allowed to go out because Mom says I'll wreck the carpet. Dad is still in the army, and he's out somewhere training. Bored, I sit in the living room and watch some awful show Mom enjoys until she gets tired from watching TV and says she's gonna go take a nap with Gracie. She also says that under *no* circumstances am I allowed to go outside and tells me to sit *right there* and watch TV.

I whine that there's nothing on TV!

Annoyed, she points at a stack of VHS cassettes and says then pop in a movie!

She goes to take a nap and I grab a VHS tape. It has three X's scratched onto the face. It's *supposed* to be He-Man and the Masters of the Universe, except it isn't. It's *a* man and *a* woman and they're naked!

I don't really know what's happening, but I *do* know that the women I'm seeing on TV right this minute are *so* beautiful! I marvel at their nude bodies and all the things they're doing, my eyes wide eyes and my mouth hanging open. I wonder if all women look like this with no clothes on, 'cause Mom sure doesn't.

These ladies have huge boobies, like basketballs, and their skin is almost orange like a basketball too, and they have so much hair! They have more hair down there than I have on my head!

Roland Amariah Gonzales

I watch a guy with curly blonde hair and a big mustache play with his penis and it gets *huge* and his lady friend seems real happy about it. I look down and try to make mine big too, but nothing happens. I yank on it a couple of times, like the guy in the movie is doing, but it's not working right, and pulling on it just hurts, so I stop.

I get bored after a few minutes watching them do the same thing. I turn it off and put the video away then rotate the knob on the TV to change the channels.

A few days later Mom and Dad are talking in the kitchen while Grace is asleep. I sit and watch TV in the other room. After I see a pretty lady in a shampoo commercial, I decide it's time to test out what I learned. I pop in the naked-people movie and go to town tugging on my penis. The conversation in the kitchen dies off as Dad hears what's *loudly* playing on TV. He looks over then does a double-take, not believing or comprehending what he's seeing.

I'm startled as he rushes over and turns off the movie, and it must be my lucky day because there's *another* pretty lady in a *different* shampoo commercial! Mom puts her hand over her eyes, shakes her head, heaves a great big sigh and says fuuuuuuck.

Dad looks at me with great concern and says uh, hey son! Uh...what've you got going on down there, champ?

I look up and say with a shrug I don't know. My hand is still on my penis.

He nods as he stares at me, then says uh-huh, uh-huh. Right. Uh, say, champ, what you're doing is okay, but uh, only...go do that in your room, okay?

I look at him in confusion. There're no pretty women in my room. What's the point of tugging on myself in my room all *by myself*? That's not going to impress anyone! I ask him why.

Dad blinks and pauses for a moment, furrows his brow, then says well, because I say so, and don't ask why.

I shrug and say okay, Dad! and run off to my room, tugging away while I go.

Amariah The Boy

Not everyone is as devout as or loves Jesus as much as Renee. When I go to school, no one really cares about Jesus at *all*, and I don't make any friends for talking about Jesus in the first place.

Some kids say I'm the weird kid in school 'cause I don't know a *thing* about what they talk about, and they don't appreciate my insistence that they're all going to hell for liking those things, either. Once all the kids agree that I'm weird they start to pick on me and make fun of me.

The other kids tell me my clothes and shoes are *raggedy* and they say it looks like I stole them from a homeless person! I'd never thought about my clothes *or* my shoes before, since clothes were only something I wear, and I sure don't want to walk around naked as a jaybird. As I look around I realize, much to my dismay, that everyone *is* wearing much nicer and newer things than me.

Some boy in class laughs at me during recess and says that I'm dirty, smell bad because everything I'm wearing is so old, *and* I'm ugly to boot! He points at his shoes and shows me how the heels light up *every* time he takes a step. All the kids say wow!

My shoes are a faded blue and gray with grass and dirt stains, the same ones that Uncle Alex and Aunt Tami got for me in first grade. There's a hole starting where the big toe is, and it's clear to everyone that my shoes are in fact the *worst* ones in the entire school! I try not to look it, but I'm red in the face from shame as he and all the kids laugh at me.

I pick up a four-square ball and throw it as *hard* as I can at his stupid face, but it goes flying past him and hits the recess teacher in *his* balls. The recess teacher's face shows absolute agony as he lets out a loud Oof! He starts coughing and doubles over in pain as he curls into a ball. I *immediately* start walking in a random direction to try and get away, but he manages to blow his whistle and loudly sputters w-who the fu... who just threw that ball!

All the flashing-light-shoe kid's friends point at me and yell out RJ did it!

When Renee picks me up my teacher tells her that I nailed the recess teacher in the junk and it doesn't *matter* what the other kid said to me, violence is *never* okay.

Renee throws me in the car, slams the door so hard I think it'll break, then races home in absolute fury.

And now I'm back in that fucking corner.

Roland Amariah Gonzales

Hours go by before she tells me I have to write "I will not pick fights at school because fighting is wrong and violence is never the answer" a hundred times.

I sit at the table and as I write the sentences, I find it easier to write I-I-I-I trailing all the way down the page a hundred times, then w-w-w-w a hundred times, and so on. She sees me writing this way then gets angry and says that I'm not doing it the *correct* way, so she calls Dad while he's at work. She tells him I got in trouble at school because I picked a fight with some other boy before assaulting a teacher.

I hear Dad yelling over the phone and I feel the color drain from my face. Dad sounds *really* fuckin' angry.

Renee talks to Dad for a bit about how *bad* I am, then hangs up and says oooh, you're gonna *get it* when your dad gets home. She's got this awful smile on her face before she goes to her room and shuts the door. I hear her strike the lighter, followed by coughing and choking while I glumly write out her sentences.

Dad gets home, puts down all his equipment from work, then heads straight to me and Grace's room. He pulls down my pants before I can say a word then swats me hard five times for misbehaving and tells me not to do it again, then leaves because he's so mad. He comes back ten minutes later, after he's showered and calmed down, and loudly asks why? Why are you starting fights and being bad?

He looks toward the doorway before he leans in close and whispers to me were ya winnin', son?

I shrug as I think about it, my ass still sore from the spanking, and say...kind of?

I tell him what happened and he starts to laugh, then quickly stops. He listens and nods while I tell my story, frowning and angry, and by the end he's frowning and angry too. He brings Grace into the bedroom, quietly shuts our door, then goes into *his* bedroom, then shuts the door.

Me and Grace hear shouting, and it reminds me of living in Georgia with Mom.

If I thought Dad was pissed at me, I was wrong. He's *furious* with Renee and the yelling gets louder. He shouts why the hell do Grace and RJ have such old, worn-out and beaten-up clothes? Why is my son going to school looking like he's homeless? What are you *doing* with the money I'm busting my ass for *every day*? Are you spending it all on *this*? This bullshit you're smoking all the time?

100

Amariah The Boy

Renee shrieks put that back down and don't you touch that! Her voice sounds like nails on a chalkboard, and I *hate* it. She shouts that she's giving to the less fortunate and buying the other kids in the neighborhood shoes and things they *need,* and if Dad was furious before then I don't even *know* what he is now. Grace and I are trying to be as quiet as we can so we can listen to Renee get yelled at, grins on our faces...but also because Dad gets *scary* when he's angry.

Dad tells her again how he busts his ass to provide for everyone and how he expects Renee to take care of everything at home, and how much she *sucks* at it.

Renee says she doesn't *need* to take this, that she *deserves* respect. Then she stomps out of the house and goes to her car.

I hear the tires screech as she peels out of the driveway and it makes me think of Aunt Tami.

Renee, unfortunately for my sister and me, feels divinely inspired to help the other kids in our neighborhood more than us. The neighbor parents always shower her with praise when she brings their kids shoes or a jacket or something like that. They never say *no* to the gifts, and no one cares if Grace and I walk around looking like homeless people. Renee tells the neighbors she's just doing the Lord's work and the neighbors nod and smile. They say the world would be better with more people like her.

Renee's gone for a couple of days. I ask Dad where she is and when she's coming back and he says she's at her grandma's place down the road. We're all pretty happy when she's gone and I do the best I can to wash our dishes and keep everything clean. If I do well, Dad will have time to go find a new wife and throw Renee in the trash, 'cause *none* of us like her.

Renee comes back during the weekend and calls me into the living room. Dad is out working one of his jobs. He tells me, before he leaves, that I'm the man of the house and to watch after Gracie.

I go into the living room, where Renee is watching TV and the room *reeks* with the smell of weed. She says to have a seat and pats a space next to her on the couch.

I feel *real* uncomfortable next to her. After a few minutes, she tells me that I'm a burden to *everyone* and no one wants me here.

Just like my cousin Mary.

Renee says she and Dad *never* fought before I arrived and they're only fighting now because he can't think of a way to get rid of me and send me home.

I don't believe her and yell nuh-uh, that's not true! Dad loves me very much!

She looks directly at me with her bloodshot eyes and says no RJ, no, he really doesn't! Kenney just feels *sorry* for you because Kathleen doesn't love you *either* and neither does your *real* father! No one loves you, not even Gracie! Why do you think everyone tosses you around from house to house? Your mom, your Uncle Alex, then here? Who knows where you're going *after*?

I *am* tossed around from house to house...she's right! My cheeks are burning hot and I start to sniffle as my bottom lip begins to quiver. I try to fight back my tears but I can't.

Seeing me cry, she smiles down at me sadly and says oh, you didn't know?

I sob and start crying.

Renee says hey, hey, it's okay, RJ. It's okay! Even if your mommy and daddy *don't* love you, *Jesus* still does, and if you let Jesus into your heart you'll go to an eternal paradise when you die. You'll go to heaven!

Renee strokes my head and pats it a few times as I hiccup, sob and rub at my eyes with my hands. After a few minutes she says okay, you can go to your room now.

I quietly walk to my room and shut the door. Grace is taking a nap on her bed across from me. I turn away from her and face the wall. I stare blankly as tears stream down my face. I wonder if they're going to kick me out on the streets, like Mom said Alex and Tami would.

Grace hears me crying, gets out of her bed, comes over and says RJ are you okay?

I shove her away.

Amariah The Boy

It's nearly summer and we head to the beach on the weekend, about ten minutes away by car, now that the weather is a bit warmer. I love the beach. The sound of waves gently lapping or crashing against the shore. The smell of salt in the air. The feeling of sand, both fine and coarse underfoot. There's an energy here that is palpable, and I drink of it deeply.

Dad teaches me how to bodyboard and it's scary at first, because even the *smallest* waves seem gigantic when you're flat on the water. I swim around without my bodyboard too, my time spent training as a deep diver with Alex and Tami having prepared me. I never see any sharks, though the thought crosses my mind from time to time. Dad says people in charge of the beach put up a great big net to keep all the sharks out, and I feel safer.

When I'm not swimming I make sandcastles with Grace. I like to frantically dig a moat and build an interior wall to divert the ocean water while Grace builds the castle itself. Sometimes *long* cords of seaweed wash up on shore and I pretend I'm Indiana Jones. I practice cracking the seaweed like a whip, until I snap myself in the face. Stunned and in stinging pain, I drop the seaweed and decide I'll stick to building sandcastles.

Dad tells Renee he's going to walk around a bit with me and says come on, Rol, let's go!

I get up from whatever I'm doing and run to be next to him, then we walk away from everyone. After five minutes or so Dad asks me how I'm doing in school but when I respond I can see that he's not really listening, he's looking at something important instead.

I follow his gaze and see all *kinds* of pretty ladies wearing tiny swimsuits. I can see their *butts* and almost *everything*! I blurt out woooow! and Dad, startled, looks at me and laughs.

He asks if I think they're pretty.

I say oh, *yeah!* and when I give him a *double*-thumbs up, he barks out a laugh.

Dad says hey, why don't you go ask if they need help putting on sunblock?

I look at him in suspicion and fear. Stephanie in Missouri told me that I'm *disgusting*. I don't wanna hear that again.

He pushes me and says go on, it'll be funny. Maybe they need help!

I think about it for a moment...they *are* really pretty. I don't need any more encouragement. I say okay! and run right up to one of the

103

pretty ladies. She's lying on her stomach and wearing a dark red bikini. She's got fair skin and *long* curly black hair. I grin and stare, then blurt out a mishmash of words crammed into a single breath: hello how are you? Do you need any help putting on sunblock because my dad says it's important to wear sunblock and I can help you if you need sunblock because there's so much sun out here and you don't want to get a sunburn and I'd probably be really good at it too. I don't know!

She rolls onto her back and sees I'm not looking at her face at *all* but staring at her legs and her little red toenails. She's got a gold anklet too, and it's *shiny*.

I say woooow! again.

The beach lady raises her eyebrows at me from behind her glasses, and then first smiles then breaks into a laugh. Her laugh sounds like wind chimes on a day when all the leaves turn gold and fall to the ground and I really like it. She says well hello there, cutie, what's your name? Where are your mom or dad?

Dad appears out of nowhere and says oh hey, there you are, son!

The lady looks at us both and says to my dad, he's *your* son? She laughs and says she guesses she can see how much we look alike.

I look at my *giant* of a Dad, then at my *very* tanned arms and chest, then look at her and say what? No, we don't.

Dad and the beach lady start laughing and then they talk for a while. She has red lips and earrings too. I can't stop staring at her but get bored after a couple of minutes, since no one is talking to me. I ask her again so do you need help putting on sunblock, because I can help if you need help.

The beach lady laughs again, smiles at me and says maybe when you're a little bigger, champ.

I get real excited and say oh! Really? Okay. That's great!

She giggles and nods with her eyebrows raised.

I stop for a moment then say wait, how much bigger? I'm *real* small right now, but Dad says I should shoot up any day now!

The beach lady shakes her head and smiles at me, then says to hold up my hand. She places her hand against mine and says when your hands are *bigger* than mine, okay?

I feel disheartened...my hands have got a *ways* to go, but I nod confidently and say mhmm, right, okay. Okay, I'll work on it!

She stares at me for a moment, laughs and says to Dad your son is going to be *trouble* when he grows up, I can tell!

Amariah The Boy

Dad says what, my boy? No way! He's *my* son, he'll be *fine*! and they both laugh again.

We all say goodbye to each other. Dad and I walk away before I hear the beach lady call out hey, champ!

Dad and I turn around and she blows me a kiss, then says and says for when you're bigger, don't forget about me, okay?

My jaw drops and I grin and wave back and say okay!

She lowers her sunglasses and gives me an exaggerated wink before shaking her head and laughing again, then rolls back onto her stomach.

It's the best beach day of my life and Dad says *nice*, and hey, good job, son! You're a chip off the ol' block!

We high five each other and I feel totally awesome.

When Dad and I aren't swimming, or walking along the beach, he runs along the shore and pulls me on my body board. I jet along laughing as ocean water sprays my face and I struggle to hold on. We do this on repeated visits until a well-timed wave and an untimely bounce coincide to flip me onto my back while he's pulling. My back gets scraped by washed-up mussels and seashells and I don't want to be pulled after that.

Sometimes we go to the beach on bikes and rollerblades, zooming along the concrete boardwalk. If I ride my bike then Renee, who's wearing skates, holds onto my seat and makes me pull her. She says it's good for me to exercise and I don't mind so much 'cause I'm just glad we're at the beach. Sometimes she buys a burger and fries and shares some fries with me. Beach times are good times...beach times are warm times.

At the end of a beach day I rest my feet in the sand, toes wriggling with handfuls of sand slowly pouring from my hand. I watch two opposing suns set into one another. For a moment, as the sky-sun meets its twin living in the ocean, everything is bathed in gold. I always help carry our stuff back to the car, though it always seems like I'm carrying *everything*. Renee says Grace can't really carry anything because she's too small and only five years old.

I say with a frown and my voice mimicking Renne, Gracie you're five but you can't do *anything*! You're too small! Then I walk to the car carrying *all* the things.

Roland Amariah Gonzales

I can't *stand* my sister. She can't really play so much and she *only* gets me into trouble *all* the time. She's my shadow. Wherever I go or whatever I do, she tells Renee, which means that I'm either in the corner or writing *more* sentences.

I'm playing with a GI Joe toy that Dad got me when Grace walks into our room. I take the GI Joe and say no one likes you Renee, and you should go away 'cause I don't like you either! Pow! And I smack Grace's Barbie doll into the closet.

Grace tells Renee.

Renee takes away GI Joe and says violence is wrong and now I have to write "I will play correctly with the toys that Dad bought me because he works very hard to give me nice things and violence is wrong" a hundred times. The next time Grace asks me what I'm doing and tries to play with me I tell her to go away and I don't like her.

She runs and tells Renee that I said mean things to her and now I have to write "I will be nice to my sister and not say mean things to her because she's my only sister and I should love her" a hundred times.

Having Grace around makes play time *incredibly* stressful.

Grace lapses back into bed-wetting and Dad is *real* upset and says he doesn't know why, since she stopped doing it around the age of half-past two. Dad is away at work when Grace pees the bed. Renee tells Grace as she shoves piss-stained sheets into the washing machine that she's a *baby*. Renee says Grace'll have to wear *diapers* in kindergarten so everyone else can *see* that she's a baby.

Grace starts crying and wipes her tears away with tiny hands and insists that she's *not* a baby. I'm *real* happy that Grace is crying and I hope they spank her too, or let me spank her since she won't stop peeing the bed. I call her a baby *any* chance I can get.

Grace *always* does things she knows will make me angry and it *always* looks like she doesn't do them on purpose, but I know better. She coughs on me *all* the time and says sorry afterward and says she just can't help it. I get more and *more* angry. It's *gross* and she's going to get me sick, so I tell her to stay away from me...but she won't!

When I get mad, Renee and Dad say I'm getting mad for no reason and they tell me to calm down or I'll have to stand in the corner or get spanked. They tell Grace to cover her mouth and they say don't cough on your brother and she says okay but keeps doing it!

Amariah The Boy

Kelly, Renee's niece, babysits us on occasion, even though I'm almost *nine* and I tell Renee that I'm all by myself *all* the time back in Missouri and don't *need* a babysitter.

Renee says well you're not in Missouri now, you're in California.

I say I don't see how a different place means I need a babysitter, but okay.

Kelly watches us for the night and microwaves some dinner for all of us. She and Grace sit on the couch and eat their food off the coffee table while I sit on the floor and do the same. Grace takes a bite of her food, gets my attention by clearing her throat, then looks *directly* at me and coughs her food *directly* onto me *and* my plate.

She says sorry afterward.

I'm disgusted, angry, and *so* mad that I only see red. I jump to my feet and kick the table into her leg as *hard* as I can and shout stop coughing on me!

Grace howls in pain and Kelly grabs me by the arm and throws me into my bedroom and I try to fight her but she's a *lot* bigger than me.

Kelly tells Renee, Renee tells Dad, and I get my ass whooped for hurting Grace *and,* oh hey, big surprise, *more* sentences.

I see through Grace when she *accidentally* does something to make me angry. Grace gets that *same* look in her eyes as Mom has when she's smiling, but not really. No one suspects Grace since she's so small. Renee *always* thinks I'm lying, and the first words out of her mouth when I say something are either did that *really* happen? or are you lying?

Renee has two cats and I find it hard to breathe between them and all the constant weed and cigarette smoke. When it's time for bed I have to get up and go to the bathroom to blow my nose *several* times. I can't do it in the bedroom 'cause it wakes up Grace and she starts crying.

Renee gets mad when I disrupt her sitting alone and watching TV-time. She says she needs peace and quiet. I get up to go to the bathroom for a few months until Renee runs up and screams at me to stay in bed.

I tell her, But I can't breathe.

Renee says she doesn't want to hear *any* of my excuses and I can either stay in bed, stand in the corner, or write sentences.

I don't *want* to stand in the corner and I sure don't *want* to write any more sentences, I just want to *breathe!* So, I trudge back to my room and decide to pick my nose and put it on the wall near my bed. I think it's gross but it's better than getting in trouble and *better* than not breathing. As long as I clean it, it's not a problem, but I forget to clean it and Grace sees it and tells on me.

No surprise what happens next. I'm writing "I will not pick my nose and put it on the wall because that's a very disgusting thing to do and I am not a pig" a hundred times. I think that if I had my own bedroom this wouldn't happen, and I could just blow my nose in there.

Struggling to breathe and Renee's screaming aren't the only problems plaguing my attempts to sleep. Sometimes at night I see shadow people standing at the foot of my bed and Grace's bed, too. I see them after the bedroom door is closed. I hear things moving in the closet, too. The shadow people scare the hell out of me but they never move, they just stand there and watch Grace and me.

I don't move an inch... I'm scared they'll attack me if I do. When the sun comes up, I ask Grace if she saw anything weird in the bedroom when it was time for bed. She nods and asks if I mean the shadow people, but she doesn't want to talk about it.

I'm glad she sees them too, so I know I'm not going crazy. Sometimes, I quietly and nervously sing songs from movies so I'm not so scared. Renee doesn't like that and yells from the other room to shut up and go to bed.

I don't understand why those scary things are there. I mean, we go to church more than *anyone* I know! At church they say that if demons try to get you, you can say in the name of Jesus, go away... and then the demons will leave.

I squeeze my eyes shut the next time I see the shadow people and quickly whisper over and over the now-I-lay-me-down-to-sleep prayer that Dad taught me from his favorite band, Metallica. When I open my eyes the shadow people are gone.

Grace doesn't see them anymore, either. I never talk about it with Dad or Renee. I don't want them to think it's my fault.

Amariah The Boy

Dad's family lives nearby. He's got a mom, dad, and two brothers and they're my family now, too. There are pictures around their house of all of us together when Mom and Dad got married, when I was just over two.

Grandpa Kenney is an old guy and he can be strict, but he also really likes to laugh, watch TV, and play board games.

He was in the Navy, and says he was a gunner on the 8-inch guns during peacetime, so he didn't fight in any wars like Dad did.

Grandma Jackie likes to laugh too, but sometimes she says all her kids drive her crazy. It seems like she's always *super* busy with work, trying to keep their huge house clean, and cook all the food. She's tired most of the time.

Uncle Steve is just a little younger than Dad, and he's always talking about sports and how good the players are. I don't know about any of that but he likes to play basketball and so do I, so sometimes we play together. He also collects books about a cat named Garfield. I don't always understand the funny parts, but it's nice that he shares them with me and lets me read them.

Uncle Phil is the coolest and he's only six years older than me. He's got *all* the Ninja Turtle and Transformer toys *and* a Nintendo, too! Uncle Phil isn't like my older cousin Mary, back when I stayed with Alex and Tami. He likes to share things with me and show off all his cool stuff. I like to play with him the most, but he's usually real busy with school.

Grandpa Kenney and Grandma Jackie have a big backyard that me and Grace run around and play in when we get the chance. There are big parks nearby too, and Dad or Steve or Phil take us there to play whenever we visit.

One time, Grace and I stay the night. Grandma Jackie says that Dad and Renee deserve a break. In the morning, she tells us she's gonna make pancakes and I'm excited...I *love* pancakes! My favorite thing is to put smooth peanut butter between the pancakes, then a lot of syrup on top. If I eat enough *without* drinking any milk then they get hard to swallow, like they're stuck in my throat. For some reason that feels good and choking on milk to wash it all down feels good, too.

Grandma tells me to go wake up Uncle Steve after she calls his name and he doesn't show up. I run upstairs and knock on his door and yell Uncle Steve, pancakes! but no one answers, so I open the door and go inside.

Roland Amariah Gonzales

Uncle Steve is still asleep and a devilish glee runs through me. I jump onto his bed, then bounce over and over and yell, wake up, pancakes!

Steve doesn't say anything, but he kicks hard at my legs when I'm in the air. I fall off the bed and hit my head against the wall.

I rub the pain in my head and he says to get out of his room...now!

I sniffle a bit as I leave and walk downstairs. Grandma asks me why I look so upset and I say Uncle Steve kicked me.

Grandma says well, what did you do?

I say I went to wake him up and jumped on his bed a bunch of times.

She sighs and shakes her head and says well maybe don't do that next time. I say okay.

We all sit down to eat pancakes and I quickly forget everything, because pancakes are awesome.

Amariah The Boy

Two girls live a few houses down from our own. They're sisters with fair skin, blonde hair, and blue eyes. The knock-kneed lanky sister, the older of the two, is around my age and has a smattering of freckles across the bridge of her nose. She's my best friend at the time, in that she's my *only* friend outside of school. Michelle is her name. I adore her.

I find any excuse I can to be around her. Our favorite game is called *House,* where we pretend we're married and make Grace be the baby. Michelle's younger and chubbier sister, Tabby, is also fun to play with, but I like Michelle the best since Tabby doesn't like to run and I *love* running.

Michelle and Tabby's mom takes us to the park sometimes where Michelle and I have a lot of fun running around and racing each other. I always push her on the swings and she pushes me, too.

Sometimes, I go to their home and watch movies and shows with Tabby that I'm not supposed to watch. I let her know *not* to tell Renee, 'cause I'll get in *big* trouble and it makes everything way more exciting for both of us. I don't know how Renee knows, but sometimes I go there to watch a movie I'm *real* excited about and as I head out of my house Renee yells from her room you better not watch anything you're not supposed to!

I yell back don't worry, I won't!

Before I'm even out the door, she coughs from smoking her weed then yells wait, take Gracie with you!

I say I don't want to...Grace is a tattletale!

Renee says well, you can either take Grace with you or you can stay in your room all day with her!

I take Grace with me.

We go to Michelle and Tabby's house and they've got a surprise for me...they just got a movie called *The Nightmare Before Christmas.* I'm *super* excited because I wanted to see this movie *real* bad but couldn't when it was in the movie theater. Renee said it didn't celebrate Jesus and was *full* of the devil.

I know the movie has *everything* Renee hates, so it's going to be awesome! No matter how old I am she'll never let me watch it, not even in a million years! I'm looking forward to it, but also worried 'cause Grace is with me. I make her promise *not* to tell Renee, and she says she won't.

Roland Amariah Gonzales

The movie is so *cool!* I've never seen anything like it. I love the songs and all the stuff I'm not allowed to see! Michelle's mom doesn't know that me and Grace aren't allowed to watch this kind of movie, and we don't tell her. She brings us juice and is happy that all the kids in her house are happy.

When the movie is over it's time for dinner, I give Michelle and Tabby great big hugs and they hug me back. I love my friends.

Amariah The Boy

Dad surprises me and Grace by getting home early and taking us out to eat at a place called *Fatburger*. I don't know how this day could get any better! First the movie and now this!

The food there is great, and I love their strawberry milkshakes. We're all happily munching away when Grace says to Renee and Dad hey, guess what RJ and I watched today.

I stare daggers into my sister as Dad chomps away at his burger and says what's that, hun?

I quickly say oh, we watched the Muppet Christmas Carol! I really liked it.

Renee gets a frown on her face and says I didn't tell her I was going to watch that movie, and how I need to tell her about *everything* I watch so she can approve it.

Dad smiles at Renee and shakes his head. With a mouthful of burger he says Muppets aren't that bad, Renee.

I kick Grace under the table as she starts to open her mouth again, 'cause I *know* she's gonna tattle on me, and she starts crying!

Grace points at me and says RJ just kicked me!

Dad gets an angry look on his face and says what did you *really* watch, Rol?

There's no point in lying now. My shoulders slump low and I must look like the unluckiest kid in the *whole* wide world. I tell him we watched *Nightmare Before Christmas* and Renee gasps then clutches her hand to her heart like she just caught the devil himself pissing on her cats. I quickly say it wasn't bad at all! There was a lot of singing and I really liked the songs and –

Dad holds up his hand and says stop talking, Rol. Then he says it doesn't *matter* whether the movie was *good*, what matters is that I disobeyed him and Renee and now I'm going to get spanked when we get home...and that's that.

I feel awful now, like there's a lump of lead in my gut. Today was almost a perfect day, but now it's ruined. It's hard to eat but Renee says you better eat your food or you're getting spanked for that, too. I force myself to eat and try not to throw up.

Dad says since I'm already getting spanked when we get home, I might as well tell them about *everything* else I've done so I can get spanked for that, too. He says if he finds out about it later then I'll get spanked *twice* as hard for lying, and he already spanks me hard enough as it is.

Roland Amariah Gonzales

For some reason I believe him and tell him about anything and *everything* that I'd kept secret up until then, even small things that aren't that bad, just in case! I tell him about how I put Renee's cat's poop in her shoes 'cause I thought it'd be real funny (but I don't say it's because I hate her). I tell him about how I'd separate all of the peas that Renee put into her tuna casserole then force them into my mouth before going to the toilet and spitting them out. I tell him about a bunch of swear words that I said and a bunch of other stuff, too.

I watch his eyes open wide, then narrow, then open wide again, but I can see that now he's *irate*.

When we get home he yells at me pull down your fuckin' pants, now! He yanks me over his knee and swats my bare ass in front of *everyone* ten times, *really* hard. I try to use my hand to cover my ass but he wrenches it out of the way. I scream in pain and he yells to move my fuckin' arm or he'll hit that, too.

After he's done spanking me he tells me to pull up my pants. Then he says come here, son. He hugs me and says he loves me very much and to stop getting in trouble so he won't have to spank me all the time!

I nod and try to stop crying but my ass hurts real bad and I bet it's fuckin' red like the setting sun, too.

Dad says to go brush my teeth, clean up, then go to my room...I'm still in trouble.

After I'm done in the bathroom I go back to my room and pretend to go to sleep. Hours go by until Grace falls asleep. I get up and hit her as *hard* as I can with my pillow until she starts screaming, then I jump back into bed.

I rub my eyes really hard so they hurt a bit. When the bedroom door flies open and Dad turns on the light, he thinks I just woke up. He yells what the hell is going on?

I lean on one arm and open a single eye while rubbing the other and say wha...? I don't know Dad, Grace just started screaming...maybe she's having a nightmare?

I yawn widely and rub my eye some more.

Dad looks at Grace and asks if she's okay, and then he yawns and rubs his eyes, too.

I hold up one hand into a fist then point at her with my other hand, making sure that Dad can't see. Grace sees this, understands, and tells Dad she's okay and it was a bad dream.

Dad says well, keep it down and try to think happy thoughts, alright hun?

Grace says okay, Dad, just before he turns off the lights and leaves.

I want to hit Grace again, or even push her down the stairs, 'cause my ass is *still* sore and it's all her fault. I don't think I can right now though without getting into *real* trouble, so I just go to sleep.

The next day, Renee says I'm grounded for two weeks and can't go out to play. When Michelle comes over I see her at the door, but Renee says RJ can't come out to play because he was very *bad* and needs to learn to obey his parents and the word of *God*.

Michelle looks behind Renee and sees me looking very sad and says oh, okay, then she leaves.

Renee makes me stay in my room all day and I can only come out to go to the bathroom or when it's time to eat. When two weeks are up Renee says Michelle is a bad influence and I'm not allowed to see her anymore. She says Michelle is going to *hell* because her parents don't care about her or *anything* she does. Renee says is that what you want? Do you want to go to hell and burn in an eternal lake of fire, where every day is *horrible?* Or do you want to go to heaven when you die and be with Jesus and everyone I love.

I'm *tired* of always hearing about how I'm going to hell and I'm tired of Renee's *stupid* face! I yell I hate you Renee, and I *hate* Jesus, and I hope I *do* go to hell, 'cause that's where *all* my friends are going...and if you're in heaven then I hope I *never* go there... 'cause you're a *bitch*!

Renee smacks my face hard like Mom used to. I fall to the ground because she's still a lot bigger than me, but I get back up real quick and glare at her and wish I could set her on fire with my mind. I wish for her to drop dead and go to heaven so she can go be with all the other people like her...but neither happens.

Renee stares at me, her eyes wide and enraged, shocked at what I said and maybe even shocked at her response. She quietly says for me to go to my room.

When Dad comes home I feel my stomach drop, but my fear quickly turns into anger. I want to fight. I want to hit him and I want to kick Renee in her lady balls. I hear him and Renee talking in their room, then yelling, then talking again.

Dad comes in and tells me to drop my pants so he can give me another spanking. I resist and try to fight him off but I can't because he's *huge*.

115

I don't make any noise this time. I instead grit my teeth then stare at him after, my chest rising and falling with heavy breaths, my eyes narrowed and anger in my face.

When he opens his arms and says to give him a hug, I stand there and yell I hate you, Dad!

Dad looks at me with a stone face and says no you don't, son.

I say yes I do, I really do!

He gets up, shakes his head, then looks at me and says, I love you, son. Then he turns off the light and closes the door. An hour or so later Grace comes into the room to go to bed, but she doesn't say anything to me and is extra quiet.

The next few weeks are awful and no one says anything to me except it's time for breakfast or lunch or dinner and I should stay in my room. I'm not allowed to play with Michelle anymore and I miss her terribly because she's not just my friend...I love her. I want us to run away together, but where could we go?

I've got no one to play with except Grace. I learn in school that salt kills snails, so I take her on the side of the house and we pour salt on snails. I make a circle of salt around the snails. After I watch them struggle to get out I make the circle smaller. I wonder if snails know fear. I wonder if these snails know they're about to die.

When the snails feel like they have no hope and they're full of only sadness and terror, I pour salt on top of them and watch them writhe in pain until they die, foaming and in utter agony.

I *wish* I could do this to Renee.

I pretend the snails are her and Grace likes that, since she hates Renee, too. We throw the dead bubbly snails against the wall of the house and whisper fuck you, Renee!

I feel better when I hurt the snails, when I kill them, but only for a moment. Then I feel sad. I feel empty. Horrified. I feel like I'm underwater and can't breathe. I can't get out. The circle of salt is getting closer and closer and it's going to pour all over me.

I wish I'd never been born.

I start to miss Mom and think maybe she wasn't so bad after all.

At dinner I poke around at some tuna pasta that Renee made, then ruined again by mixing peas into it. She *knows* I hate this, and now she and Dad *always* make me stay at the dinner table for ages after everyone else leaves because by now they know I'm just going to take them to the toilet. I *hate* peas, they squish in my mouth and remind me of how dog poop squishes when you accidentally step on it!

I tell Dad I want to go home. I say I miss Mom.

Renee looks up from her plate with a hopeful smile at Dad and quickly says okay, we can do that!

Dad looks real sad. He says we'll talk about it tomorrow, okay son?

We don't talk for a few days. Before I have a chance to bring it up, Dad says it's time I got my own room. He says I'm too old to share a room with Grace and a growing boy needs his privacy.

I'm surprised and ask where will I sleep? Will I go to the den? That'd be like having my own house!

Dad laughs then says no I can't move all the way down to the den, that's too far. He says he and Renee are tired of sleeping on their waterbed, so I can move into their old room and they'll move into what was the guest room.

That made me completely forget about wanting to leave and live with Mom again. I feel like I'm not drowning anymore. I can finally *breathe.*

Renee isn't happy at *all* about me taking their old room. She's stone-faced when I ask if she'll miss her waterbed and offers only a curt no.

Grace is *super* jealous of my new room and finds any excuse she can to come in and go on my waterbed. I yell get out of my room! a *bunch* of times, then she whines real loud like she *always* does when she can't get her way.

Dad walks into my room and says come on, Gracie. Don't go in your brother's room without asking!

I'm stunned. It's a small victory, and though it's the only one so far, it's big to me!

I love the waterbed, it's the coolest thing ever! It's not really that great for sleeping, but I don't really sleep that much anymore. I like laying on it...it's like swimming in the ocean.

Eventually Grace *does* get to stay in my room for one night after she begs and begs Dad, and Dad is tired of hearing her whine. Dad says okay Rol, let her stay in your room tonight.

I object and Dad says come on Rol, it's only one night.

He bribes me with pizza and a movie too. I can't complain.

We eat pepperoni pizza then watch a movie that Renee likes, and then it's time for bed. After I brush my teeth and Grace brushes hers, she crawls onto my bed to curl up and go to sleep. Not *fifteen* minutes later she throws up *all* over it! I *know* she did it on purpose! I hit her with a pillow while she's crying and yell no Grace, *no*! like she's a bad dog.

Dad comes in and calms her down. She's crying and hiccupping a lot after throwing up, so he rubs her back and says hey Gracie, hey, it's okay sweetheart, it's okay.

I just wanna hit her with a pillow again.

Amariah The Boy

Renee takes Grace to the bathroom, in case she needs to throw up some more. Dad gets a paper towel and cleans up the vomit best he can. I whine that it *still* smells awful, and I don't *wanna* sleep in vomit! I ask can't they put on clean sheets or give 'em to me so I can do it?

Dad is tired and getting pissed too. He says look here, son we don't *have* any right now. He says go to bed, we can wash everything in the morning, alright?

Grace comes back into my bedroom crawls back onto my waterbed, then turns her back to me and goes to sleep. I'm *pissed* 'cause now my bed smells *awful,* and I never wanted her on my waterbed in the first place!

That's the *last* time I let Grace sleep on my bed. When she tries again, I always bring up the time the waterbed made her throw up. Even when she runs to Dad he says nope, sorry honey.

A few weeks later, just one *day* before Grace's birthday, and early in the morning, a *massive* earthquake strikes. It *topples* buildings and snaps freeways in half like old breadsticks. It makes streets roll like waves on the beach! I'm sure that dogs outside meow and cats bark, because everything is *wrong.*

I awake mid-air before I slam into the wall, since that's where the waterbed decided I needed to go. Stunned and confused, I struggle to my feet and hear Renee screaming in the hallway.

I open my bedroom door and see her. If she's not screaming in terror, then she's saying oh-my-God, Jesus save me! over and over.

Grace is in the hallway leaning against the wall and crying, so I grab ahold of her and pull her into my doorway, like I learned in school.

As the house shakes, I think about the emergency earthquake box we made at school for my home and my fruit snacks inside. I can't *wait* to eat them 'cause there's an earthquake right now and that means I get to eat them...I hope they'll be okay and not get smashed.

Renee stops screaming when she sees us and joins us in the doorway. After she joins us, I get to hear her scream oh Jesus oh Jesus, lord in heaven save us with your grace!

She does this directly in my ear while she clutches Grace and I in absolute terror, like she's casting a magic spell.

I think to myself this sure is strange because she *hates* magic spells. She told me so a thousand times. Magic is the devil's work.

Dad's somewhere far away doing work, so it's just the three of us. Grace is still a little scared but mostly calm now and I just want my fruit snacks. Renee won't shut up though. I hope if Jesus *does* hear her, he'll drop the house *right* on her head, like the bad witch in The Wizard of Oz. Or kind of like when you notice a mosquito and say oh, what's that? and then smack it. Not that me and Grace need to be smacked...just Renee.

The aftershock hits and I'm paralyzed in fear. I was mostly asleep for the first wave and actually feel this one. I think to myself I hope Renee's voice isn't the last thing I hear.

She's screaming again.

Grace is crying and I hold her tight against me with one arm while I hug the door jamb with my legs and other arm.

Renee prays to Jesus even *louder.*

I pray to Jesus that if we *all* get squished and die, that me and Grace go to the opposite of wherever the hell Renee goes. The shaking comes to a stop as the aftershocks die away, an angry toddler kicking its legs and then finally drifting off to sleep. I immediately go for my fruit snacks. I figure I earned them, but Renee yanks me back to the doorway, terrified and squeezing my shoulder while she trembles.

We wait for ten minutes or so in silence and nothing happens, then check around the house for damage. We're really lucky: only a few drinking glasses and Renee's stupid little ceramic angels are shattered. When the power comes on Renee flips on the TV and turns it to the news. I've retrieved my fruit snacks and happily open the bag, when she calls us into the sitting room to say oh my God, look at the news! Oh my God!

I'm more interested in snacks. I munch away at them and I like strawberry best, but cherry is pretty good, too.

Renee says something about how many people probably died and how lucky we were, and then she says oh praise Jesus, thank you, thank you Jesus...and now she's crying.

I wonder why she's like this.

I make a little humming noise and find a blue fruit snack and wonder what flavor it is...it tastes *really* good! I look at the back and discover it's blue raspberry. I didn't know there were blue-flavored raspberries! Definitely my favorite.

Renee yells hey what do you think you're doing?

I pause chewing for a moment. With a full mouth I say what? We just got hit by an earthquake. I'm eating the earthquake food!

120

Amariah The Boy

She tells me that any food we have is for *emergencies* and I say well, Grace is eating honey grahams!

Renee tells me to get her a bag of honey-grahams too, then she leads us in prayer. She says to pray *extra* hard to thank the Lord for sparing us, because we're *not* worthy.

Roland Amariah Gonzales

When third grade ends, and a few days of summer break go by, Dad says I'm allowed to talk to Michelle again. He says he's tired of seeing me mope around and it's important for me to have friends.

Renee's upset about this and says she thinks it's a bad idea, but hey what does *she* know, because she's *just* a woman!

Dad looks at her then sighs and shakes his head before he says *really,* Renee?

They argue a bit. I didn't know that women knew *less* than men...but Renee *is* doing what Dad says...it must be true! That's good to know! I need to remember this for the next time Renee tells me to do something.

When I finally see Michelle she says she's going to summer camp and will be gone *all* summer. I quickly rush home and ask Dad and Renee if I can go to summer camp with Michelle.

Dad calls them and after a short talk on the phone tells me it's too late to sign up and there's no more room.

I'm *devastated.* I *finally* got to talk to Michelle again and now she's going away for the *whole* summer!

Before she leaves, we sit together in her backyard on her bench swing and hold hands when no one is around. We swing together as she squeezes my hand and says she'll come back at the end of summer. She says don't be sad, okay?

I glumly say okay, I'll try, and I hope she has a good time. I say don't forget me, okay?

Michelle gives me a little kiss on my cheek, says she won't, then smiles.

I smile back and it feels like I just laid down on a giant, fluffy, soft pillow that swallows my whole body. I'm real happy...but real sad, too. I'll miss Michelle. I wish I was going with her.

Dad signs me up for a local summer camp at the community center so at least I'm not stuck at home all day. He or Renee drops me off in the morning, then Renee picks me up about an hour after everyone else gets picked up. The camp people don't complain so much because they're busy cleaning up everything anyway. I sure do get bored though.

I try to make friends but it's *hard.* The other kids are all sixth and seventh graders, and I'm only going into the fourth grade! They sit together and talk about movies and things I don't know *anything* about.

Amariah The Boy

One day a seventh-grade boy looks over at me and asks who my favorite character is from a movie called *Tombstone.*

I look at the ground for a moment then take a guess and say uhh Mr. Jimmy?

He barks out a laugh and says who the *hell* is *Mr. Jimmy?* And then they all laugh.

My face is red with embarrassment, so I get up and check out a big ball from the rec room. I bounce it against a wall while they pretend to be cowboys.

After a few weeks a girl named Maria joins our camp. She's my age, has reddish hair and tanned skin, and she even has the same last name as me but it's spelled a little bit different. I find out that she likes to run as much as I do so we race together a lot, but I don't forget Michelle and think about her every day.

I wonder if she's having fun.

Maria and I drift apart 'cause she likes to be with the seventh graders more and she knows about the stuff they're talking about, so I'm alone again.

When all of us aren't outside enjoying free time, we're in the community center building doing arts and crafts. We make twisty keychains and stuff with yarn and popsicles sticks called god-eyes. We play games that the camp counselors start, like kickball, baseball, and sometimes we watch movies! It's usually a movie that Renee doesn't approve of so I have to go outside. The camp-counselor has to sit with me and he's *never* happy since he wants to sit and relax while all the other kids are watching the movie.

They take us to a play in a little theater nearby and it's about the Wizard of Oz. I know the movie, but I don't understand what's going on in the play and it's hard to hear what everyone says. It's nice and cool in the theater though so it's better than standing outside in the sun.

When summer comes to an end I see Michelle again and I'm really happy. I'm even happier when she gives me a great big hug and says she didn't forget me and gives me *another* kiss on my cheek. We spend a whole afternoon talking about our summer and hers sounds a *whole* lot better than mine. She was at a lake and swam and did canoes and hikes and so much else! But I don't care, I'm not jealous or anything.

I'm just happy to be around her again.

Roland Amariah Gonzales

Just after the start of fourth grade, Dad says he has a friend who might stay with us for a while, and it's our job as good Christians to help someone in need. I don't really care, but Renee doesn't seem happy at *all,* so I loudly voice that Dad is *right* and Renee should do what Dad says 'cause he's smarter than her.

They both look at me with wide eyes, then before I know it, I'm back in the corner staring at the wall. I protest since that's what Renee herself said!

Eventually they tell me to get out from the corner and say don't say that again but won't tell me *why* it was bad to say in the first place!

A week later a guy named Andrew moves into our home with his dog Kona. Andrew is okay, I guess. He lets us play with his dog and the dog reminds me of Rock because they look the same, but Rock is more like vanilla ice cream and Kona is more like caramel.

Andrew and Kona move into the den and I'm *jealous* so I offer to trade my room, but Dad laughs and says no way Jose.

I'm pissed, because all the toys and games are down there and we can't go into that room unless Andrew says it's okay.

Andrew can see that I'm bummed and he buys me a Ninja Turtle comic book. It's not like *anything* I've ever seen with Uncle Phil. There's frogs and other things in that comic book and holy cow everyone in the comic is *dying!*

Andrew sees my amazement then winks at me and says he'll keep it downstairs for me so Renee doesn't find it. Andrew is a pretty cool guy!

There's a party at our place a couple of weeks later and some girls my age, Renee's nieces, are there and they're afraid of Andrew's dog. Kona keeps growling and barking at them and I don't know why. I know Kona's a good boy so I put my hands around his snout and hold it shut, because I want them to like him too! I look him in the eye and tell him *no* and he growls at me, but I don't know why he's growling. He's never done that before so I bring my face closer to his and say no again.

When I let go he barks loudly at me. I jerk my head back when he barks, but I'm not fast enough and he closes his jaw on my face. A crimson river *erupts* from the gash and blood runs into my left eye. I shoot my hand up to hold the blood in as an explosion of horrible burning pain envelops me. My thoughts are mostly static and oh no oh no! I can't see! Oh no my eye! I curl into a ball. I shake and moan in pain. The girls scream as Kona runs off.

124

Amariah The Boy

I lie on cold pavement on the side of the house, holding my face with my eyes squeezed shut, weeping in agony. I hear Grace scream and a moment later someone sighs and says great. What are you crying about now, son?

I open my mouth to speak but the pain is so intense that I can't make words. Only moaning noises come out before I grit my teeth.

Dad says alright, let me see and he tries to pry my hands away from my eye but my body is locked up tight. I can't take my hand away. My eye will fall out.

Dad yells goddamit, Rol, let me see! He wrenches my hand away from my face and I hear him shout Oh, FUCK!

He scoops me up and I feel him running and telling people to get the hell out of the way. People cry out in shock. I can't think and I can't see. Everything hurts. I hold my hand against my face. Dad puts me in the car and buckles my seatbelt, then races through the streets to the hospital. I hear a police siren.

Dad says FUCK! Again then yells come on, come on. I hear him telling someone that a dog bit out his son's eye and I'm scared because my eye must *already* be gone.

He says something about the emergency room. I hear the police siren get even *louder*, and it doesn't stop until our car slams on its brakes and I hear Dad shout thank you to someone nearby. He scoops me up and now he's running again.

Dad must be real angry because he's yelling at people. I can feel warm blood pouring around my hand and down my elbow. I try to open my right eye and all I can see is a pool of blood on the floor. I scream, then squeeze my eyes shut again. I start to feel dizzy and say Dad I don't feel so good.

Dad yells someone get the *fuck* out here and help him!

I hear gasps and then a lot of people are saying Oh, shit! And Oh my God! Everyone is yelling for a doctor and I hear someone rush up to us. They tell Dad to follow them and he runs with me to another room.

The doctor pulls my hand away and looks at the bite. He says that I'm *very* lucky. I whine that I don't feel lucky at all.

The doctor tells Dad to hold me down and then he says he has to hurt me to help me.

The doctor starts his bloody work. His needle pierces me repeatedly as he weaves a tapestry with the torn flesh of my face. I grit my teeth and squeeze my eyes shut, pushing back into the bed as hard as I can. Dad holds me down and tries to calm me as my body racks in pain.

My fists clench and my fingernails dig into the palms of my hand with such force that I bleed from there as well. I alternate between moaning, sobbing and screaming. Dad sounds mad and tells the doctor to use *some* kind of anesthetic, but the doctor says no and explains some doctor reason that sounds really complicated.

After an eternity the doctor puts a bandage around my head and says he's done.

Dad tells me I can open my eyes.

When I do I see out of only one, my right eye. Dad tries to smile and says the ladies at the beach are going to miss me for a while.

I laugh weakly and say that's not funny.

The doctor tells me I'll need to come back to get all the stitches out after a long time. And then he gives me some shots, telling Dad that the last thing I want is an infection. By the time we get home the party is over and everyone's gone. Dad tells me to be *extra* careful with the bandage and to put a plastic bag over my head when I shower so nothing gets wet.

A short while later I hear a dog screaming and yelping in pain and run to see what all the noise is. I find Andrew in the den kicking Kona repeatedly as hard as he can. Kona tries to get away, but Andrew just follows him and keeps kicking *hard.* Kona yelps and screams and I throw my hands over my ears and start crying.

Dad runs into the room and yells why all the noise then sees Andrew and yells hey, *hey*! What the hell are you doing? Are you going to kill the damn dog or what?

Andrew stops kicking Kona, who yelps a couple more times, then limps to the corner.

Andrew looks in Kona's direction, breathes heavily, then looks at Dad and says no, man.

Dad says then leave it the fuck alone and stop torturing the thing.

I slowly approach Kona. I'm scared but I know he didn't mean to hurt me, he just wanted me to go away. I'm the one who messed up, not him. Kona whines when I get close and shuffles against the wall nervously, like he wants to get away but he's got nowhere to go.

I sit down some distance from him and he watches me. I hesitate for a moment then nervously call come here, boy...it's okay.

Amariah The Boy

Kona doesn't move, he just whimpers. With more confidence, I call out louder come on boy, it's okay!

Dad and Andrew silently watch as Kona whimpers, gets up, pauses, then slowly limps to me and curls up on my lap. I hold him and say I'm sorry, Kona. *Everything* is my fault.

He licks my arms and face.

Dad tells me later that he grabbed a baseball bat and was ready to bash the dog's head if it tried to bite me again. I'm horrified, but nod my head and say thank you, Dad.

The kids at school think my bandages are really weird and ask me what happened. I tell them a dog bit me and leave it at that.

Roland Amariah Gonzales

My ninth birthday rolls around and my eye has healed. I've got an interesting scar to talk about and I can still see fine. Andrew didn't stay long after his dog almost bit out my eye and I wonder if Kona is okay.

Dad tells me there's going to be a family party for my birthday and he even has a surprise for me. I'm surprised indeed when I answer the door to see Michelle. Even though I'm allowed to go to *her* house, I thought she wasn't allowed over here, around Renee.

Renee is polite to her but I can tell her politeness is forced and she's not happy.

I'm super-excited to see Michelle! We grin at one another and hold hands before I pick her up and squeeze her tight against me. She bursts into laughter then does the same to me and I laugh too. I love Michelle.

Renee looks over and yells that we shouldn't pick each other up because we could get a hernia.

Grandpa Kenney and Grandma Jackie arrive and so do Uncle Alex and Aunt Tammy! ...though no one else from the Gonzales side of my family shows up.

Grandma Margaret comes too but says she can't stay long. She says she's got an AA meeting later.

I get presents from nearly everyone and most of them are five-dollar bills inside a birthday card because people say they don't know what to get me.

Renee gets mad at me and says I'm opening presents *too fast* and I'm making a mess.

I say I don't understand what difference it makes. Won't all the wrapping paper go in the trash?

Renee walks up to me in a huff and snatches a present from my hand. She says if I can't do it right then I can *wait* until I learn how to open them all properly, and the presents can sit up in her closet.

Dad looks exasperated and says really, Renee? He points at me and says Rol's right. All the wrapping paper is going in the trash anyway.

Everyone looks at Renee like she's got a banana growing out of her nose. Renee looks down her nose right back at them for a moment then says she doesn't *care* about their opinions one bit, because they're all going to *hell* anyway.

I feel really bad now and people are either glaring at Renee or trying to look anywhere but *at* Renee. It feels like everyone is about to fight.

I quickly say I'm sorry, I'll open the presents right and can she show me how to do it?

128

Amariah The Boy

Renee carefully peels back *every* small strip of tape then folds the tape in on itself until the wrapping paper forms an even and flat sheet.

I mimic her and *carefully* open the wrapping paper and try to fold the tape in on itself, then gently unfold all the corners before laying the wrapping paper out in a somewhat even sheet.

I hate it. I *agonize* over how *slowly* she makes me unwrap each and every present, so I do it *even slower* than I'm supposed to, so everyone can see how much I hate it and we all suffer.

If the wrapping paper doesn't form a somewhat even square or rectangle after I unfold and lay it out, she scoffs, shakes her head, and mutters how can people *not* wrap things correctly?

When I finally unwrap the gift from Grandpa Kenney, I see...a box of sticks?

I look down and study the box and see a smiling little boy looking at a little log cabin. I mutter son of a bitch, then look up at Grandpa Kenney in confusion.

Dad clears his throat and glares at me. He says hey Rol, say *thank you.*

I look at Dad and, oh shit, he must've heard me and he's *pissed.* I quickly look at Grandpa Kenney and say hey, thanks Grandpa, this is great!

I try to smile and carefully set the box of sticks to the side. Grandpa Kenney looks hurt and everyone is real quiet. I feel bad now. I can tell that I hurt his feelings, but I'm pissed too. Who gives someone *sticks* as a present?

The day went from okay to bad to stupid... and now I hate my birthday.

After I unwrap Renee's present and lay out the wrapping paper, I see that the paper forms a near-perfect rectangle. Everyone is talking amongst themselves because watching me unwrap something for ten minutes isn't as exciting as it sounds.

Renee loudly says *see, RJ?* Look at how nice that wrapping paper is? It's an even rectangle!

Dad rolls his eyes and shakes his head.

I nod and put on a smile. I look at her present and see...coloring books. Renee's been giving me coloring books since I first got to California and *I'm not five anymore,* but no one told her. I put on plastic smile and say to Renee yeah, but it's what's on the inside that counts, right?

129

Renee's jaw drops and everyone looks at me in surprise before they burst out laughing, including Grandpa Kenney.

Renee storms out of the room and slams the door.

I put the coloring books on top of the box of sticks.

Dad laughs so hard that he has to wipe a tear from his eye. He says I shouldn't say things like that.

I say indignantly that Renee says that to me all the time.

Dad points to a bigger box and says right, well, how about you open that next one?

I start to carefully peel away the wrapping paper before Dad leans in close and says Rol, tear that thing up.

I excitedly tear the wrapping paper to shreds while my family cheers. When I see that Dad got me a Lego castle, I'm so happy! I *love* building things and it looks really cool! I give Dad a great big hug and say thank you! And he says no problem son, and then he tells me he loves me and tousles my hair.

Michelle smiles at me then hands me her gift last, in a small bag. It's got a necklace in it. It's nothing special. It's not big or shiny. It doesn't light up or tell the time.

It's from her though, so I love it.

I love Michelle. She helps me put it on then grins at me and shows me that she has a matching one. I hug her and we both hug for so long that Dad laughs and says okay you two, okay. Let's all eat some cake!

After everyone goes home Dad pulls me to the side and says that I really hurt Grandpa Kenney's feelings. He says I should at least *try* to play with what he got me 'cause it's the thought that counts.

I say what, play with sticks?

Dad says first off Rol, they're not *sticks* they're Lincoln Logs, and I got them as a boy too. Secondly, they're not that bad and you might be surprised.

I say oh, okay.

I play with the Lego castle first, and it's a lot of fun to look at the how-to pages that come with it and put it all together. When I finish the first castle, I'm so proud and show it off to Dad. He's grinning before he points at me and says don't forget about the Lincoln Logs, and I say okay.

I have a blast holding imaginary battles in my castle for about two days until Renee smokes her weed, gets really high, and comes into my room. She tells me I need to stop playing and clean up my room. I sigh

130

dejectedly and say I will, then I move to the other side to pick up some clothes I left on the floor.

Renee picks up my Lego castle by the *very top* of a castle tower.

I yell wait, Renee! Don't hold it by that part! But she ignores me. The part she's holding breaks off in her hand, and the rest of the castle explodes onto the floor in a million pieces.

I cry out no!

Renee says oh, *sorry* and I should stop overreacting. Then she says anyway, now you can put it together again...isn't that the most fun part? She says to make sure I pick up *all* the pieces 'cause she doesn't want to step on any, then she leaves my room.

I'm angry and try not to cry. She always ruins *everything*. I push all the pieces into a pile in the corner of the room. I don't want to put it all together again right now because it takes *forever*.

I sit on the bed and look out the window. I listen to the birds while I sniffle a bit then get up to blow my nose and notice the Lincoln Logs. I decide to give them a try and oh hey, these things fit together real easy. After I make a little log cabin, I pick it up and out of curiosity drop it on the floor. It doesn't explode like the Lego castle did and I like that a lot.

Dad gets home and hears what happened from Renee then comes into my room to check in on me and ask if I'm okay. I'm playing with little Lego castle people who are now in the Lincoln Log houses that I made, and I'm making them battle.

I look up and say yeah Dad, I'm okay!

Before he sees me playing with the Lincoln Logs, he says he's sorry that Renee broke my castle. When he sees what I'm doing he says oh hey, you're digging those Lincoln Logs, huh?

I say yeah they're a lot of fun, Dad!

He's happy about that. He goes and calls Grandpa Kenney who's happy to hear that, too. Grandpa Kenney even calls me later to ask how much I like them and laughs after I say that at first I thought they sucked, but they're actually really cool.

Roland Amariah Gonzales

Fourth grade is *awesome.* We do all kinds of neat stuff, sometimes *really* gross, but still really cool. We learn about how owls throw up their food and the bone-clumps are called owl pellets. I raise my hand and shout to the teacher does that mean that owls don't poop and they don't have butts, or do they poop from their mouths? And everyone laughs because I said *poop* and *butts.* The teacher smiles wryly and says *yes* they have butts, this is just the way they eat little critters.

We dissect owl pellets and then reassemble the bones to figure out what the animal used to be, and I learn that owls eat all kinds of small animals. I love science! We also learn about Native American tribes and use papier-mâché, cardboard and lots of colorful feathers to make tribal war shields.

Dad signs me up for some kind of special education class after school and I notice that the other kids are *really* different from me. Some of them are wearing helmets, some of them are drooling a bit, and some are stuck in wheelchairs. One kid thinks it's real funny to pick his nose and try put it on me and I don't think it's funny *at all.* When he shoves his hand in his butt and tries to touch me, I scream and run away.

The classes aren't always bad and sometimes we do fun things like bounce a huge ball on top of a big sheet trampoline or watch a movie. Other times we get granola bars and juice which is cool, I guess.

I tell Dad that I don't like that class but he says that I need to give it a chance. I start to dread it every day because a lot of the kids do gross things all the time and I don't want drool or snot or *anything* on me! One of my normal classmates sees me in that class after school and makes fun of me during normal class and says I'm a retard.

I yell back nuh-uh, *you're* a retard! But he just laughs and says he's not the one in the retard class!

I'm angry and sit in class and think about how I *know* I'm not retarded but...wait. Do the other kids in that class *also* not think they're retarded? Because they *definitely* are. One of them bit my arm when I was looking at the trees and not listening to him and – oh shit.

Am I retarded?

My grades are all pretty good, but I do get in trouble a lot for talking in class and I hate sitting still in one place. I mean, I don't bite anyone but sometimes I want to. I laugh at fart noises but so does everyone else! I start to get really worried and I have *more* trouble sleeping, but

Amariah The Boy

Dad pulls me out of that class before I have a chance to say anything. I don't bring it up in case he decides to put me back.

Roland Amariah Gonzales

Mom calls the house and tells me that she's coming out to California to be with me and to see Gracie. I'm excited to see her again 'cause I forgot about how horrible she was before, and this means I can watch the stuff on TV that I used to!

Mom says even though she missed my birthday she'll be here in time for Halloween. I think to myself maybe I won't have to go to another Christian Harvest Festival!

Mom drives out but Randy isn't with her anymore. There's a new guy now and she says his name is Rowdy. I think about how the names Randy and Rowdy sound almost exactly the same.

Rowdy looks like Randy though he's a bit scragglier. He's got longer black hair under a faded and worn trucker hat, a similar mustache, and a big nose.

Mom gets a job at a Fatburger nearby and I'm excited, because that means free strawberry milkshakes.

Both Dad and Renee aren't happy to have Mom in the house, Renee being *especially* pissed, but she allows it so Mom can see Grace.

Mom stays in California for a couple of weeks until Dad and Renee tell her she can't live at their house and has to find a place of her own. Mom looks around for a day or so then says that everything is too expensive and we're going back to Missouri. She tells me we're leaving in two days.

I try to convince her to stay and look harder. I tell her I've only got a bit of the fourth grade left, even though it just started, and I'm doing really well in school.

Most importantly, I don't want to leave Michelle! I beg Mom to find a place out here. Maybe we can live with Grandma Margaret? Mom says it ain't up to you, and that I can visit Michelle if I ever come back.

I can feel my heart ripping apart. I don't want to go back to Missouri! I don't want to leave Michelle.

I go to my room and collapse onto my bed, scream into my pillow, then lay there and stare at the wall.

Dad comes into my room and says he's really sorry and that it's not up to him. He says hey Rol, why don't you go say goodbye to Michelle?

I go to Michelle's house and we sit on the bench swing together. I try really hard not to cry, but it's not easy because I'm leaving in a couple of days and I don't think I'll ever see her again. When I tell her that my mom is taking me back to Missouri she starts to cry, and that makes me cry, too. She squeezes my hand really hard and we're not swinging anymore.

Michelle's mom comes out when she hears us both crying and asks what's wrong. Michelle sobs and says RJ is going away and never coming back.

Michelle's mom sees us holding hands and looks heartbroken, and says aw, I'm so sorry, you two. I'm so sorry. Sometimes this happens in life. She says hey, do you want a picture together? So you don't forget each other?

We both wipe away the tears on our faces and try to smile.

Her mom goes into the house and comes out with a camera then tells me to sit on the swing and Michelle to sit on my lap. I hug Michelle tightly and give her a small kiss on the back of her head and then I'm crying and so is she, but at least I'm not sobbing anymore.

Michelle's mom says aw, come on now. She tells us to *try* to smile so we can remember each other happy and not sad. She says it's *really important* so we try to put away all of our sad feelings and smile.

That day, Michelle's mom takes in the film to get it developed. Two days later, on the day I'm leaving for Missouri, she hands the photograph to me.

I hug Michelle for a short eternity. I bury my face in her neck and inhale her scent deeply. She smells of jasmine flowers and a bit of sweat. I don't want to forget her scent. I don't want to forget her, not ever. She puts her hands on my shoulders and we share a kiss for the first and last time. I say I love you very much and she says she loves me, too. We're both about to cry again, so we say goodbye to each other and she runs home.

I feel like there's a tree growing out of my throat.

I say goodbye to Dad and Grace. Renee is inside the house and Dad says she doesn't feel well. Dad tells me to come back soon. I nod my head and wipe away my tears, and then I get in the car with Mom and Rowdy.

Roland Amariah Gonzales

CLINTON II

The drive back to Missouri is long, absolutely boring, and entirely uneventful. It's winter of 1994 and I struggle with a deep sense of sadness and a loss of the warmth of California weather, a sharp contrast to the *increasingly* frigid weather the farther we drive east.

We get lost a couple times along the way as Mom has trouble reading the map she got at a gas station. In about four days, we journey from Redondo Beach to Kansas City, and then we arrive in Clinton.

It's a couple of weeks before the Thanksgiving holiday and Mom says I'll go back to school afterward. I remembered the cold sweeping winds of Clinton but had forgotten the familiar, biting sting. It latches onto me the moment I step out of the car and refuses to let go, a dog hungry for the kill. I squint and struggle to see ahead as the howling wind robs me of my senses.

Rowdy and Mom push me toward a house. We go in and he introduces me to his mom, Dena.

Dena says I can call her Grandma Dena. I say okay but think to myself great, grandma number...four? Five?

Grandma Dena has wrinkly skin that's fair in color, curly gray hair, and always wears sweaters because she's cold all the time. And she's real tall.

Mom and Rowdy say we'll stay here for a while until we get our own place. I look around and realize that Rock isn't here. I ask Mom about Rock and she says she gave him away to a nice family. She says like it's the most obvious thing in the world that she couldn't bring him with her when she went to get me in California. She says we can go visit him if I want.

Rock was my best friend when I was here before. In fact, he was my *only* friend...he saved my life. Mom just...gave him away?

I feel tears welling up in my eyes, but I don't want Grandma Dena to see me cry. I just met her. I don't want her to think I'm a crybaby, *especially* because Dad says I cry all the time.

Amariah The Boy

I nod, tell Mom okay and then swallow the lump in my throat. I ask Grandma Dena where the bathroom is and run in there. Mom laughs and calls out yells looks like that boy's gotta go!

I sit on the toilet lid and think of Michelle's pretty smiling face, how she said she loves me, too. I think of Rock furiously licking my cheeks while I struggle to push him away, laughing so hard that my belly hurts. I think of Grandpa Irish's warm smile as he looks around to make sure no one is watching before he sneaks me some candy. They're all gone now.

I'm all alone.

I turn on the water then bury my face in a hand towel so no one can hear me cry. I take off my clothes and hop into the shower and let the warm water cascade over me before making it so hot that thick clouds of steam limit my sight. When I walk out of the bathroom, I'm handed a red onesie pajama that Grandma Dena got for me. I object at first, complaining that onesies are for *babies.*

Mom echoes this when she sees it and says in a sickly-sweet voice there's nothing wrong with wearing baby clothes, RJ.

Grandma Dena frowns at my mom, shakes her head, then says they're not *baby onesies*, RJ. They're long johns, a kind of full-body underwear. All the men wear them.

I look up at her in suspicion, but then she pats me on the head and says trust me, you're gonna need it in this cold weather!

My bedroom is next to the kitchen, and opposite the stairs leading to the basement. Rowdy says there's no insulation *and* no heater for my bedroom. I try to sleep without the baby onesie the first night but I wake up at the witching hour, my body shaking and teeth chattering. I look at the long johns for only a moment before I don them. I am not about to freeze to death.

Mom takes me to see Rock the next day. I'm sad to know he's not my boy anymore, but I'm hopeful, too. We pull up to an old and faded blue house. As I exit the car I gaze at the trees around me, covered in those gold and red leaves that I'd missed during my stay in California. The sky has an orange glow as the sun trails in the distance, its work done for the day.

Rock sits behind a big white wooden fence and he's chained to the ground next to a dog house that looks much too small.

I grin then yell out Rock! and his ears perk up.

Roland Amariah Gonzales

He first barks out a small inquisitive woof or two before following with louder borks. He runs back and forth in his yard, tail wagging. When he tries to jump up against the fence he gets yanked back by the chain, falls to the ground and coughs, then barks again and happily wags his tail.

A family comes out of their house, lets us into their yard, and unchains Rock who was straining against his chain. I crouch down and clap my hands and Rock runs up and starts licking my face. He gets real excited and jumps up, knocking me over. I can't stop laughing when he keeps licking me like I'm an ice cream cone. I wrap my arms around him and squeeze him tightly before I wrestle him to the ground.

I never want to let go.

While Mom and Rowdy are talking to the people at the house. Rock's new boy yells out Rock come 'ere!

Rock doesn't budge. The boy yells out angrily Rock, *come. Now!*

Rock jumps off me and runs up to his new boy and sits. The boy pets Rock's head and tells him what a good boy he is.

I smile and try to call Rock back to me, and he starts to move toward me, but the boy holds his collar so Rock can't move. I clap my hands and call louder but Rock is held back.

The boy smiles at me triumphantly and tells Rock what a good boy he is, and isn't he the best boy? Then rubs his head some more.

The boy throws a ball toward me and tells Rock to fetch it and Rock bolts after the ball then brings it back to the boy, who then loudly says to me Rock is just the best boy ever, ain't he? Rock rolls over and the boy rubs his belly.

Now Rock is wagging his tail like he's trying to put out a fire, his tongue lolling out the side of his mouth. This boy doesn't want to share Rock with me.

I'm not Rock's boy anymore.

I walk over to Mom and ask if we can go home.

She says oh, already? We just got here!

I tell her I'm really tired and just wanna go home.

Mom says alright kid, wait a couple of minutes.

Mom and the boy's parents talk for about ten more minutes while I watch the boy play with Rock. The boy keeps his back to me and throws the ball away from me so Rock can't go anywhere near me.

After a while Mom yells out alright Rol, let's go home so you can have your nappy nap! and laughs at her joke.

Amariah The Boy

The boy's parents say I can come visit Rock any time. Their son says yeah, anytime! and waves at me and grins a big toothy grin.

His dad rubs his son's hair and smiles down at him.

I never see Rock again.

I mope about the house, not wanting to go outside, not knowing where to go even if I did. I spend most of my time in my bedroom. Grandma Dena knocks on my door, enters, and says I can't sit in there up 'til Thanksgiving. She says it's only a few days away, you know! She asks if I'd like to come and sit with her and watch figure skating on the TV.

I don't know what figure skating is and I'm tired of sitting in my room and being sad, so I say okay.

I watch people slide and fly around on the ice. Sometimes they do really neat tricks like jumping up and spinning around or skating backward *fast*. Some of the ladies wear really pretty costumes and I can almost see their *hoo-hahs*...and I say so.

Grandma Dena looks down at me in surprise, looks back up at the TV, then lets out a cackle and says yeah RJ, I guess you *can* almost see their hoo-hahs! Then she says but that's not what this is all about, so try to appreciate the other stuff too, okay?

I look at her thoughtfully then say mmm and nod my head.

After twenty minutes or so she asks if I'd like some cheesecake and tea and I don't know about tea but I *do* love cheesecake and excitedly say yes.

She smiles and takes me into the kitchen then cuts a slice of cherry cheesecake. It's probably the *best* thing I've ever eaten and I ask her where she bought it.

Grandma Dena looks at me and raises an eyebrow and cackles again. She says buy? No way, silly goose, *I* made this!

I say wow, nuh-uh!

She cackles again and then asks if I'd like to learn how. I nod enthusiastically and we spend the next few days in the kitchen while she shows me how to bake cheesecakes, make coffee caramel twists, rock candies, breakfast candies, and apple butter.

I ask how she learned to do all this and she taps my nose with her flour-covered finger as she says her grandma taught her, just like she's teaching me right this minute.

Mom sees us baking up a storm and laughs that it's a good thing Thanksgiving is only a day away!

Roland Amariah Gonzales

Thanksgiving comes around and Grandma Dena is a *whirlwind* in the kitchen all day! I ask if I can help and she says maybe next year, because she has to move really fast and doesn't want me to get hurt by any flying pans or falling into the oven. She laughs that cackling laugh and says I'm sweet and everyone will gobble me up, but I won't like it!

I laugh and tell her I *really* wanna help, so she tells me I can get some stuff from the basement. I smile and say okay.

Grandma Dena sends me to get jars of apple butter that she had made a couple of months ago. I turn up my nose in disgust and say ew, Grandma Dena, won't they taste old and moldy?

She eyes me, gives me a frown and says nonsense, they age very well, just like me! and then she laughs again. She says now git! and shoos me off with her kitchen towel.

I laugh and run out the kitchen door that leads directly to the basement. I look into the dark murky abyss below me and have second thoughts. I swear I can hear something moving around down there.

Grandma Dena says from the kitchen close that door, RJ, it's cold! And make sure you're real careful coming up those stairs. Only carry what you can safely, okay? Those glass jars are fragile and don't like to be dropped on the ground – just like me!

She cackles again and I flip the light switch next to me. A dim yellow light illuminates cobwebs and spider webs around me as I look down with an uncertain frown, and steel myself. I say to myself okay RJ, we can do this. We're doing this for Grandma Dena, so we have to be brave, okay?

I think back to when Grandma Dena showed me the basement. There's a pull-string for another light switch at the *bottom* of the stairs. If I can get there quick enough to pull the string then nothing can get me...*those are the rules.*

I slowly descend the stairs and freeze in place after I hear the ancient wood creak underfoot, my presence trumpeted for all to hear. A sinking feeling hits my stomach as any hope I had of stealthily retrieving the jars is dashed.

My right hand traces the wall for support, the stairs lacking any sort of handrail. I feel about in the dimly-lit dark and pray that the sticky strands of spider webs entangled on my hand bear no venomous hosts. I frantically wipe my hands against my pant leg. My thoughts become darker as I journey forward and flirt with oblivion. Did the shadow people in Redondo Beach follow me here? Are they down in the basement? What if there's something new and terrifying down here? Would anyone be able to get to me before I'm dragged away to some place terrible...or devoured?

I try whispering, In the name of Jesus, go away a few times but it does nothing to alleviate the overwhelming feeling of despair that threatens to swallow me whole. I'm almost at the bottom of the stairs now. I hear something skitter under the stairs directly underfoot and gasp. Was it a mouse? A snake? The long, barbed tentacle of some great monstrosity poised to strike? My heart is pounding and my breath is shallow as I slowly arrive at the bottom and step onto the cold concrete floor.

I realize only now that I should have worn shoes. The ground is *freezing*. I cautiously snake my hand up to the light's drawstring and hear movement again. I pause and realize that I'm not doing a very good job of quickly doing *anything*. Just before I pull the drawstring, I experience a moment of terror as I notice all the jars on the shelves in front of me. They're dimly lit by the light at the top of the stairs. Each one looks like it holds some kind of wriggling abomination desperate to break free and slop, crawl, and writhe toward me, eager to consume my flesh.

I pull the drawstring, my chest heaving with my labored breathing. The light comes on and everything reverts to normal. I slowly relax and my shoulders drop as I take in a deep breath and let it out slowly. I balance four jars of apple butter against my chest with one arm, then look to pull the drawstring and turn off the lights.

I pause for a moment and think no way in hell, then make my way back up the stairs. I fumble with the door up top and finally get it open, eager to close it after I pass through.

Grandma Dena exclaims oh, so many! and asks if I turned off the light at the bottom and I say that I couldn't with all the jars in my hands.

She says oh, well can you go turn it off? We can't light up the world from the basement, can we? and then lets out another one of her cackles.

I nod and tell her I'm going to leave the kitchen door open in case I fall, that way she can hear me.

She looks at me for a moment then smiles knowingly and says alright then, RJ, but be quick!

I make my way to the bottom of the stairs as briskly as I can, turn to face the upper door, plan my escape, then deftly pull the drawstring and run up the stairs as fast as I can. I jump through the door, close it, and desperately lock it, imagining something thundering after me, but that something is unable to open a locked door.

Grandma Dena laughs and says so fast! Were your feet cold?

I look down and wriggle my toes then laugh and say yes, my feet are very cold, so I'm gonna go put on socks!

Rowdy's cousins, his uncle, his sister and her son arrive at the house a few hours later. I go to change into the nicest clothes I have, since it's Thanksgiving and everyone is supposed to wear nice things. They're not comfortable at *all*, but Grandma Dena tells me I'm such a handsome little man so that's nice, I guess.

I don't talk much with all the new people. I don't know them so well, and I don't like talking to people I don't know because they usually make fun of you.

Grandma Dena introduces me to her grandson Robert and says she calls him Rob.

Rob is four years younger than me and he's small.

Grandma Dena tells us to give her space because she's got a lot to do. There's no one else around, so I play with Rob.

We go outside in our big warm winter coats, then we explore a bit. There's a large pine tree in the front yard, and under it is a bed of pinecones. We pick them up and toss 'em around, making a game of who can hit the most *whatever* with a pinecone. We make our way to the backyard, just outside the basement.

Grandma Dena has a garden in her backyard. This is which she grows vegetables, but nothing is growing now because it's too cold. As we walk around, I enjoy the frozen grass crunching underfoot.

The neighbor's house is *huge* and their backyard is *gigantic*. I ask Rob if he wants to explore the neighbor's backyard but he says he can't because he'll get in trouble.

Having no concept of private property beyond *don't get caught,* I shrug and say suit yourself.

I crawl through the fence which is easy to do because it's only got two wooden logs connecting each fencepost. It's more art than it is a barrier to keep people like me out. Convinced that the fence is more an invitation than a safeguard, I walk around free of worry.

The neighbor's backyard is *so cool!* It's a world unto itself, set with dark-grey stone paths lined with knee-high light-grey stone walls, and these lead to many different plants, bench swings, little ponds, and gardens for growing food. It's the size of a park! I enjoy sneaking around, that feeling of a heightened sense of danger. The sounds of every scrape, drip, shuffle, and movement become intensified.

I look back over my shoulder to see Rob staring at me with wide eyes, scared as hell. I motion for him to join me and mouth come *on,* but he shakes his head and whispers loudly *no!* He looks like he's about to cry. I roll my eyes and keep exploring until I hear a door nearby open. I drop to the ground and freeze.

I wait a minute or two, my body pressed flat against the cold, hard stone. I listen for heavy footfalls before slowly lifting my head above a stone wall and peeking through a bush. I see a little old lady peering over her balcony in my direction, and then she scans her entire backyard in all its familiarity, her face suggesting that she's got an intruder.

I remain motionless, taking shallow breaths and hoping their frosty trail won't give me away. The old lady lingers a moment longer, but then a bitterly cold gust sweeps across her garden.

I stifle a laugh as I watch her surprise at this wind, and I hear her yelp as she quickly retreats.

When she's inside, I quietly exhale, the crisp air sending a shiver down my spine.

I look over my shoulder to see that Rob is gone. I frown and shake my head as I think ah, he must've run away when the old lady emerged.

I keep low to the ground as I crawl back toward the wooden fence, the chill of the stone burning my hands. I stop and peek over the wall for a moment to see if the old woman is perhaps spying through the windows. I see nothing.

Satisfied that no one is watching me, I take a few short quick breaths then make a mad dash toward the fence, tumble through the opening, and then run around the far corner of the house. When I get to the other side I take a moment to catch my breath and brush the leaves and frosty grass off my clothes.

I make my way to the front door then go inside and take off my coat. I wince as a blast of hot air from a nearby heating vent lashes across my face. Was it *that* cold outside?

Rowdy notices leaves on my clothes that I missed and says oh? What happened bud, you fall?

I look down, laugh, and say yeah, I slipped out there on the grass 'cause it's so icy! Hey, is the food ready yet? I'm starving!

Rowdy says that everything is just about done, and that I'd better go clean up and then come to the table.

I wash my hands and face in the bathroom, check that my clothes don't have any leaves or twigs, then make my way to the dining table. When I see that all the chairs are taken, I say hey Mom, where am I supposed to sit?

Mom laughs and says whaddya mean, boy? You go sit at the kids' table, you're a kid!

I look over and see Rob waving at me with a smile on his face. He's sitting at a small, plastic, pink and blue table decorated with elephants holding onto balloons. There's *no way* I'll fit on that chair, and I'm not even that big! But this table? It's for babies!

I say to Mom, I don't think it's big enough, and Mom says well that's all ya get, so sit down already.

I carefully sit on the tiny, plastic, bright blue kiddie chair and try to scoot up to the table so I can reach my food. My legs are too big to go under it, so I have to spread my legs like a stretched-out crab. It's real uncomfortable.

I eat as quickly as I can, thinking how sitting at the kiddie table *sucks*.

The food is great, and I eat turkey, honey-baked ham, mashed potatoes with gravy, some green bean casserole that Mom forces me to, cranberry sauce from a can, candied yams, and blueberry cheesecake for dessert.

The adults all drink wine and me and Rob get sparkling grape cider. I'm so full after dinner that I can barely breathe, and I'm also super sleepy. Everyone says their goodbyes and promises to visit for Christmas.

I hop in the shower and dry off, then put on my red onesie pajamas. Grandma Dena was right. These things are lifesavers. Time for bed.

Amariah The Boy

I've got one last free weekend before school starts and decide to explore the neighborhood. I walk down the road, having been forcibly pulled from my pit of despair by the unfaltering optimism of Grandma Dena. There's a small cluster of single-floor apartments nestled together at the top of a hill, about five minutes south of Grandma Dena's house. My ears perk up when I hear sounds of kids laughing and a basketball thumping against pavement.

I pick up a light jog, a slight smile on my face, until I come around a building's corner and see a bunch of kids playing basketball. Only a few are my size, most are much bigger. I see a kid that I suppose is my age and ask if I can play, too. One of the bigger kids, a boy, comes over and slams the ball against my chest and says he don't want me touchin' *his* ball and I *can* go fuck myself.

I kick myself mentally for trying to talk to new people. I should've known better.

I pause for a moment as I cough and rub the pain from my chest. Confused, I look at the ground and say oh...okay.

A young girl, no more than four or five, yells out yeah, *you* don't belong here! The other kids echo similar lines.

I take a step back and notice for the first time that *all* the kids are Black, they've all stopped playing, and they're all staring at me and the bigger boy. Another boy, the same age as the young girl, yells out get the fuck out of here!

A memory flashes in my mind of the Johnson kids throwing rocks at me a couple of years prior.

I quickly leave the area, crestfallen, then walk toward our temporary home then past it in the opposite direction for ten minutes or so. No one is playing outside and hardly any cars are driving down the road. Those that do are filled with people who glance at me with raised eyebrows, making me wonder if I've got something on my face.

I discover nothing interesting except a large dairy factory opposite Grandma Dena's house. After an hour or so of not seeing anyone, I give up and go home. It seems that no one lives around this part of town, or if they do, then their kids don't go outside. Maybe it's too cold?

I tell Grandma Dena that there's nothing to do around here and that there's an old dairy factory across the way, maybe I can explore it?

Grandma Dena says she used to work in that factory and that's no place for little boys. She suggests maybe I could build a puzzle?

145

I sigh then look at the floor then mumble yeah I guess so, and sulk to my room. Mom gets back from the store and I tell her I'm real bored. I don't tell her about the kids up the road though. Mom says I can go with her to the Newsroom. I remember that place from the last time I was in Missouri, she and Randy went there all the time. They seemed to really like it. My interest is piqued, so I go with Mom.

The Newsroom is a dusty old bar southwest of the town courthouse. It's filled with music from the 1970s and enough cigarette smoke that one could be forgiven for thinking someone threw a cloud inside. I can hear a couple of low conversations and occasional laughter inside. Everyone is focused on their drinks, whether staring into them wordlessly or actually drinking. And no one seems to mind a little brown kid running around, so long as I keep out of everyone's way.

I spend my time listening to classic rock and playing arcade games like Centipede, Dig Dug, and Galaga. The bartender switches the games to free play, so I'm glued to the seat. I pinch my fingers when I play Centipede though, because they're too small and get caught on the ball sometimes. Mom is in a good mood and buys me bar food. I eat 146rench fries, chicken strips, and potato skins, which are my favorite. Dad *rarely* let me eat this stuff, because he said it was garbage, but Mom doesn't seem to care and neither do I!

The bartender, an older woman with fading gray hair matched by a fading raspy voice, makes me drinks but only if I sing her a song and because I like to sing, I get as many free drinks as I want! I prefer Roy Rogers more than Shirley Temple. Even though I'm fond of the lemon-lime flavors of a Shirley Temple, I *really* like the maraschino cherry in a Roy Rogers.

Mom and I walk around a bit after we leave. She says it's always good to walk it off. I don't know what *it* is, but *it* beats sitting in the house. Mom says everyone calls this area The Square, because it's a huge square of businesses surrounding the town courthouse. It's a Sunday, so most businesses are closed. Folks are busy going to church. As I enjoy the silence, I think how great it feels to not be stuck in a stuffy church with a bunch of people crying, screaming, and laughing.

Me and Mom quietly walk and don't say a thing. I'm careful to avoid the occasional patch of ice. I peer through the shop windows and see lots of clothing, crafts, decorations, tools, and other stuff for sale. We pass by a pawn shop and it's open, so Mom takes me in. I'm thrilled as I gaze at all the guns, knives and musical instruments. I say to the man

146

running the place that his shop is so cool and he has so many cool things!

He's a big guy with fair skin and dark brown hair streaked with gray, drawn back in a ponytail. He's got big arms and a deep, rumbling voice. He smiles back at me and says his name is Pat and that he and Mom go back a fair ways. I nod, say uh-huh, and ask if I can hold one of the guns.

He says you most certainly may not, but here's a drumstick. Knock yourself out, kiddo.

It's not as cool as a gun. I absentmindedly walk around and tap it against stuff until he and Mom are done talking and Mom says alright Rol, time to go!

I run up to Pat and return the drumstick and he says thank you and waves, then calls out see you around! I wave back. We make our way to the car then drive to Grandma Dena's house. I make a mental note that The Square is actually *really* close. I can probably walk there if I want.

Roland Amariah Gonzales

Monday rolls around, it's early morning, and I wait for the school bus under the pine tree in front of Grandma Dena's house. Snow blanketed everything the night before. I pass time throwing pinecones at the branches above to knock snow to the ground.

The bus arrives and I notice it's much larger than the one I had ridden last time I was in Missouri. The ride through town is around fifteen to twenty minutes. I first recognize the apartment cluster filled with mean and angry Black kids, then The Square, and eventually the Newsroom, as we pass by my landmarks.

I arrive at the school then blindly follow the other kids as they trudge to the cafeteria to eat breakfast. I sit at one of the tables by myself. There's an older lady walking around who looks like she just ate a lemon. None of the kids look at her, and when she gets close they get real quiet.

I don't say anything to the kids who sit next to me. I fumble a bit with my chocolate milk. Unable to open the correct side, I opt to open the opposite. Can't do that either. Dammit.

I raise my hand and yell out to the lemon-faced lady hey miss, can you give me a hand? I can't open this thing.

She stares hard at me, the interloper, then begrudgingly walks to the table and opens my milk carton.

I smile up at her and say thank you miss.

She says man.

I pause, confused, and say uh, thank you, man.

She says *no*, my name is *Miss Mann.*

I immediately think to myself Mister Lady and laugh out loud.

Miss Mann slams her hand against the table and all of the kids, myself included, jerk back in surprise. Miss Mann looks at me and says you're new here, right? No talking.

A lot of kids look at me in wide-eyed confusion, though none ask my name. The bell rings about twenty minutes later. I empty the trash on my tray into the garbage, then go to the main office and ask where my teacher's room is. They ask my name and an adult escorts me to my classroom.

When I arrive at the room the teacher first looks at me in confusion and then says oh! You must be Roland Gonzales, our transfer student! I'm Mrs. Sammons. Class, say hello to Roland who just arrived from California!

Some of the class drones hello Roland, and I say hello back.

148

Amariah The Boy

I tell Mrs. Sammons that I used to live here in Clinton and that I was visiting my dad out in California, that's why I was gone.

She nods and says uh-hunh, that's nice, now go ahead and take a seat.

I'm surprised to see that some kids actually remember me as "the boy from California," though remembrance does not equate to enthusiasm. The attitude of most of them toward me is at *best* indifference. I don't spot Stephanie anywhere and wonder if she left for a different school. Ah well, wouldn't matter much anyway, I suppose.

Over the weeks, I become accustomed to sitting by the window and gazing outside while my classmates pass notes or whisper to one another. No one talks to me much, if at all. I watch kids from younger classes during their recess period and smile at how much fun they have chasing each other and playing around.

I ponder what few leaves remain on skeletal trees before the chill wind gives them one last funerary dance, carrying them to join their kin on the cold hard earth. I envy the flight of birds as they flutter about on the playground, having reclaimed it from screaming children now absent and returned to class.

I think about the time that boy stole my swing and I threw rocks at him and smile. I remember hiding out in the art teacher's room for as long as I could, and I grin to think of how absurd it was to hide from writing such a *small* number of sentences, when compared to the *novel* I had to pen for Renee. I think of Redondo Beach and absentmindedly reach up to feel the gap in my left eyebrow from Kona's bite. My smile fades.

I draw in a deep breath and sigh. I'm nine years old and already nostalgic of what was, to me, a simpler past.

Occasionally, thick rain comes down in heavy sheets, or pelting hailstones in waves, and we're not allowed outside for recess. Instead, we stay inside and play with board games, puzzles, and the like. Mrs. Sammons steps out of the room during one such recess to go make copies for an exam.

I find a spot on the floor to work on a puzzle of a fox jumping over the moon. After a few minutes, a shoe roughly kicks my hand, then stomps on the puzzle. I look up and see the big Black boy, the one who had told me to go fuck myself when I asked if I could play basketball.

I try to stand up and he pushes me back down. I try again and he pushes me down again, and then smiles and laughs. I've got tears in my

149

eyes because I'm angry, and I've never done anything to this kid! Why is he being so mean? I grab a book and intend to throw it at his stupid smiling face and then kick him in his junk so hard that he can't pee for a week...when Mrs. Sammons suddenly returns.

She looks first at him with his foot on the puzzle pieces and then at me with a book raised behind my head, arm cocked to throw, and says Jeremy, RJ, what is going on here?

Jeremy looks stone faced at Mrs. Sammoms, and says nuthin' Mrs. Sammons, and I echo the same.

Mrs. Sammons eyes us both for a moment then tells us to go sit at our desks.

I *hate* Jeremy and he's *not* my friend. When I get home I try to talk to Mom or Rowdy about it, but they're both too tired and tell me they need a break and they actually work all day.

Mom has gotten a job as the assistant manager at a convenience store called Casey's, and Rowdy is working at a print shop. Sometimes, Mom brings back day-old or two-day-old donuts and they're not all that bad, I guess. The day-olds are a bit tough but there's usually some yummy strawberry or chocolate donuts. Apple fritters are my favorite but those are never in the day-olds. Two-day olds are like a rock and Mom says to put water on 'em and throw 'em in the microwave so they get soft.

They're still awful.

Mom and Rowdy say they don't have time to hear about *my* problems, they've got their own and they just want to relax.

I talk to Grandma Dena about Jeremy and she gets a frown on her face before she says well, just try to avoid him, okay? Some people just aren't nice and there's nothing you can do about that.

I say but he's in the same class as me and he's so much bigger!

Grandma Dena smiles sadly and says well RJ, *everyone's* going to be bigger than you because you skipped a grade!

I have no idea what she's talking about, and she explains that I *just* turned nine and I started fourth grade at the age of eight. She says all the other kids are already nine or ten!

I look down, feeling dejected, and think to myself that I don't *remember* skipping a grade. First, second, third, and now fourth? What grade did I skip? My shoulders slump.

Grandma Dena pinches my cheek and says it means you're one smart cookie, RJ!

Amariah The Boy

I throw up my arms and complain loudly well, then that means I'm going to be smaller than everyone else forever!

Grandma Dena laughs and says when you get older it'll be *good* to be so young, and you won't be so small forever, don't you worry.

That makes no sense to me, so I just nod and say okay, thank you Grandma Dena.

I think to myself I wonder what Dad would tell me to do about Jeremy, then realize Dad would make me go to Jeremy's house and punch him right in his stupid face. I decide I like Grandma Dena's idea more and just try to stay away from Jeremy best I can.

The days plod along and before I know it, it's nearly Christmas. Mom and Rowdy have saved up a bit of money and say we'll be finding our own place soon. I'm sad to leave Grandma Dena and tell her so, but she cackles and says she's got a few years left in her yet!

There's no school at Christmas break, and I haven't even made any friends yet because no one wants to play with me. The only kids nearby tell me to go fuck myself and I don't wanna. I spend my time alone.

I love Christmas break and all the decorations around The Square. Beautiful green, blue, and red lights line most of the business windows, and there are ugly yellow lights in others. The blue lights are my *favorite*, then the red and sometimes the green. Mostly blue, though. I *hate* orange. Shiny silver and gold tinsel wraps around streetlamps. Everyone's a lot happier and the smell of apples, cinnamon and other sweet things hangs in the air.

Grandma Dena decorates the outside of her house with colorful lights, and the inside with neat miniature houses that she sets up on a small table. They light up and play music. Everything feels warmer even though it's so cold outside, and I'm not even that sad that I have no friends, because at least Grandma Dena is nice to me.

Grandma Dena and I spend a lot of the Christmas break making sweets and when Christmas day comes, Mom and Rowdy have a surprise for me. They give me a big box that's all wrapped up, then tell me to open it while they sit on the couch and smile at me. I start to peel each tiny piece of tape off the wrapping paper as carefully and meticulously as I can, when Mom speaks up and says what the hell are ya doin', boy? We ain't got 'til next Christmas, go crazy!

I laugh and tear the wrapping paper to shreds, glad that Renee isn't here, and gasp in surprise. They got me a Super Nintendo and I can't believe it! I'm thrilled and jump up and down and they both hug me. I get some warm clothes from Grandma Dena and I say thank you.

I'm *really* excited for the Nintendo. Mom says I can only play with it when my homework is done and *after* I've done all my chores *and* Grandma Dena says it's okay to use the TV.

I say okay! and ask Grandma Dena if I can use the TV right away.

Grandma Dena cackles and tells me *after* she watches A Christmas Story. She says why don't you go and get some hot chocolate for us both and the come and sit right next to me.

I happily run off to the kitchen and bring back two mugs. I have a hard time paying attention to the movie when it starts, but I start to laugh when I see that the boy is my age and now I want a bb-gun, too. When he beats up the bully I think of Jeremy and how I want to hit him in his stupid, ugly face.

I tell Grandma I really like that movie and she smiles and says she does too. I enjoy the rest of Christmas break.

New Year's celebration is nothing special, just staying up late to count backward from ten and I don't see why adults think that's fun. I have to count backward from twenty at *least* once a week and it's never been *that* great.

Soon enough it's 1995, the vacation is over, and it's time to brave the cold and wait for the school bus once more.

Amariah The Boy

Valentine's Day approaches and a sense of malaise overtakes me. My last experience with love hadn't been pleasant, with Stephanie wholly rejecting me. I find Valentine's Day cards pinned to my backpack with an attached note. It reads: For cuties in your class!

I can't recognize the handwriting. I feel uneasy and place the cards in my backpack, then leave to get the school bus. There's a pretty girl named Carrie in the same class as me who shows up at the bus stop sometimes. She's much taller than me and has brownish curly hair. She doesn't talk much, and I never say much to her. She just so happens to be there this morning and I offer a good morning along with a smile.

No response. A good start.

I arrive at school and see paper cutouts of red hearts, mischievous cupids, and lots of pink lining the inside of all the classrooms. Mrs. Sammons says we'll take a break ten minutes before lunch to pass out cards and candies to those we like. The girls in my class giggle and look at one another and the boys they may like. The boys smile and laugh too, some leaning back in their chairs with their hands on their heads, confident of cards and candies to be received.

One of the popular boys says loudly maybe RJ will pass out some of his mom's two-day-old donuts and all the kids laugh before Mrs. Sammons tells them to hush.

After, a bunch of, lessons, on the importance of, comma placement, Mrs. Sammons clasps her hands and announces everyone, clear your desks, let's begin! We each have desk mailboxes, named *heart homes* by Mrs. Sammons, that we had crafted two days before. A flurry of activity ensues as my classmates scramble from desk to desk. They quickly drop cards off, eager to be unseen. I'm nervous because no one's dropped anything off in my heart home. I tell myself that maybe girls aren't coming 'cause they're shy?

I get up and walk around the room and put my mysteriously gifted cards in the heart homes of girls I fancy.

After five minutes, the teacher loudly claps her hands and everyone returns to their desks. The room is buzzing in excitement. My classmates dump the contents of their heart homes on their desks and I look around nervously as I hold my own. The popular boys who have nice haircuts and expensive clothes have *huge* piles of cards and candies, practically from every girl in class! The girls, for the most part, have the same. I take a deep breath and upend my heart home and a single solitary card hits my desk.

Roland Amariah Gonzales

It reads: You Sure Are Swell and has a picture of a monkey inflating a blue balloon in the shape of a heart. I turn it over and see there's no name on it. One of the popular and pretty girls loudly speaks in my direction, right after I look for a name, and tells her friend that her mom forced her to give *everyone* a card, even people she *doesn't* like.

I look out the window and focus on the birds dancing around the playground and how happy they are. I wonder glumly what I did to make everyone hate me. Is this because I *didn't* bring two-day-old donuts? Those things are awful, they're like trying to chew through a sugar-coated brick!

Mrs. Sammons says for everyone to put all their cards and sweets in their heart homes and take them home. And no eating candy in class! She listens to the groans then says okay, one piece each.

I wish I could fly like the birds. I would fly far away from here and go back to California and see Michelle. I bet she'd have a nice card for me, one that she made herself, and I'd make one for her too, and we'd sit on the bench swing together and hold hands when no one is looking.

I feel a gnawing pain deep in my stomach and a lump in my throat every time I swallow. I try not to cry. It's time for lunch, so we all line up at the door and I'm at the back. My eyes are drawn toward the trash can. I look into it and see all the cards I had given out in the trash.

As we walk to the lunchroom, the same popular pretty girl who had given me her obligatory card whispers loudly to her friend, did you see those *crappy* cards that the California kid gave out? They looked like they came from the dollar store!

Her friend says ewww, did you get one too? I threw mine in the trash! They both look back at me and giggle before Mrs. Sammons says no talking in line, girls.

I swallow again and choke out to Mrs. Sammons that I need to use the restroom.

She says okay. Hurry up, you don't want to miss lunch. And wash your hands!

I duck out of line as the girls continue to giggle. I briskly walk to the restroom, go into a stall, and sit on the toilet. I hug my knees and cry into them as quietly as I can so no one hears me. I try as hard as I can to remain blank and emotionless for the rest of the day, as the kids in my class sneak candies into their mouths and Mrs. Sammons pretends not to see. I didn't get any candies.

154

Amariah The Boy

I quietly walk back to my room when I get back home at the end of the day. I don't want to talk to anyone.I hear a knock on my door and Grandma Dena is there. She asks if the girls in my class liked my cards and did I get a whole bunch, too? She says she bets I did because I'm a cutie and she's sure all the girls think so, too.

I struggle to put on a smile. I say yeah Grandma Dena, yeah, I got a whole bunch. Thank you so much!

She squeezes me in a warm hug. I wrap my arms around her waist and bury my face in her sweater, close my eyes and deeply breathe in her scent. Grandma Dena smells like flowers and food from the kitchen. We squeeze each other again and then pull away. Grandma Dena smiles down at me and says any time dear, then sees me wiping away at my eyes and says oh, are you tired?

I nod and am glad she can't see me crying. She tells me to have a good nap and she'll make me a snack when I wake up. I smile and say thank you Grandma, then close the door and fall onto my bed, burying my face in my pillow. I hate Valentine's Day.

Roland Amariah Gonzales

At the end of the school year, Mom and Rowdy find a new place to rent on the southwestern side of town, out near the train tracks. The house isn't anywhere near as nice or big as Grandma Dena's, but it has a basement like hers. Kind of.

I ask Rowdy why our basement is filled with *dirt* when Grandma Dena's is concrete.

He says we ain't got a *basement*, we got a *storm shelter*. He says a storm shelter is a big open space under the house for when tornadoes come to kill us all, then he laughs.

I say oh, well I think Grandma Dena's house is a lot nicer than ours.

Rowdy looks at our house wistfully for a moment then says yeah, yeah that's true, I grew up in that there house, ya know, but in *this* house, your new room has a heater connected to it, *and* insulation!

I say yeah, but it's June *and* hot as hell outside! What good does a heater do me now?

He laughs and says just you wait until winter. Shoot, you'll see how useless it is!

Rowdy and I don't talk much, but when we *do* he usually complains about his job and how his boss doesn't respect him. He smokes some weed then looks at me and says don't my boss know I can do the work of *three* different people? Rowdy says he *really* deserves a raise because he's so great. He takes another hit from his bong then coughs a bit and says his boss ain't a fan of him takin' off to California with Mom. He clears his throat and says his boss is being a *real* dick about it.

Rowdy mostly complains to Mom who voices her support and encourages him to demand a raise, though sometimes he complains to me and I nod, as if I understand the plight of the modern worker.

Mom takes me to visit her friends on occasion, an older couple she met at the Newsroom. They're probably ten years her senior, but she seems to have as much trouble making friends at her age as I do my own! Connie has long, wiry, graying hair drawn into a ponytail, a gaunt near-skeletal appearance, and prefers blue flannel shirts and blue jeans. Lee is more or less Connie's mirror image, except he also wears a faded and dirty trucker's hat.

Lee and Connie like to laugh and they like to get high. When Mom and I visit, they all sit together and smoke weed, drink beer, or smoke something that smells like burning plastic but kind of sweet.

I play in the front yard or sit on the couch next to them if the heat outside is sweltering which is often the case. Weather in Missouri follows *extremes*. I heard Mom say that winter is so cold that dogs pissin' get stuck to fire hydrants. In the summer I hear Rowdy say it's about as hot as two rats fuckin' in a wool sock.

After Connie smokes from her glass pipe, she lays back into the couch and says she feels *real* good and then laughs. She likes to joke around a lot and I hate it. She digs her fingers into my leg and squeezes it just above my knee, or roughly drags her fingers over my ribcage while she laughs and asks how much it tickles.

I get angry and say it doesn't tickle at all! I tell her it hurts as I try to bat her hands away.

Mom laughs, smokes from the glass pipe, and sometimes joins in with Connie's jokes.

Connie thinks it's really funny to try and burn me with her cigarettes and she laughs when I get up from the couch and try to run away. If I get too upset or whine Mom tells me to calm down. She says ain't no one gonna burn you with a cigarette.

When everything settles down I return to the couch. Mom and Connie start talking again and I try to watch cartoons on Connie's TV. The thing is so old I can hardly see anything. And hell, the show I'm watching has got to be as old as the TV!

While they're talking Connie grabs my arm and stubs out her cigarette on it. I scream in pain and run out the front door. I hear my confused mom say oh? before they both start laughing, like it's the funniest thing in the world.

I've got tears in my eyes from the pain. I hate going outside— it's so *hot* out there and it's hard to breathe! But I hate being burned by cigarettes even more.

There's nothing to do out here, so I walk up and down the street a few times. After about an hour, Mom comes outside and seems surprised to see me. She blinks a few times then clears her throat, spits, and says come on, Rol, let's go home.

I look at my arm while she drives and I wince in pain when I touch the burn.

I wonder if this will make a new scar. I hope not.

I also wonder what kids from my class are doing right now. Do they get cigarette burned by their mom's friends, too?

Mom drives with a goofy grin on her face like she just heard a great joke. I gaze longingly at the green leaves of trees and birds flitting about. Occasionally I see the brilliant red feathers of a cardinal, or the striking blue of a blue jay. I think to myself how pretty they are, how much I'd like to fly.

When we pull into our driveway, a patch of gravel, I see a woman across the street chasing a dog. Mom gets out of the car then squints and watches the scene for a moment. She wobbles a bit before unsteadily before going inside.

The woman calls out Lady! Stop, Lady! You git back here right now, you darn dog!

I crouch down and call out to the dog while clapping my hands together. She perks up her ears then runs over to me. Lady wags her tail, licks me and nuzzles me. I laugh and pet her until she nuzzles my cigarette-burn and I hiss in pain. I move her away from my burn and take hold of her collar as the woman runs up and thanks me for helping her with her dog.

The woman introduces herself as Mary. Mary is an older lady with fair skin and dark hair mixed with a bit of gray. She wears glasses over beady little eyes and reminds a bit of a ferret. She invites me over to her place and I call out to Mom to ask if it's okay. No response.

I say to Mary my mom must be asleep and she seemed real tired on the drive back.

Mary says well, is it okay if you go over to my place?

I shrug my shoulders and walk in that direction. She takes me inside and shows me a *huge* pantry full of cupcakes and sweets that she got from the store. She says I can help myself, my reward for helping her catch Lady!

My jaw just about hits the floor and I can't believe it! I ask are you sure? and she says uh-huh, go for it.

I cautiously take a single brownie.

Mary says my, what a gentleman, here ya go kid. She hands me two of everything. She smiles at me and says make sure you hide all that, y'hear? And you didn't get that from me!

I laugh and hide it all under my shirt as best I can then cross the street to my house. I think to myself it's good that Rowdy's away at work or he'd tell me to hand these over to Mom.

I sneak inside and hear Mom snoring loudly in her room. With a smile on my face I tiptoe into my room then quietly deposit my prize in my closet in an old jigsaw puzzle box.

Amariah The Boy

A few days later, I explore down the road and hear some kids shouting and laughing. I walk toward the noise and hide behind a tree, just in case it's more angry Black kids who throw rocks at me or tell me to go fuck myself. I find four kids playing hide and seek, and after three or so minutes of hiding in my spot, the youngest one runs behind my same tree. We're both startled by each other and after a moment he asks if I wanna play, too.

I smile and say yeah, sure!

He yells time out! And then walks me over to the other kids.

I say hey everyone, I'm RJ.

I'm introduced to Logan, a chubby kid with blond hair and squinty blue eyes. His younger brother, the kid who found me, says his name is Ricky. He's skinnier than Logan, though he also has blonde hair and wears glasses. They've got a stepbrother named Tyler who has tanned skin like me and dark hair, and there's another kid named Wyatt, who has freckles and light brown hair.

They all say because I'm new I have to be "it."

I laugh and say okay!

I learn that I'm two grades above everyone because I was skipped ahead or something, but me and Logan are only a year apart in age. I don't mind at all that I'm hanging out with kids in lower grades, I'm just stoked to have finally made some friends.

Logan introduces me to his mom and her name is Renee too, just like my dad's awful new wife out in Redondo Beach! I don't say this to her but I'm amazed that two people share that same name.

We play for a while until Logan says he's hungry and they're gonna go eat something. My face lights up and I say hey wait a minute! I've got something! I tell them to wait right there.

I run back to my house while they all wait in the shade. Mom and Rowdy are gone now, off at the Newsroom drinking, probably, so I rush into my room and grab some goodies from my stash. I run back and share them with everyone and just like that, I've made friends for life.

Mom is glad that I made some friends and says it'll be good to see me not mope around the house all day like someone shot my dog.

My new friends and I spend the summer exploring the woods. Logan's got an old bicycle he lets me borrow. We go to the nearby Artesian Park and have a blast riding around. The park has two entrances. The first goes to the public swimming pool, the volleyball court, and the giant twisty-slide. The other one leads to the lake, the National Guard post, and a small playground.

We prefer the lakeside with its steep hills and zoom down on our bikes, heedless of danger or consequence. We bike off the main road and ride on trails, stopping to hide our bikes behind trees while we explore the forest and creeks. Less people come around here than the other side, so it's like we have a private reserve all to ourselves...meaning there are *rarely* any adults around.

Occasionally we find an abandoned camp or other signs of people living in the wilderness. We love to scare one another with spooky stories, most of them retellings of the same old tales that everyone has heard in their neighborhoods at one point or another. We whisper of packs of cannibals who roam the forest, witches who skin little boys alive, an escaped murderer from the local prison, and devil-worshipping cults that need virgin blood...anything to feel that *awesome* tingle of fear and excitement.

The more scared we get, the more our awareness heightens. Every sound in the forest becomes deafeningly loud, making the hair on our necks stand on end. One of us always yells or whispers they saw something before we run screaming for our bikes. We trample over brush and jump over fallen logs in a desperate effort not to be the last one (and therefore most likely to be eaten/ killed) to get to the bikes. We ride away laughing, swearing that we *all* saw or heard something.

The game often involves leaving Ricky behind because he's the smallest and slowest. But when he catches up to us, he gets *real* pissed and has angry tears that usually end with a series of Fuck You! And I Hope You Burn In Hell! ...though he doesn't hold any grudges.

We're all quick to forgive and forget any slights made against one another, as that's what boys do. We'd rather play than be angry and tomorrow is always another day.

Over the summer we go swimming in the lake. That is, until one of us spots a snake swimming along the surface. High-pitched shrieks follow and we high-tail it back to our bikes.

We talk about bringing innertubes and floating along the river and seeing where it goes, but we never follow through.

Probably because of the snakes.

There's an Army National Guard post nearby and they have an old Korean War tank out front, completely gutted. We climb on top and pretend to shoot the school or the church and laugh at other things that we imagine blowing up, until a guardsman comes out and shoos us away. He shouts hey ya dumb kids, there's a dang hornet's nest in that there tank! He waves his arms wildly and shouts don't y'all *see* them hornets? The hell is wrong with you boys? Git on out of here!

We look around us and for the first time notice there really *are* a dozen or so hornets swarming about. They've likely become enraged by our talking about blowing up the church and they're no doubt here to mete out divine retribution. We all scream and run for our bikes and Tyler yells don't worry, the hornets'll get Ricky 'cause he's so dumb and slow!

I yell out hey you better run, Rick! I can see 'em closing' in on you!

Ricky screams in terror as he runs for his bike and we all ride away laughing. In short order he's caught up to us and has a fresh round of I hope you all burn in hell!

Roland Amariah Gonzales

We make our way to the giant twisty-slide and lay down our bikes. The slide is a two-story-tall. old-ketchup-and-mustard color that somehow has a gleaming aluminum surface area, despite its nasty exterior. Climbing to the top is an exercise in pain endurance because the handrails are *flaming* hot. I reckon by the time a particular individual descends from top to bottom that their ass will be on fire. If the damn slide is a frying pan then your ass is ham.

We're all wearing short shorts and no one wants to go first. Logan pretends to be nice to his younger brother. He says hey Ricky you can go first! But Ricky sees through Logan's kindness and shakes his head and says nuh-uh!

We play rock-paper-scissors to see whose ass is gonna go up in flames first. Tyler is the unlucky winner. We have to push him onto the stairs and up the handrail, because he's wearing such small shorts and he *really* doesn't want to be the winner. We all kick and yell at one another but *especially* at Tyler. Logan shouts hurry the hell up and go down the damn slide, you chicken!

We cluck at Tyler like a chicken and shout obscenities, just as some lady walks by with her kids. I imagine it's a ridiculous sight to see—four boys clucking and pushing against a singular boy up the stairs as he angrily cries and shouts no!

The lady shakes her head and keeps walking.

We get Tyler all the way to the top and he tries to push back one final time. He yells out, I don't wanna go first and you can't make me!

I yell out bullshit, you're the winner, jackass, and them's the rules! You hafta go!

We all strain and push against Tyler until he slips and his bare leg touches the hot slide and he howls in the pain. He does a little dance as the frying pan cooks his ham and we yell out, go, already! It's hot up here, asshole!

Logan kicks at Tyler's hands as he desperately tries holding onto the top of the slide. Tyler loses his grip and goes down the slide on his *belly*. He screams the whole way down as the slide roasts him, then jumps up and down in pain when he gets to the bottom.

Having heroically absorbed most of the fire, we all follow Tyler's brave example and fly down the slide.

Though not on our bellies because that's dumb as hell and why did he do that, anyway?

Amariah The Boy

When we're all at the bottom we see Tyler splashing water from a fountain onto his belly. At the same time he's yelling out all *kinds* of awful things at us.

I say boy is *he* mad! Y'all shouldn'ta forced 'im down the slide!

Logan looks at me and I look at him and we both laugh. A rock slams against my foot and I yelp in pain. Tyler chucks rocks at us so we throw some right back at him. After one hits his arm he yelps in pain and starts crying.

We all say uh-oh and drop our rocks then run to him. We tell him sorry over and over except for Ricky who says he didn't hit shit.

I stare daggers into Ricky and whisper shut up, Rick!

Logan looks at Tyler and says we didn't mean to hurt you. Let's all go back home and cool off.

Tyler looks at us with hurt in his eyes and says we can all go kiss snakes for all he cares.

I say hey look, you nailed me with that rock, so we're even! And then I exaggerate a limp, to show him how much it hurts.

Tyler looks at me limping then shakes his head and says he gets to hit Logan, and Logan says no way! before we talk him into it.

Tyler rears back his arm and slams his fist into Logan's gut. Logan lets out a whooshing *oof* noise then doubles over and vomits.

When Logan's done puking we all threaten to tell on each other. Everyone runs to his bike and we're all racing back to Logan's mom to see who will get in trouble the least.

Ricky is dead last because he's smaller and slower than the rest of us. The rest of us are all neck and neck, hurling expletives at one another as we race our bikes down the road, narrowly avoiding angry drivers who honk at us.

I get to Logan's house first and quickly jump off my borrowed bike while I zoom along, sending *it* flying into their front yard bush. Within a heartbeat I run inside but don't see anyone. I search while yelling out hey Renee, Tyler threw rocks at us and he hit me in the foot and...

Tyler is right behind me yelling nuh-uh! The idiots threw me down the slide and the slide was hot as hell and look at how red my belly is! Then he pulls up his shirt, but there's no one there to see! Just as he's saying it burned the hell out of me and...

Logan shows up and hollers, Tyler punched me in the stomach and made me throw up... and we didn't even do nothin'! All we did is push him down the slide and...

163

And then Ricky catches up to us and jumps inside and yells out, Mom, Logan hit me upside my head and Tyler was throwing rocks and...

Renee suddenly appears, too overwhelmed from drinking a cool beer under the air conditioner to hearing four hysterical shouting boys. Her eyes dart about as she sees us pushing each other, pointing and yelling and screaming. She yells EVERYONE SHUT THE HELL UP! and we all go quiet. In a somewhat elevated voice she barks out everyone go to your room!

The brothers all yell out aww! but I didn't do—

Renee cuts them off and yells NOW!

The brothers say humph! and sulk off to their rooms...but I don't have a room to go to 'cause I don't live there. I stand in confusion and look around as the doors slam shut, then I turn to Renee and say uh, where do I go?

Renee looks at me with her eyes wide in surprise.

Maybe she forgot I was there?

She puts her hands on my shoulders and says *you go home!*

I walk outside to pull the bike out of the bush but Renee yells and leave that bike there since you done such a good job of planting it in the bush anyhow!

I walk home which sucks, 'cause my foot hurts from stupid Tyler's stupid rock. I don't say a thing to Mom or Rowdy. They're watching TV and I can see they're both high as hell. Lucky for me Renee doesn't say anything to them...probably because she's too busy going room to room, tanning Logan's and everyone else's hides.

Mom looks up from the television and sees me limping, even though I try to hide it, and asks me what happened. I tell her I stepped on a squirrel and it ran off with my foot.

Mom says oh okay then pauses and says wait a minute, what? But she's too high to figure it out and doesn't care so much anyway. She says Rol, be more careful and don't do that.

I nod and go into my room.

Amariah The Boy

I go to Logan's house the next day to see if they can play but Renee says everyone is grounded for a week. I say oh okay. I walk back home and am bored out of my *mind* for a week.

When they all get released from home-jail we agree not to tell on each other anymore if we can help it, 'cause we all end up paying for it and it isn't worth it.

We go back to the park and still have a great time playing on the slide. This time we bring a piece of cardboard so our asses aren't set ablaze.

Every now and then a boy from the nearby trailer park shows up and he's got a mouth that looks like a horse, so we call him horse-face.

Logan squeals in both excitement and panic and says if horse-face touches you you'll get the gay *and* the retarded. He yells not even gay guys will want you 'cause you'll be a retard too!

We all gasp in shock at this revelation and since none of us wants to be gay *or* retarded, it turns into an impromptu game of tag...and horse-face is *it*. Horse-face doesn't seem to mind and runs around trying to touch everyone while laughing hysterically.

Now, I'm *pretty* sure getting the gay isn't something you get from touch. I was *especially* sure you couldn't become retarded from touching a retarded person because I high-fived a *bunch* of retarded kids back in school in Redondo Beach and I didn't turn retarded...did I?

Horse-face runs at me and I don't have time for difficult introspective questions. I scream before I run away laughing.

We do our best to keep away from horse-face. That is, until he tags Tyler who screams oh no I'm tuuurning into a gaaay-retaaard!

Tyler starts to moan like a zombie and shuffles-runs after people. We all laugh and try to keep away from both horse-face *and* Tyler until we're finally all tagged and become zombie. We moan I'm gaaayyy while we shuffle around.

We bump into one another then fall to the ground and wrestle in the dirt which goes on for a while until Logan gets hurt and yells quit it, I don't wanna play no more! He hits Tyler, Tyler yells out and hits him back and then Logan pushes over Ricky for the hell of it.

We all go home.

All of us like to watch wrestling on TV though I'm not into it as much as everyone else, especially since I was smaller than *all* the other boys in fourth grade. I can only imagine they're gonna get bigger. These

Roland Amariah Gonzales

friends are about the same size as me though and when there's nothing else to do, we all sit and watch wrestling together. I like some of the costumes and the flying acrobatic movements are pretty cool, but I get bored when they're beating each other or talking for a long time. Hulk Hogan is my favorite, probably because he reminds me of Dad.

Tyler gets the most worked up after watching wrestling and always wants to do what he sees on TV. He tries to wrestle with me and I hate it because I *hate* being in pain. I complain daily to Rowdy that Tyler keeps hurting me and I don't like it, but Rowdy says the only way to get Tyler to stop is to hurt him back.

A few weeks go by and Tyler keeps hitting me, and I don't wanna hit him because the last time I hit someone they bled all over the place, and I'm pretty sure they died because I never saw them again. I get tired of it all after he pins me down and gives me a wet willy. I jump up and tackle him to the ground and at first he laughs, but then is crying out for me to stop because I punch him in the ribs in the same spot, over and over.

From that point on I wrestle him to the ground and punch him in his sides until he goes away. Once or twice he gets real mad and tells on me to Renee and his dad, but they know that he always starts it and his dad says don't start what ya can't finish, boy!

Tyler stops horsin' around with me after that and I'm happier for it.

Sometimes we have sleepovers at their house, which isn't that big a deal because I live a stone's throw away. The best part is *definitely* the food, because Renee orders pizza from a family-owned spot called Pizza Glen and their pizza is the *best*.

We watch movies or play board games and thankfully *Missouri* Renee is *way* better than California Renee. Living here, I'm no longer limited to Christian-friendly films. We're not allowed to watch anything rated R, but we *can* watch from a wide variety of topics rated PG-13 and below.

I ask Mom if I can invite them over for a sleepover and she says no. She says the house is too small for even just *one* of my friends and she doesn't want a bunch of kids over *anyhow*. Rowdy says mhmm and nods in agreement before taking another long hit from the bong.

I frown and think to myself I *guess* that all makes sense. Mom and Rowdy are always on the couch smoking weed or drinking...so yeah they're right, there's not much room at all.

166

Amariah The Boy

The summer of 1995 zooms by and with its end comes fifth grade. Mom says she doesn't have money for school stuff, and she needs to call Grandma Margaret.

Grandma Margaret doesn't seem too keen on sending *any* money to Mom, but then Mom motions me over. She covers the mouthpiece and tells me to talk to Grandma. She hands me the phone then sits back on the couch and lights up a cigarette.

I chat with Grandma Margaret for thirty minutes or so, tell her I miss her and I miss California, and hope I can come out and visit soon.

Grandma Margaret says she'd love for me to visit during the summer and asks me if I need money for school supplies. I tell her yes and she wires money to Mom.

Mom takes me to a thrift store in town the weekend before school starts to get some clothes. She says I only grew an inch over the summer, so I don't need much. I'm excited when I see a couple of shirts that the cool kids wore in fourth grade. Mom says they're half off and they'll do just fine.

I also find some shoes that don't look *too* beat up and a pair of pants.

I'm anxious about the start of fifth grade. I didn't see *anyone* my age over the summer and all my friends are two grades under me. I don't have *any* friends in school.

Monday rolls around and the school bus pulls up in front of my house. The trip is much shorter than from Grandma Dena's so I arrive at school in no time.

I go to the cafeteria same as any other day and the lemon-faced lady is still there walking around, looking mean. I sit down with my breakfast tray and a girl with blonde pigtails wearing a pink shirt says in a low tone ew you can't sit here, you're gross.

It's the *first fucking day of school* for crying out loud! I look over my shoulder to see if the lemon-faced lady is far enough away then whisper back *fuck you, you pigtail-headed fuck*!

The girl looks at me in absolute shock like I just kicked her puppy then, without looking, raises her hand and calls out Miss Mann, this boy just said bad words at me!

The lemon-faced lady slithers over, practically *hissing* as she moves. A scowl deepens the pre-existing lines on her face before she snarls if you want to be bad then you can go be bad over there!

She points to a spot where I'll have to eat standing up.

I look at her in disbelief. How could she possibly know what I said one way or another? Why'd she immediately take the girl's side?

Miss Mann orders me to get up and go or she'll go and *get* me up!

I pick up my backpack and food tray then cast one last look at the girl with pigtails. She sticks her tongue out and makes an ugly face, then checks over her shoulder before flipping me the bird.

I gasp first in anger then surprise. I raise my hand and yell, Miss Mann! As soon as she hears me she shouts back no talking!

I stand against the wall and choke down school eggs that are greyish in color. When the bell sounds I go to my assigned room and see a few familiar faces. Our fifth-grade teacher, Mrs. Anders, explains that we won't have *all* of our subjects in this room because she doesn't teach math. She says we'll have to walk to another room where the math teacher will teach us.

As a class, we're introduced to cursive writing and more complex reading materials, the kind I'd read by myself in the past.

Mrs. Anders has us read John Cristopher's series, The Tripods. I resonate with the protagonist, Will Parker, surviving and seemingly alone in a world set against him. It's my first exposure to the post-apocalyptic genre and I *devour* it. My imagination races with the prospect of discovering long-lost civilizations, fighting against an alien menace that everyone else worships, meeting a group of people who become my steadfast friends, leading a double-life, experiencing the danger...all of it.

My life is so utterly mundane compared.

At the end of the school day I spend what time I have in the library, much the same as in Redondo Beach. Whereas in second grade you're taken by the hand and led to the gym to wait for the bus, in fourth and fifth grades you're expected to either be there on time or walk your ass home.

I pore over the school's library and search for books that resemble The Tripods but have a hard time finding anything. I ask the librarian, an 800-year-old grannie who's more dust than woman, if she has any books like the Tripods. She puts a hand to her ear and says the try what? Try who?

I explain The Tripods and being met only with a blank stare, explain science fiction in general. Her eyes glaze over before she flatly tells me no, then points at a shelf and says use the Dewey cards, that's what they're for.

I sigh and say thanks...I guess.

Over the coming weeks I search for books that I may like, but to no avail. This school library has a bunch of stuff, sure...but it's *severely* lacking, compared to the school library in Redondo. They don't even have any Choose Your Own Adventure books! It's either dull non-fiction, dusty old tomes filled with historical texts, or single-sentence books for babies in second grade. Dejected, I resolve to give up completely until one day I come across something a bit different from science fiction...but also kind of similar...fantasy!

I hold a faded book in my hands and look at the cover. I run my finger along the surface of a half-bull, half-man fighting a man armed with a sword. I crack the book open to a random story and start reading. What follows are weeks of tales about gods, goddesses, mythical creatures, magic, and all kinds of moral lessons. I learn that a long time ago people worshipped these ancient gods and had temples all over Greece.

I find the Greek gods, monsters and heroes *fascinating*. They're *much* more interesting than what I read in the Christian Bible. I realize that I don't really *care* about bible stories or how many goats or sheep some guy in the desert begat to another guy anyway!

There's hardly *any* magic in the Bible, just Jesus making a lot of fish or turning water into wine. No one is hurling thunderbolts, defeating hydras or shape-changing into a bull to get a lady pregnant that he turned into a cow. Some of the Greek books even have pictures of *boobies* and *butts*! I smile when I see them, before quickly turning the page whenever someone looks over at me and is wondering why I'm grinning like a fool.

I begin to collect books and amass somewhat of a library at home. I already had a few from Redondo Beach. Sometimes there's a book fair in school and, if I'm lucky, Mom gives me ten dollars to spend...though it's only after I call Grandma to ask for book money. I start to go with Mom to the thrift store any time I can in hopes I'll find a book on sale and she'll feel generous. Mom never checks any of the books I get and doesn't care *what* I get, so long as she doesn't see any nudity on the cover, because nudity and sex are bad.

I quickly become fond of *any* books that talk about or depict sex as my interest in women begins to develop more, *especially* because I'm not allowed to have them. I'm not interested in girls my age, of course...they're all mean as hell *and* gross, but rather the older ladies in high school as well as our school counselor.

All my teachers are for the most part middle-aged and egg-shaped, except for my math teacher. She's hamburger-shaped! But not the school counselor...she's *beautiful*. She walks the hallways wearing black stockings and a long black skirt, and she *always* wears high heels that click-clack on the floors so you can hear her coming.

When I see her walk down the hall I stop talking and stare for a moment before my brain kicks in and I remember to breathe. I smile, wave, and say happily hello Mrs. Brookes, you look very pretty today!

She smiles back and tilts her head to the side before she says why thank you, RJ!

I'm *thrilled* she knows my name, though I guess it's not that hard to remember since it's only two letters.

Her smile grows broader as all the boys say hello and she says hello back. The boys glare at each other afterward, sure that each of them likes her the most.

Every kid—well, all the boys— seems to love spending time in the counselor's office. Mrs. Brookes has long, dirty-blonde hair, pretty blue eyes and an even prettier smile. She's got painted fingernails that are usually dark red, plus perfume that smells like sugar *and* flowers, and a laugh that makes my heart flutter. She's the same lady who made me write all those sentences back in second grade. I used to be really mad at her about it but don't care so much anymore.

I remember when I first started second grade, how I was scared and didn't know where to go, until Mrs. Brookes led me to Mrs. Cook's classroom. I remember standing next to her in uncertainty and squeezing her calf muscle, how it felt elastic and squishy but also firm. I wish I could do that again but I know I'd probably get smacked and in a *lot* of trouble... 'cause you're not supposed to touch ladies without their permission. Still, I try to remember that elastic, squishy feeling, and sigh to myself instead.

HARD LESSONS

I frequently get into fights at school that always seem to be *just* out of any teacher's view. I don't know *why* the other boys hate me so much. I never say anything mean to anyone and I'm always nice unless someone's mean to me first. Maybe it's because I'm too little?

I raise my hand to go to the restroom in Mrs. Anders' class and she says after you finish your cursive exam. I struggle with writing the letter Z, it's always a pain to write. I *finally* finish, turn my exam over, then head out of the room.

I don't even have to use the restroom really, I just want to get out of the classroom for a few minutes. Sometimes, it feels like I can't breathe with all those people in the room.

After washing my hands and splashing some cool water on my face, I make a wet-paper-towel noisemaker that I'd seen another boy make the week before. I blow it up, then pop it and smile at the loud noise it makes in the quiet bathroom.

It's been about five minutes. I need to get back to the classroom, because I'm really pushing it.

I toss the noisemaker into the trash and head for the door, but I'm knocked back as three boys violently enter. I recognize the smallest boy, a third grader, and he pushes me against the urinal. I bounce off it and tell him he better not mess with me because I'm a *fifth grader* and push him back.

There's a big kid with him who looks like he took the day off from *eighth grade,* just to come to this school and beat my ass. And that's exactly what he proceeds to do.

First, he pushes me hard and I slam into the wall, hitting my head, then fall onto the floor, hitting my head again. He holds me down while the smaller one punches me and kicks me in the gut, my back, and my head. I try to get up but I can't because I'm pinned against the floor. I can't do anything but curl into a ball and cover my face as they beat me. I try to yell out stop! a couple of times but they don't respond. They never say a word.

Roland Amariah Gonzales

Eventually they get bored of beating the hell out of me and leave.

I stand up after I'm sure they're gone, tears in my eyes, both angry and ashamed. I breathe heavily. I'm so mad. Murderous thoughts fill my mind and I think about stabbing the big kid with a knife just like the hero slew the Minotaur.

My thoughts cool off after I splash water on my face and slow down my breathing and then I'm filled with a sense of overwhelming sadness. Why did this happen?

They didn't even say anything, they just hit me over and over. I look in the mirror and try to fix my hair. I try to clean up as best I can, but my shirt is real stretched out and my face is red from being hit a bunch of times.

When I get back to class Mrs. Anders is ready to give me an earful for taking so long but sees my face and disheveled appearance. She raises her eyebrows then stays silent.

A week later I wear one of the cool shirts I'd gotten at the thrift store. I think to myself maybe kids will think I'm cool now, too.

It's lunch time and Miss Mann steps out to use the restroom, ordering us to stay put and shut up or we'll eat against the wall. When she's gone, a boy sitting across from me in the cafeteria laughs and says I'm wearing his old shirt.

I look at him in confusion and say there's no way, my mom and I bought this at the store.

The boy says his mom *donated* his old clothes to the less fortunate, then laughs and points at me and says that means I'm a less fortunate.

I say I don't see what the problem is because I like the colors on it. I say it's black and neon green and it almost glows in the dark.

The boy comes around to my side of the table and before I can stop him, grabs the back of my shirt, looks inside and yells out holy shit, my initials are *still* on the tag!

The cafeteria bursts into laughter and I'm red in the face with embarrassment. The boy announces to everyone that he used his shirt to clean up his dog's piss and that's why he donated it!

The kids in the cafeteria are in tears from laughing so hard. I hide my face in shame under my arms and cry in anger. Someone yells that Miss Mann is coming back. Everyone hushes up and the boy runs back to his seat.

When I get home I run and throw the shirt in the trash, first chance I get.

172

Amariah The Boy

Mom gets a black Labrador she names Rex. I hadn't asked for a dog after she gave away Rock. In fact, I hadn't even *thought* of another pup devastated as I was.

Rex is an average-sized puppy, about five months old. He isn't allowed to stay inside the house because he tears up the carpeted floor or chews on the wooden doors when we leave. Mom beats him and throws him outside when she sees this. Rowdy attaches a steel cable between a couple of trees and chains Rex to it, so he can run around the backyard a bit.

I show Rex off to my neighbor, Mary. She sees the cable between the trees and says oh, that right there is a *swell* idea. I ought to give that a try for Lady.

I laugh and say but you ain't *got* no trees, Ma'am!

Mary glances at her yard then back at me with wide eyes. Feigning surprise, she says holy shit! Coulda sworn they were right there! She smiles at me and says maybe if I plant 'em again they'll be ready in, oh, about 14 years, and then we laugh a bit.

She turns to go home then pauses and asks if I want any cakes from her cupboard, and I say no thank you, Ma'am!

She trudges along some more, before stopping again and calling out and don't call me ma'am! I ain't *that* old! Call me *Mary*!

We laugh again.

I walk over to Rex and, after a brief struggle of snatching his ball from his mouth, toss it in the backyard where he can reach it. Rex brings it back and licks me in appreciation. After my hands are thoroughly covered in slobber, I head inside to wash off.

I try to take Rex out for walks but he's *so* big that I can hardly keep a hold on the leash. If he sees a squirrel or rabbit it's game over for me, because he takes off and I go *flying* through the air before *slamming* into the ground and getting dragged across dirt and rocks, yelling REX NO, REX! STOP!

I prefer to play with him in the backyard though he likes to jump on me a lot and I always get scratched up. I tell Mom I wish he was smaller or I was bigger.

She laughs and says I'll get there someday...*maybe*.

My tenth birthday comes half-past October and we have a little party in the Artesian Park, on the lake side. The sun is shining and doing its part to take the edge off the October chill. It's an odd environment where being in the sun makes you sweat and sitting in the shade makes

173

your teeth chatter. Logan and his brothers come but Wyatt can't because he says he's got something else to do.

No one from my class shows up even though I invited everyone and told them I was having a birthday in the park that weekend. I get a flying disc and a football from Logan and his brothers. We all play together and throw the football and flying disc *at* one another, trying to nail each other in the head.

It's late autumn now and either Grace asks to visit us or Dad feels that it's necessary. Mom says Gracie is on her way out to stay with us for a while. She says me and Grace will have to share a room.

I think to myself *again...*and I'm bummed that I won't have privacy. I think for a moment then realize something and say to Mom hey, if Grace can live with us *forever*, how come my friends can't stay the night for just *one* night?

Mom says because I said so.

I frown and go to my room.

I get home from school one day and see that Rex is gone. I find Mom sitting on the couch, a bottle of beer in her hand and ask her where did Rex go, Mom? Is he at the vet?

Mom says she gave Rex to a farm so he can run around and be a barn dog.

I'm not as sad as when she gave Rock away but I'm still pretty broken up. I ask why she didn't ask me first, 'cause I love Rex.

Mom lowers her beer as she's about to take a drink and says impatiently boy, he weren't never your dog in the first place. He was mine.

I look down at the floor and say oh, well can we go visit him?

Mom gives a snort and laughs before she says *that* ain't gonna happen.

I quietly say oh, okay, then walk into my room and shut the door. I sit on my bed, hug my pillow, then look out the window and wonder if Rex is happy.

I never got to say goodbye.

Amariah The Boy

Mom drags me to the airport a couple of weeks later to pick up Grace. Mom is *ecstatic* when she sees Grace exit the plane. She runs up to Grace and picks her up high in the air, then spins around and kisses Grace all over until Grace is laughing hysterically. Mom looks over to me with a grin on her face and says isn't Gracie the most precious thing in the whole world?

I roll my eyes then walk to the airport window and watch planes take off. I wish Grace and I were trading places, that I was going back to California.

Mom is *never* this excited to see me, even when she drove all the way out to California to come get me! I think to myself that seeing Grace this time is less exciting than back in California. Maybe that's because Dad isn't here, it's just Grace.

Memories of her being a tattletale are *still* fresh in my head. She's going to be nothing but trouble.

In the coming weeks, I grow to *hate* having her around with me and my friends or being forced to take her with me to the park. Logan and his brothers don't mind Grace so much and Logan's youngest brother Ricky has a crush on her. They're nearly the same age.

Ricky likes to sneak around with Grace and practice smooching when no one's looking. Me and my friends catch them a few times and laugh as they run around trying to find a new hiding spot to smooch some more.

I think to myself how crazy it is that she's kissing other boys already. I mean hell, she *just* finished first grade! I didn't smooch Michelle until I was in fourth grade!

I wonder whether I'm lagging behind everyone in life if my little sister is already way ahead of me. Then I think of Michelle. Michelle. A pang of sadness shoots through me as I realize I hadn't thought of her in a long time. I can hardly remember what she looks like. I go to my room and find the last photo we took together hidden away in one of my books. If Mom finds this photo, she'll *accidentally* lose it, like she did Grandpa Flavian's Gentleman's Box. I need to hide it. Protect it.

I trace Michelle's face with my finger and try to remember the sound of her voice, her laugh, her scent, and find that I can't. I wonder if Michelle has grown a lot since last I saw her. Grace pulls me from my reverie when she announces that she wants to go to the park. And then Mom raises her voice and tells me to take her there.

Roland Amariah Gonzales

I sigh, give Michelle's smiling face a little kiss and put the picture back in my book. I wonder if I'll ever see her again. Does she think of me?

As soon as Grace and I get away from the house she starts whining. She's *always* whining. She complains loudly if she's cold or bored or hot and she throws fits if we go too fast or do something *she* doesn't want to do, like we're all there just to entertain her. If I don't *try* to steer the group toward something *she* wants to do, she'll tell Mom I was mean.

If she tells Mom I was mean, Mom either hits me or takes away the Super Nintendo for a week. I *swear,* Mom bought that thing only for the sole purpose of having something to take away from me. It spends more time on a shelf at the top of her closet than it does connected to the damn TV.

Grace *never* listens to a word I say and often does the opposite of anything I tell her *just* to spite me. If I complain to Mom, she says that Grace doesn't know any better and I need to be nicer to her.

No one has *ever* once said oh it's okay, Roland doesn't know any better and you need to be nicer to him.

When I was Grace's age and made even the *smallest* mistakes, I got hit on my mouth with a wooden spoon or whipped with a fucking phone cord. I hate the way Mom has one set of rules for Grace and another set of rules for me.

I hate Mom...and I hate Grace.

I get a reading lamp in my bedroom that Rowdy finds on the side of the road after someone threw it out. He and Mom don't want it anymore for some reason, so they give it to me. He says it works just fine and it's even got a new lightbulb! I know beggars can't be choosers, but I wish for once that I could be the latter and not the former.

The lamp has a dirty coffee-or-something stained-canvas shade and the frame is bent so it always sits at a weird angle. I don't mind that so much— I just turn it away from me. I can still use it to read and I *love* reading. What *does* bother me is the plug doesn't sit right in the outlet and I always have to push it back in! I get a nasty jolt of electricity *every single time.*

And I holler real loud every time, too.

Mom eventually hears and yells what the hell are you doing in there?

I say the damn lamp just zapped me!

Mom laughs and says well, don't play with it!

176

Amariah The Boy

I place my burnt finger in my mouth after getting zapped for the thousandth time, because Grace wanted me to plug in the radio so she can listen to music. She walks in the room and laughs that I'm sucking on my finger like a baby. I snap at her and say well I ain't doin' it for fun, the damn lamp just zapped me!

I point at the plug and say be careful and don't touch that or it'll zap you, too!

The *first* thing she does before she breathes, blinks or *anything* is reach down and touch the part I *just* touched, staring at me the whole time in defiance! She of course *immediately* gets electrocuted and screams in pain. I burst into laughter after she screams and pulls away. That's gotta be the *funniest* and *stupidest* goddamn thing I've seen in a long time.

Grace is crying and Mom walks into the room and hollers at me what did you do?

I say I didn't do nothin', Grace touched the damn lamp and got zapped! And then I say to Mom I told you that lamp keeps zapping me, didn't you listen?

Mom looks at the lamp, frowns then says the lamp is dangerous. She goes to unplug it then gets zapped and screams in pain. She yanks the thing out of the wall and throws it in the trash, then she goes to Grace, who is *still* crying, and tells her RJ got zapped a *bunch* of times. Mom points at me and says how stupid I am because I kept touching it.

She says to Grace look at me, I'm RJ! and she mimics touching the outlet and getting electrocuted before collapsing onto the bed.

Grace stops crying. She starts laughing and says yeah, RJ *is* dumb! and they both laugh together.

It's always like that. When all else fails, Mom humiliates me in front of Grace to make Grace laugh. Those two are buddy-buddy at my expense, and I hate it.

177

Roland Amariah Gonzales

Grace has been with us for a little over a month and is enrolled at a small school nearby. We regularly wait for the school bus in the morning and ride it together, her school stop being before mine. All the kids are making large plumes of frost from our breaths when someone calls out to me, hey, isn't that your neighbor's dog?

I see Lady wandering in the street and realize that she got out again. I look past Lady and see our school bus some distance away as it zooms toward us on its approach. I yell out oh no, Lady!

The other kids see the dog walking back and forth but don't try to help or *anything*! They just *watch*. I drop down to my heels and frantically call to Lady, clapping my hands. Lady happily runs back and forth across the road, enjoying being out of her fenced yard. Oblivious.

I'm screaming at her now. The bus is almost on top of her and it isn't slowing down. I yell out Lady, Lady! *Please*! Come *here*, Lady! *Come*!

Time slows to a crawl as Lady perks up her ears, as if hearing me for the first time. She runs toward me, but she's too slow. Time returns to normal as the school bus rampages over Lady's small body. I hear her cry out first in surprise, then agony. Over and over her mournful wails penetrate the otherwise silent bus stop.

Grace is in shock and doesn't say a thing. My vision is blurred with tears. I see Lady's guts splayed all over the ground and it's so cold outside. She looks so cold and I want to help her but I don't know how. How can I help her, what can I do? None of the other kids say anything. They're quiet and either look away silently or on with seeming indifference.

I tell the bus driver angrily that she hit Lady. In a cigarette-stained voice she absentmindedly throats hunh, what?

I'm crying now and I yell you just hit my neighbor's dog!

She looks at me for a moment and says hm, sorry. Hurry up and get on the bus, it's cold out there.

I look at her eyes and see they're real red like Mom's when she smokes or drinks a lot. I ask the bus driver if I can tell my neighbor that her dog got hit.

She glances at the house then at the steering wheel, her brow furrowed and her head wobbly. She blinks a couple of times then snaps at me and says no, we ain't got time! Hurry on up and get on the bus or I'm leaving you here!

178

Amariah The Boy

I look back at Lady and she's whimpering now and I want to go to her, I want to help her and I'm so sorry Lady, I'm so sorry. I'm sobbing now. I want to go help. Mom said if I miss the bus in the morning and she has to drive me there that she'll whip me good and hard in front of *everyone*.

I quickly yell out Mary, Lady got hit! as loud as I can before the bus driver yanks me into the bus and floors it. I run to the back of the bus in defiance of the bus driver who screams at me to sit down. I watch Lady lie on the cold hard road, her small black furry body with a burst of red coming out of it. I watch Lady and hear her in my mind whimpering, alone and afraid as we drive away.

I feel nothing at school. No one says anything. No one cares. When I get back home I run to Mary's house. Maybe she got to Lady. Maybe she saved her? I bang on the door. Mary sees me and slowly opens it. She stares at me dead-eyed for a moment before she quietly says Lady is dead. Mary says the other kids told her *I* called Lady to get hit by the bus. On purpose.

I yell out *no*! No that's not true!

Mary stares at me coolly and says to *never* bother her again. She slams the door.

Thanksgiving arrives a few weeks later and I've put Lady and Rex far from my mind...I have to. I see Grandma Dena the day before Thanksgiving and she's really happy, like always. Being around her makes me feel better. I help her make sweets like the year before. She lets me help her in the kitchen the day of Thanksgiving because I'm older and a little bigger now.

I'm not so scared of the basement anymore. I show Grace around there and then the backyard, too. We go back inside where it's warm and drink hot cocoa.

Rob shows up and he's a little bigger. I bring Rob and Grace to my old room then whisper that we should all sneak around the neighbor's backyard.

Rob says he doesn't want to go back there and that it's boring, but *I* know better why he's saying that. He's a scaredy-cat!

I say come on Gracie, all the *babies* can stay here.

Grace and I step out of the house and walk from the front yard around the back. About ten seconds later, Rob runs out the front door to follow us and says he's *not* a baby and he's coming, too.

I grin and say okay, you can be the lookout!

Grace is as amazed by the backyard as I was the first time I saw it. I tell her to stay low and stay out of sight, because the neighbor is an old witch. Grace looks at me with wide eyes, then nods and follows me as we sneak around the yard for a while. That is until, just like last year, the old lady comes out her back door and searches for us from her porch.

Grace and I drop flat to the ground and we hear the little old lady call out hello? There better not be anyone back there or I'll call the police!

I think to myself doesn't this old hag have anything *better* to do than make sure no one enjoys her awesome backyard?

Grace and I look at each other then smile and laugh as quietly as we can. This is super exciting. I slowly poke my head up and see the old lady go back inside. Grace suddenly squeals *run*!

My jaw almost hits the dirt because I was *just* about to say the same to her! I gasp in surprise then scream and run for the fence. Grace giggles hysterically and I laugh too. Rob is already around the far corner of the house motioning for us to hurry with a panicked look on his face.

About ten minutes later, Rowdy calls all three of us into the sitting room. The guy's positively *livid* as he points at the ground and says you three just go ahead and park yourselves right here and listen. Now, I just got done talking with Agatha and she says y'all keep poking around her backyard, *and* she saw you run back over *here* afterward. If I hear about this again I'm gonna tan your hides, understand?

Feigning innocence, I say I don't know any Agatha and I don't know anything about Agatha's backyard.

Rowdy looks up away from us as he impatiently says she's the lady next door!

I say ohhh, yeah we were definitely all over that place. It's awesome.

He frowns at me and points his finger at each of us and says, not. One. More. Time, ya hear?

Grace and I say sure, okaaaay before he huffs off. Rob is practically in tears and says *see?* I *told* you we'd get in trouble!

I look at Rob then shake my head and say *that* wasn't trouble, that was an ass-chewing. I feel fine! What about you Grace?

Grace shrugs her shoulders at me as if to say what's the big deal?

Grandma Dena calls for everyone to come eat and we happily dash in her direction.

Grandma Dena says because I'm bigger now I can sit at the adult table. Grace is pissed because she wants to sit there too, but she's still too little and has to sit at the kiddie table. Mom tries to make space for Grace at the adult table and I object and say hey that's not fair, I had to sit at the kiddie table last year and Gracie is *half* the size I was a year ago!

Mom says tough! and laughs at me, but after a few minutes it becomes apparent that Grace can *barely* see over the tabletop because she's so small. I look at her with a smug smile and she sticks her tongue out at me and makes a nasty face.

We all say our thanksgiving prayers and soon eat together and are happy. Grace and I gorge ourselves with mashed potatoes, candied yams, cranberry sauce, and cheesecake, choking down green bean casserole as needed.

The return to school after the Thanksgiving holiday is relatively uneventful. With Christmas approaching, most people are in high spirits.

Logan and his brothers wait at the bus stop with me one morning because their mom can't take them into school. While we're standing there, they teach me a song about Miss Mann whom I learn they also hate:

Roland Amariah Gonzales

Jooooy to the world, Miss Mann is dead,
We baaaarbecuuuued her head,
And what about her body,
We flushed it down the potty.
And round and round it went,
And round and 'round it went,
'roow-hooound, and roow-hoooound,
Fuck you Miss Maaaaannn.

We laugh hysterically at the song, and we all agree that Miss Mann is probably the *worst* person in the *whole* world. Logan says he heard that Miss Mann had a son, and he hated her *so* much that he blew off his head with a shotgun just to get away.

Most of the kids at the bus stop say whoa, no way!

Logan insists it's true, then he points at a house nearby and says no, I'm serious and it happened right over there! He says that the police were all over the place and everything and that's why she's even *more* of a bitch now!

I nod thoughtfully and say hmm, yeah. That makes sense. She *is* real bitchy now.

Logan points at me and says there ya go!

We all get on the bus and there's a new driver now. She's an older lady who looks like she needs a bath...but at least her eyes aren't red. I sit down and wonder how awful it must've been at home to make that kid blow his own head off. I wonder how bad my mom is compared to Miss Mann, and why I haven't shot myself in the head yet.

The hallways and classrooms are decorated with Christmas things, cutouts of Christmas trees and Santa made from construction paper. Lots of tinsel. The other boys stop picking fights with me, which is great. No one invites me over to play or to any birthday parties or anything like that, but I guess not getting my ass kicked on a weekly basis is a nice enough present.

I overhear a boy in class named Todd talking about a Christmas party. He invites a girl next to me and, feeling pretty good thanks to Christmastime, I turn around and quickly ask if I can come too.

Todd yells out haha no *way*, you're a loser!

I yell back no, *you're* a loser!

The class laughs. Mrs. Anders had been writing something on the chalkboard about transitive verbs or some other boring English

182

grammar rule before she turns around and snaps at the class. She yells who's talking in class?

Looks like she's having a bad day.

The kids point at me. I complain loudly that it wasn't just me, Todd was talking, too!

She tells us *both* to go stand outside. When we get outside Todd says *this* is why you can't come, you fuckin' loser!

I angrily tell him *he's* a fuckin' loser.

Todd raises his hand like he's going to punch me and I flinch and cover my face. I hear the click-clack of Mrs. Brookes' heels coming down the hallway. Todd and I quickly stand on either side of the door. Mrs. Brookes stops in front of us and smiles at us, but there's concern on her face. She asks why we're outside the classroom and I say we got in trouble.

She shakes her head, smiles at me, then frowns. She tells me that I'm *always* in trouble and to be better. She says it's Christmas time! There's no reason to get in trouble during Christmas *or* any other time of the year!

I say okay and she walks off.

I think for a moment and I realize that Mrs. Brookes is right. I *am* always in trouble. I'm always in trouble for doing the same stuff that other kids do and they *never* get in trouble. Why the hell am I always punished for stuff that everyone else gets away with? That isn't fair at all!

Mrs. Anders steps out of the room and addresses us both and says she's going to have to call our parents.

Todd laughs and says okay then folds his arms over his chest.

If Mrs. Anders calls my mom, she'll whip me outside in the snow with a switch and it hurts a lot more out in the cold. I burst into an emotional rant and say it's not fair Mrs. Anders, everyone hates me and everyone likes *him*. I *always* get in trouble for things that no one else gets in trouble for. You only ever send *me* outside the class and I'm just a...a pariah!

We'd just learned that word a couple of days ago.

Mrs. Anders blinks for a moment and looks uncomfortable. She swallows and tells us through her teeth to be quiet for the rest of the day and if she hears anything more she *will* have to call our homes.

Roland Amariah Gonzales

We both agree and I sulk back into the room, my shoulders low. A lot of the kids look at me with either wide eyes or they laugh at me for my outburst. Todd's head is held high, like he just won a contest.

Amariah The Boy

A couple of weeks later, the teacher tells us we're going to have a special guest. A girl in my class, Kelsey, has an older sister, Kristi, who's in high school. It's her sister's freshman year and she's coming to talk to *our* class about our futures as part of some outreach program. Kristi pops in the day before her scheduled talk and reminds us all to have questions ready for her. She hands out little pamphlets and says they go into detail about everything our town's high school offers. She smiles as she informs us this way we'll be aware of our options!

I'm confused and think to myself we have *options?* I didn't know our town had more than one high school...

As Kristi hands me the pamphlet I reach out for it and my bored *thank you* comes out as thank... uh...!

I gasp as we make eye contact. She's *gorgeous.* In stark contrast to Kelsey who has dark hair, brown eyes, and fair skin, Kristi has *blonde* hair, *blue* eyes...and the same fair skin. Her polite smile turns into a grin as she crinkles her nose and giggles at my reaction, seeing her profound effect on me. I stutter and say I-I'm thank you. I'm RJ...you.

She tilts her head in mock confusion while smiling and says R-J-U?

I laugh and say no, I'm RJ. You're pretty. I mean you're Kristi. Hi Kristi, you're pretty! I smile, my face burning red.

She giggles again before nodding politely. She holds out her hand and says hello RJ, nice to meet you.

I awkwardly reach out and take hold of her hand as she gently-but-firmly shakes my own. Her hand is so *soft.* She releases my hand then moves on to the next desk. I reach up to brush something out of my hair and realize my freshly shaken hand now smells strongly of peaches.

Wow. What an amazing lady! I bring my hand to my face and inhale that scent some more.

It's then that I notice the boys and girls in class are looking at me. I hear a girl a couple of seats behind me whisper in disgust ew, what is he doing?

I cough lightly then look down at my desk to read the pamphlet.

When Kristi leaves the room to return to her school I wave and loudly say goodbye Kristi!

She turns around smartly. With a grin she waves and says goodbye, RJ!

I take the pamphlet home and pore over it. Maybe I can find something that'll impress Kristi? On the back page, I find the Clinton

185

High School alma mater and commit it to memory. I barely sleep that night in anticipation of the next day.

Kristi returns to talk about high school. She plays a video on the classroom TV about the Junior Reserve Officer Training Corps program (JROTC). Afterward, Mrs. Anders steps out of the class to give Kristi the floor. Kristi walks around and engages the class in open discussion about their hopes and futures. I start humming a simple tune from the video and notice that the tune's melody matches the word pattern of the alma mater.

Kristi talks to another student before she gets distracted by me. She looks over as I pretend to look at the pamphlet, quietly singing her alma mater to the same tune I heard in the video. She walks over to my desk with a grin on her face and says oh my goodness, did you memorize our alma mater overnight?

I smile then say yes and ask if she'll be in high school when I get there.

She offers me a sad smile and says she doesn't think so but she's *sure* I'll have no problem because I am a *cutie!*

She leans over my desk and tousles my hair.

The class laughs at my messed-up hair and I'm upset for just a second. Then I look up and see Kristi's face. It isn't mean like the other kids. It's warm. Kind. *Sincere.* I smile back at her and nod. I never see her again but never forget her kindness, all the same.

THE BIKE

Christmas break arrives and Mom says Grace coming out to visit us was *everyone's* Christmas present, not just Mom's, so I shouldn't expect a whole lot this year. I think to myself Mom's gotta be *shitting* me. I didn't ask for this present! Send it back!

Mom sticks to her word and doesn't get me anything, but *does* take me and Grace to the pawn shop over in The Square to see Pat.

Pat says because it's Christmas I can pick out a game under ten dollars for my Super Nintendo.

I say quietly...but Pat I don't have any money.

I'm confused that he'd give away something for free, since no *one* is this nice, even during Christmas! And especially not nice to me.

He laughs then says boy, I am well aware that you don't have any money. He says it's Christmas and to hurry up, then starts to count down from five to one.

I frantically look at the games and see a fighting game, some boring old *golf* game, a racing game, and then another game with a weird-looking white cat-thing with red wings, standing on a sword. It looks different and, compared to the other game cartridges, feels *heavy* in my hands.

Pat loudly says one! He says alright, that's it! Merry Christmas! He waves me away then laughs and says to get out of his store.

I wave back at Pat with a broad grin on my face and call out, Merry Christmas!

We all walk out of the store.

Grace complains that she didn't get anything from Pat.

Mom says well, there wasn't anything in there you liked, was there? She says she'll get Grace something from a different store.

I think to myself but didn't Mom *just* say we didn't have any money?

We walk around The Square until Grace finds a store she likes and we go inside. It's warm and smells like pumpkin pie and other sweets. I look around with a feverish glee in my eye but don't locate the mysterious pie. An old lady sitting behind a counter sees me searching then laughs and says there ain't no pie, boy. Just this here candle.

She points at a scented candle and I ask if it *tastes* like pumpkin pie, too?

She says well, you're welcome to try. She says she ain't never tasted the candle herself and she s'poses it tastes like burning, likely.

I say ah, no thanks.

Grace gets some girly pink thing and as we drive back to the house I carefully study my game. "Final Fantasy 3." It *sounds* interesting. I look at the cover and can't figure for the life of me what in the hell the game is about. Is it a game about fighting or shooting evil flying cats?

When we get home, I ask Mom if I can play with my new game.

She says it's fine until dinner.

I pop the game in and the introduction is pretty cool. There are big robot things walking through the snow. Maybe I use those to shoot the cats? I get to the main menu and see there are already three saved games. I pick one and start to play it and it *looks* interesting but I have no idea what's going on. I'm not shooting evil cats at all and none of it makes any sense. I quickly get bored, sigh, and turn it off. Maybe I'll try it later, when there's nothing else to do.

Christmas comes and goes and I get some more warm clothes from Grandma Dena. I'm a bit glum because I know that other kids will have really cool stuff that they'll talk about or show off. I thank her all the same though. I love Grandma Dena.

Christmas is nearing its end and I don't have anything, really. Man, I just *know* the other kids are going to make fun of me.

Mom comes into my room one day and says she got me a real good present. She says Grandma Margaret sent her money to get me something special.

Mom normally isn't this happy about *anything* that involves me, but now she's *real* excited...and that makes me nervous.

She tells everyone to get in the car and we drive to a neighborhood that I rode a bike through with Logan and the others. I think to myself these are rich people's houses. These are where the popular kids live. I feel uneasy and then a little bit sick as the car slows down.

What present could be all the way out here?

Mom suddenly stops the car in the middle of the street. As I look around in confusion she reaches down and pops open the trunk. She motions behind us and says take a look, Rol!

188

Amariah The Boy

When I look out the back window I see the handlebars of a new bike. I'm thrilled, I haven't had my own bike since second grade! My jaw drops as I gasp in surprise and say in giddy disbelief is that a new bike? For me?!

I move to get out of the car and am stopped when Mom locks the doors. I look at her in confusion and she smiles cruelly and says not yet, boy, you gotta *earn* this bike!

I say what? How? How do I *earn* a Christmas present? A present from Grandma Margaret?

Mom looks at Grace and says what do you think, Gracie? What should we make him do?

Grace looks at Mom in confusion while she tries to process what is happening and says uhh.

Mom laughs and says should we make him walk outside with his pants around his ankles? Or maybe walk behind the car and holler that he's a big fat baby?

Grace looks at her and smiles then says in excitement make him cluck like a chicken!

Mom laughs at this shared game with her daughter and says alright boy, you heard Gracie. Get out of the car and cluck like a chicken! And nice and loud, so everyone can hear you!

I look at Rowdy in desperation. He laughs and says come on kid, get goin'!

I'm *mortified.* I can't move.

Mom snaps when she sees I'm ruining her fun. She shouts if you want that bike, you better get your skinny ass out there or I'll return it and spend the money on Gracie!

Rowdy sits in the front seat and chuckles at the coming spectacle.

I'm a whirlwind of emotions as I try to understand what's happening. I'm confused, angry, and ashamed. I'd love a new bike, but I don't wanna go out there and make a fool of myself, *especially* not out here in front of all the popular kids' homes. They'll *never* let me hear the end of it.

Mom starts to count down from five after she unlocks the doors. When she gets to one I fumble with the door, open it, then fall outside onto the road. I stand up and slowly walk around to the back of the car. I try to quickly snatch the bike *before* I have to humiliate myself, but Mom is watching and steps on the gas.

The car lurches away. As I run after it, Mom rolls down the window and shouts cluck, you cluckin' chicken!

She laughs along with Grace who's giggling in the back of the car.

I feel a deep lump in the back of my throat and let out a few quiet clucks.

Mom calls out louder boy, everyone needs to hear!

She pushes down on the car horn. My eyes go wide in shock as I look all around and start clucking louder, reaching for the bike again. Mom steps on the gas again and drives away a bit, cackling madly out the window while Grace watches me and laughs herself to tears. I run toward the car clucking as loud as I can with my eyes closed before it comes to a screeching halt.

I slam into the car and hurt my knee. I cry out in pain and try to remove my bike but it's stuck. The car lurches forward and I hold on this time, getting dragged as the trunk comes slamming down on my arms. I yelp in pain and let go then grab at my arms and fall onto the road.

Tears are streaming down my face, beet-red in shame. It's Christmastime. Why can't I have anything nice? Why can't I have it *easy* like the other kids? Just once? Other kids don't have to do this for Christmas. Mom didn't get me this bike, Grandma Margaret did! I wonder what Grandma Margaret would say if she could see Mom's behavior right now.

It's not fair.

The car comes to a stop before Mom looks back and sees me crying. She laughs a bit more then yells don't be such a baby, Rol! She snaps go and git your damn bike already you big baby!

Rowdy chuckles and shakes his head from side to side as he wipes away a tear from laughing so hard.

I cautiously approach the car again and gingerly pull the bike from the trunk, just as Mom lays into the horn. People are looking from the windows of their homes at this spectacle. I yank my bike out so hard that it falls on the same leg I'd hurt a moment before. I climb atop my bike and pedal away as fast as I can, wincing in pain from the strain on my leg. Mom peels away, everyone laughing as she yells see you at home, ya big baby!

I ride as fast and as far from that neighborhood as I can, keeping my head down so no one can see my face filled with shame. Now that I'm away from Mom I take time to appreciate Grandma Margaret's gift. I ride to the top of a large hill and notice my bike has multiple gears. It's a *lot* easier climbing a hill than with the other bike Logan let me borrow.

I look down the hill toward the bottom, breathing heavily. I release the brakes and head downward until I *zoom*. I cluck with wild abandon, flying through cross-traffic, past faces both confused and angry. People in their cars honk their horns angrily and slam on their brakes. I make it through in one piece.

A shame.

I ride to Artesian Park, hands-free, laughing as the crisp wind courses through my hair. I find a frosty spot under a tree and carefully set my bike against it, then collapse onto the ground. Some time passes until I sit up and gaze at the trees. The wind howls through the gnarled and empty branches. I watch a scant few families spend the day together. Happy kids playing with gifts from their happy and loving parents. I draw in a deep breath and fight back tears.

I sit under my tree, cold and alone, until the sun sets. I watch all the *happy people* as they laugh, get into their cars and drive to their happy fucking homes. I'm angry at all of them. I even hate them! I don't know why. It's Christmas.

I sit alone, cold and full of hate, hugging my knees as the chill wind cuts through my clothing. I wait until everyone leaves and I'm in the park alone.

And then I weep like the baby I am.

I hold off on returning home until I can't bear the cold any longer, then grudgingly pedal back. I put my bike in the washroom before entering the living room. Mom and Grace see me and break into laughter. I refuse to look at them and go straight to my room then close the door.

Mom calls out there's cold meatloaf on the counter...it was warm a few hours ago. She says if I hadn't had a temper tantrum I could've had it hot. She offers to microwave it for me.

Like she fuckin' cares.

I don't respond and after a few minutes she stomps to my room and slams the TV remote against my door and says if I wanna act like a baby, then so be it! She says I can be a baby and sit my ass in my room for a week and maybe *then* my attitude'll go away! She says hell, maybe she should return that bike right now. Spend that money on herself!

I don't respond and go to sleep.

Roland Amariah Gonzales

Christmas break comes to an end and after another boring New Year's celebration it's back to school. Boys and girls brag about going on trips with their families to St. Louis or Kansas City, or some other place out of state. I'm starting to think I'm the only kid who doesn't go anywhere or do anything.

I tell Mom about it and she says well we ain't got that kind of money, Rol. We're poor.

I say but you and Rowdy both have jobs, so doesn't that mean we have double the money? A lot of kids in class only have their dads working, and their moms just sit at home!

Mom takes a swig from her beer and looks at me with a sour face then says it don't work that way. It ain't about how *many* jobs a house's got, it's how *much* that job pays.

I say well how much do you and Rowdy get paid?

Mom says that ain't *none* of your business, now go play outside with your sister.

After that, I start to notice how *much* and how *often* they spend money on beer, cigarettes, and weed. Mom buys a carton of cigarettes at least twice a week, a six-pack of beer every day, and a big bag of weed once a week. The next time she buys some weed from her friend, I see she pays around twenty dollars.

I go to school and ask other kids if their parents smoke or drink. Only a couple actually answer me, and when they do they say not as much as mine probably do.

I do some math in my math class then figure that Mom spends almost a hundred dollars every *week* on all that stuff, and that's four hundred to five hundred every *month*. The rent for our home is only two hundred and fifty!

...that means they spend more on booze, smokes, and weed than they do on Grace and me or...hell, more than they *ever have* on just me alone!

I think back on all the times the boys in my class made fun of my clothes or told me I looked like a homeless person. I think of that boy in the cafeteria and how he said I was wearing his dog's piss-shirt. I think of the girls who told me I was disgusting. I think of all the times I was beaten in the bathroom or somewhere else.

Was it all because my mom couldn't afford to give a damn about me?

HANGIN' AROUND

Mom gets another dog, this time she says it's for Grace. His name is Cyan and he's a little black puppy, not even two months old. Cyan is super tiny and he's *super* cute. He squeaks out tiny yips, extra-small barks, and he's got a great big ol' belly. I tell Gracie that Cyan is more belly than puppy and she laughs.

He's too little to go on the same chain that Rex used, the one hooked up between the trees, so Mom chains him up next to the storm shelter entrance outside. I ask if Cyan can stay inside with us because it's cold outside, but Mom says she doesn't want Cyan pissin' and poopin' all over the place.

Me and Grace take off Cyan's chain and play with him in the backyard. He chases us back and forth and wags his little tail hard enough to take off into the sky if he had wings. Me and Grace collapse onto the ground in mock exhaustion as Cyan runs all over us with his tiny puppy feet and licks our faces.

Sometimes I see Mary standing in her backyard. She watches us with a grim look on her face. I know she's still upset because she thinks I killed her dog. Maybe if she comes and plays with Cyan she'll be happier? I wave at her and yell out do you want to come see our new puppy?

Mary watches us for a while, doesn't wave or anything, then goes back inside.

I have a *bunch* of chores that Mom and Rowdy task me with, not the least of which is picking up all of Cyan's poops in the backyard. Grace never helps and I hate doing it by myself.

Why does Cyan poop so much!

I've gotta wash the dishes, sweep the floors, wash the cars, vacuum the carpet, take out the trash, then anything and everything else they can think of. Mom says it's only fair because she and Rowdy work so hard and I don't pay *any* rent. Mom gives me two-fifty a week and after a few months I've saved up enough so I can go out to a nice restaurant.

Roland Amariah Gonzales

Unfortunately this means I've gotta take *everyone* because I can't go by myself. It's too far to walk and I can't drive a car. I'm only ten. I don't think it's fair that I have to pay for everyone because no one else helped me with all my chores, but it's this or nothing.

The restaurant is a buffet place called Golden Corral. I can't *wait* to eat all the pizza, mashed potatoes and ham. They've even got an all-you-can-eat dessert table with ice cream and the gooiest chewiest chocolate-fudge brownies I've ever had! I always make sure to save a *lot* of room in my stomach for dessert. If I'm extra lucky, they bring out a fresh tray of hot brownies straight from the oven.

When we get ready to leave the house, I ask Mom if we can put Cyan inside while we're gone because it's so cold outside.

Mom says don't you worry about Cyan, Rol. He's got fur, he'll be just fine. She says to make sure his collar is tightened while we're all gone so he can't go and run off. Don't want him getting' run over like Mary's dog!

I walk up to Cyan and see him curled into a tight little black ball of fur. I call his name softly and he looks up and licks my hand. He whimpers when I tighten his collar and I whisper it's only for a little while, okay? You be a good boy!

I kiss him on his head and Cyan licks my nose in response. He whimpers and barks at us as we drive away. Grace and I wave at him while he barks and strains against his chain, trying to get to us.

Everyone is in a good mood as we gorge ourselves on all our favorites. Mom and Rowdy stick to fried chicken and baked potatoes while Grace and I go for pizza, french fries, and other stuff. Mom makes us eat a plate of veggies and afterward says we can eat whatever. Grace and I race one another to the dessert bar. She goes for ice cream and I go for the brownies. When we're done eating I proudly pay the bill and give our waitress a nice tip, even though she didn't really do anything.

All the plates, cups, and flatware are up near the buffet tables!

I've spent all my hard-earned money but it was worth it. We drive back as the sun sets, casting a deep purple across the night sky. When we pull up to the house, me and Grace run straight to Cyan...but he's not there.

We search around the house, in the backyard and up the street. I call his name over and over but I don't hear anything, not even a whimper. I'm really worried that he ran away somehow. I think to

194

myself I *knew* we should've put him inside...where could he *be*? And then I hear Grace scream. I run to her and see Mom and Rowdy there, too.

Mom says oh, my god.

I look into the storm shelter and see Cyan's body dangling at the end of his chain. He's not moving. Mom reaches in and carefully pulls out his limp little body.

I fall to my knees and sob as I repeat his name over and over. A million thoughts shatter my mind as tears run a river down my face. Cyan's little puppy tongue that licked my face is hanging out the side of his mouth. He's never gonna lick me or anyone ever again. Now he can't chase us or anyone anymore.

I'm the one who tightened his collar...if I hadn't done that he would've been able to slip out. He'd be running around our storm shelter. He'd still be alive...this is all my fault.

I'm so sorry Cyan. I'm so sorry and I wish I was dead. Not you.

Grace is devastated. She's crying and shaking. Mom tries to give Cyan mouth-to-mouth, as if she knows what she's doing. I glare at her. If she would've let Cyan stay inside, if she would've listened to me, he'd still be alive.

I hate my mother. I hate how she *never* listens and someone *always* gets hurt. Someone or something I love dies.

I pause in my grief for a moment. Wait a minute. Cyan wouldn't be running around the the storm shelter if the collar was loose. The door was closed. It's *always* closed, how did it get open? Cyan couldn't have moved it. It's too heavy.

The sight of Cyan's lifeless body placed gently against the ground robs me of any further thoughts on who to blame.

Mom gives up on trying to bring Cyan back from the dead. She holds Grace close to her and rubs the back of her head, as she tries to shush her crying. Rowdy stands there with one hand in his pocket and the other rubbing the back of his head as he shakes it from side to side, lost on what to do.

I sit next to Cyan's body on the cold hard ground and look at him, hugging my knees. I weep.

No one comforts me.

Roland Amariah Gonzales

HIDE AND SEEK

Time passes. A couple of weeks or more, I don't know. Mom and Rowdy numb their pain with booze, smokes, and weed, and soon enough it's all back to normal for them, but it ain't so easy for us kids. They don't talk about what happened and there's no consoling words from them, either. Mom says she's sick of seeing me mope around the house. She says I need to get over it, then takes another hit from her bong. She says she's sick of my attitude and my Super Nintendo finds its way onto her closet shelf again.

Fucking Valentine's Day. *Again.* I don't bother asking for money to buy cards. I just go to class and stare at the wall. One of the popular boys says maybe I'll get twice as many cards as last year and everyone laughs.

I stare at my desk and say yeah.

Everyone is in a frenzy of activity and some girls even get singing candy-grams from boys who have money to spend on that stuff. They're all laughing and having a great time and the room is full of aww, you're so sweet, thank you...and hugs. No one comes to my desk.

When class is settled down, that same popular boy says hey RJ, how many cards did you get this year?

The class snickers and Mrs. Anders smiles at the joke. I pick up my plain, undecorated, brown cardboard Valentine's box from my desk, carry it to the front of the room then toss it in the trash. I walk back to my desk and put my head down. Some kids gasp, some laugh, some say what's *his* problem?

A popular girl says in a mocking tone aww, you threw away my card!

Mrs. Anders chastises me and says what I just did was *incredibly* rude.

I don't lift my head and say yeah.

She says I need to apologize to popular girl.

I don't lift my head and say yeah.

She says maybe she needs to call my house.

I don't lift my head and say yeah.

Amariah The Boy

Mrs. Anders grabs me by the wrist and takes me to the front office after class. She calls my house but no one answers. She demands that I give her Mom or Rowdy's work telephone number.

I say yeah and stare blankly ahead.

With a furrowed brow she slams down the phone down and writes an angry note. She tells me to give it to my parents and return it signed or I'll be suspended and then thrusts it in my face.

I don't move to grab it and say yeah.

She shoves the note in my backpack and sends me toward the gym, telling me to hurry up or I'll miss my bus.

The sky is a patchwork of dark gray and white. The bus pulls up to Grace's school. She gets on the bus and sits across from me then stares out the window wordlessly. I do the same.

When I get home I crumple up the note and throw it at the couch. I walk to my room then lay down and stare at the wall for a while before I close my eyes and go to sleep.

Grace doesn't bug me. I wake up to the sound of Mom getting back from work. She tramples like a big fat elephant announcing her presence to a circus. I continue to stare at the wall.

Mom calls me for dinner. She yells Rol, don't make me go in there and get you, I've just about had *enough* of your bullshit attitude.

I get up and walk to the kitchen and poke at my food. I eat what I can. Afterward, I look on the couch for the crumpled-up paper but it's gone. I glance at the trash can and, sure enough, it's in there. Oh well, I tried. *Someone* touched it. Good enough for me.

I return to school the next day. Mrs. Anders stands outside the classroom and watches me walk down the hallway. Before I enter she stops me and demands the signed note.

I say my mom took the note, crumpled it up and chucked it in the trash. I raise my eyebrows and say I don't think she *cares* about your note, Mrs. Anders.

Mrs. Anders is *furious*. She tells me to sit outside the classroom all day. When we all go to lunch I have to stand against the wall and eat by myself. Afterward, Mrs. Anders tells me to sit right back where I was in the hallway. After an hour or so I hear the familiar click-clack of Mrs. Brookes's high heels as she walks down the hallway.

She looks at me with concern and, after talking to Mrs. Anders, pulls me into her office. I melt into a large, soft chair, much more comfortable than the concrete floor and brick wall, while Mrs. Brookes tries to talk to me. After some time passes, and with her gentle prodding, I tell her I'm not happy. Mrs. Brookes asks why and I tell her. My words are a slow trickle, quickly growing into a deluge as they punch through the dam that is my lips.

I tell her how Cyan died. How it's all my fault. How my neighbor's dog died before that and my neighbor blamed me for that, too. How I can't do *anything* right. How no one's given me anything for two *years* on Valentine's Day. I tell her how much I *hate* Valentine's Day. I tell her how much everyone hates me and how much I hate everyone. I tell her how I feel tired all the time and I just want to sleep forever. Maybe wake up in a hundred years when everyone is dead.

Mrs. Brookes listens patiently to my rant. Sometimes her eyes go wide and her brow creases. She gasps when I go into vivid detail about Cyan's body at the end of the chain, or Lady's guts splayed out on the freezing road. After I'm done talking she hands me some tissue and I realize my face is wet.

Dad's right, I'm always crying. I'm just a crybaby.

Mrs. Brookes's voice cracks as she excuses herself from her office and is gone for a while. Ten minutes? Maybe more? I'm not sure. I drift off to sleep on that comfy chair in her warm office that smells like her perfume. The scent of sugar and flowers.

When she returns, I see that she's re-applied her eyeliner. Her eyes are darker than they were before. She sits down, takes a deep breath, and asks if I tried to talk to my mom or dad about any of this.

I bark out a laugh then quickly silence myself. I tell her my dad lives out in California. I say my mom has a boyfriend right now but the two of them ain't good for advice and they're always...

I say they're busy working all the time.

I don't tell Mrs. Brookes how they go straight from work to the couch and are either smoking or drinking, and that's about all they're good for. Mom warned me in second grade that I'd be snatched away by Child Protection Services if I ever told *anyone* about our home life. She said I'd end up in an *awful* foster home *way* worse than however bad I thought *I* had it.

Mrs. Brookes says she thinks it'd really help me and it's important for families to communicate when they have problems.

I protest loudly and tell her not to worry, and I'll talk to my mom when I get home, but Mrs. Brookes calls my house anyway. The phone rings for about a minute and I breathe a sigh of relief because I'm sure everyone's at work, but then my mom answers the phone.

Mrs. Brookes says hello and finds out that mom is sick right now and that's why she's at home. Mrs. Brookes says she's sorry for bothering her and for her not feeling so well...and she needs to talk.

The phone call goes on for about five minutes as Mrs. Brookes tells Mom about all my difficulties, how I'm getting into trouble, why she thinks that is and how Mom can help.

There are lots of uh-huhs, okays, and oh, I sees. By the end, Mrs. Brookes has a genuine smile on her face, says thank you, and hangs up the phone. She looks at me then smiles and says see that wasn't so bad. Your mother is really nice!

I force a smile and say oh hey, that's great to hear.

Mrs. Brookes says now that she's talked to my mother, we can all have a nice chat when I get home and that everything should be fine now.

I feign sincere gratitude and thank her, after which she leads me back to class. Mrs. Anders lets me back in after she and Mrs. Brookes talk for a few minutes in private. She tells me not to disrupt the class and we can go from there.

When school is over I'm full of dread. In fact, I'm terrified. I don't know what's waiting for me at home, but I *know* it isn't good.

Grace sits next to me on the bus and we both look out the window. When we get home, Mom tells Grace to go play outside then calls me to her room. She lies on the bed and says in a weakened and sick voice something that I can barely hear. She tells me to come closer and I hesitate for a moment. She weakly says come on, Rol. She coughs and says she can hardly talk.

I slowly shuffle closer to her bed. Her arm shoots out and snatches my arm then digs her nails into it. She yanks me close to her face and hisses at me what did I tell you, boy? What did I say about getting into trouble...about making trouble? Huh? What did I *say?*

The stench of booze and cigarettes on her breath is so powerful that I fight back a wave of nausea. She pulls out that damn wooden spoon from under her pillow and beats my arms and legs not at *all* like a sick and weak person could.

I hop up and down in pain and try to get away but she won't let go of my wrist as she hits me with her free hand, wielding her wooden spoon.

Roland Amariah Gonzales

I yell over and over I'm sorry, I'm sorry Mom, please! I won't do it again! After a good fifteen seconds of getting my ass whipped, I grab her nearby incense holder, a small wooden rectangle thing covered in ashes, and throw it at her face. I then pull my face close to her arm and bite her hand as *hard* as I fucking can.

Mom screams in pain and releases my arm then violently swings her wooden spoon at my face. I've already turned around and am running for the door as the spoon glances off the back of my head. I fly past Grace out of the house while Mom screams you little shit! You get the *fuck* back here right *now!*

I hop on my bike and speed toward Logan's place, then hide my bike inside. This isn't a very good hiding spot because it's the first place Mom looks. Logan's mom and her boyfriend aren't there and when my mom comes poking around looking for me, Logan and his brothers say she can't come in 'cause no one's home.

Mom *fumes* outside and shrieks Rol you better get your ass home right fucking *now* 'cause I *swear,* the longer you make me wait the worse it's gonna be! She shrieks I'm gonna tan your fuckin' hide, you hear me, boy!? YA HEAR ME!?

I don't say a thing and after a minute or two she leaves. Logan looks at me with eyes that say *oh shit,* then says man, what did you *do?*

I tell him I had to talk to Mrs. Brookes in school today and she called home, so my mom is *pissed* 'cause she says I'm making trouble. I ask if they can go to the park with me and say I wanna get away from here.

They shake their heads before looking out the window then back at me and say nuh-*uh.*

I nod... I understand.

Ricky looks out the back window as my mom storms away, swearing to herself all the while. I sneak my bike out the front when he says it's clear and ride away.

I pedal furiously to the lake side of the park. I'm real anxious and constantly look over my shoulder. I go to a good spot where I can see the entrance from behind some trees. I feel like Mom is watching me.

Not fifteen minutes go by before I see a car enter. It's Mom's car.

My breath hangs in my throat as I peek out from behind a tree. I can see her angry face in the distance and think to myself shit, I need to hide!

Amariah The Boy

I quickly move back to my bike and follow a trail that my friends and I had gone down before. I find a familiar spot to move my bike off trail, cover it in leaves, then do the same for myself. I breathe into the sleeve of my jacket because I figure she can see my breath—it's real cold out.

If Mom catches me I'm *dead*. I hear her voice faintly in the distance as she yells out Rol I know you're out here, you little shit! You best get over here *right now* or I'm gonna beat your ass so hard that—

She stops yelling for a second and I can barely hear her a moment later when she says what do you *mean* calm down? I don't tell you how to raise your kids. I'm looking for my boy. You can fuck off! Fine, call the police!

Then silence.

I wait for a good thirty minutes under that pile of leaves. I freeze my ass off but am at least *somewhat* protected from the wind. I leave my bike under the leaves then get up, brush myself off, and creep forward from tree to tree until I can see the main road. I stay crouched low and peek out from time to time. I don't see her car anywhere.

Satisfied, I make my way back to my bike, pull it out of the leaves and brush it off a bit, then start riding toward the main road. The sun is setting and cars have all got their headlights on.

My whole body tingles as my arm hairs stand on end. My scalp feels like it has electricity running through it. I stop riding and pause to look behind me as I see a car driving on the back-country roads. It's still light enough so I can make out at least the *shape* of the car. I think to myself God damn, woman, give up already!

I quickly ride back to Logan's house and ask if I can stay the night. It's a Friday.

Logan begs his mom to let me stay over. At first she's against it but I desperately say *please*, Renee?

Renee looks me over from head to toe. She sees my disheveled appearance and the pleading, frightened look in my eyes. She raises her eyebrows, then nods and says alright.

A bit later, my mom pulls up in her car and asks in that sickly-sweet, nicest voice in the world, if anyone's seen her baby boy.

Renee tells Mom no, she hasn't seen me, and that Mom might try Wyatt's house across town.

Mom says oh, I'm just *so* worried about my boy. and if you see him, please let me know.

Roland Amariah Gonzales

Renee says in a flat tone sure, I'll do just that.

Mom leaves. I emerge from hiding and try to keep myself together as I choke out a thank you to Renee for her hospitality. I can't say much else. I'm completely exhausted physically and otherwise.

Renee pauses as she looks at me with a sad and concerned face then quietly says hey, no problem...try and keep the noise down tonight, okay?

I nod, try to smile and say I'll be very quiet.

I keep away from the windows in case Mom might shoot her arms inside and snatch me out. Or reach inside to try to stab me with a knife for my insolence, for daring to bite the hand that feeds me. I try to sleep, but I'm too scared.

Saturday passes and I hide inside. Mom doesn't try and find me. The next day, Renee says I can't hide here forever and that Mom is probably cooled off by now.

I tentatively retrieve my bike from their shed and pedal around town for a few hours before heading home. I take a deep breath then cautiously poke my head through the door. Mom and Rowdy are sitting on the couch and the pungent smell of weed in the living room *reeks.* Mom is high as *hell* as she stares at the TV and doesn't get up from the couch. She asks in an amused tone where were you?

I say I was sleeping in a ditch around the corner.

Mom barks out a laugh and says it serves me right! That's where I belong, not in a bed in a loving home but in a ditch, in the *mud.*

She and Rowdy laugh at her joke and now I'm pissed. I say you know what? I'm leaving. I'm running away!

Now Mom and Rowdy are laughing even harder. Mom says hey, by all means go right on ahead!

I go to my room, say goodbye to Grace, then put a bunch of clothes and stuff in a suitcase and walk out the front door. Mom laughs and says have a nice trip, boy! And send a postcard!

I exit the house and consider my bike for a moment but can't pedal and carry the suitcase at the same time. I walk down the road a bit and it starts raining. I don't have any idea where I'm gonna go. I can't go back to Logan's house and...well, I don't have any other friends. I stand on the corner in the rain. I feel hopeless and lost. A police car pulls up and an officer rolls down the passenger window to look at me and my suitcase. With a mixture of concern and amusement he says hey boy, everything okay?

Amariah The Boy

I look at him then back at my house and say yessir, I'm just headed back home right now. I just wanted to go for a walk. In the rain.

He says well, alright then. You need a ride?

I shake my head then tell him thanks, but I'm alright. I live close by.

The *last* thing I need is for the police to show up to my house. I'd be *dead* if that happened. I walk slowly until I hear the police car drive away and am certain they don't know where I live, then I walk back to the house.

After I enter the house Mom laughs and says well, that was a short trip, Rol! You weren't hardly gone for a minute! I didn't even get a postcard!

I say I made it to the end of the road before the policeman stopped me and sent me back. I lie and say the police said I can't run away unless I want to run my ass into jail.

I'm soaked from head to toe and look absolutely pitiful. Mom looks at my miserable state and my angry demeanor and bursts out laughing. I pull my suitcase into my room then shut the door.

Mom seems happy enough that someone else threatened me and leaves it at that.

I gain a measure of understanding how my mom thinks. She *needs* to believe she's better than me. She needs to believe that I'm *nothing* compared to her so she can feel better about herself. She's just like the boys in school, the ones who put me down and puff out their chests to the applause of the other kids. I suddenly feel that I understand *so* much more about my mom, about the rich kids. Hell, more about people and life in general.

Grace goes back to California just before summer break starts and I breathe a sigh of relief. Now Mom will be less of a sadistic bitch.

Roland Amariah Gonzales

SUMMER OF LOVE

The summer of '96 kicks off. I go over to Logan's house and Tyler is in a foul mood. He says Jessica, his stupid older sister, is coming out from their mom's house in Idaho. Tyler glumly tells me that Jessica *always* tries to boss him around and she's going to be there the *whole* summer.

I laugh and say shoot, she can't boss you around if *all* of us throw her in the lake!

He laughs then says hey, you're right! His face lights up and he says and you're a lot bigger than her, too! You could probably beat her up!

I think to myself that I'd grown *maybe* two inches since I got back to Clinton two years earlier, and hell, I've gotta *still* be the smallest boy going into sixth grade!

I laugh and say yeah, ya think so? Hell, maybe!

Jessica arrives a week later and I don't get why Tyler is worried because she seems just like any other girl. She's super shy for some reason and no one can figure out why because she already knows Logan, Tyler and Ricky.

What's her problem?

She *always* avoids being alone with me and is real awkward around me. Renee notices and says I need to stop picking on Jessica and be nice to her.

I tell Renee I haven't ever said a word to Jessica one way or another!

Renee eyes me like she's studying something only she can see for a moment. She smiles then says oh is that so? Hmm...well, just be nice when ya do.

Not a few days later, Jessica grabs me by my wrist and *yanks* me into her bedroom. I'm thinking we're gonna fight so I put my fists up only to feel her small boobs squish against them as she pushes me against the wall. She looks in my eyes with a crazy look on her face that I've *never* seen on a girl before.

Jessica says she *really* likes me and I'd better like her too or she's gonna beat the hell out of me. She grins and laughs.

Amariah The Boy

I gulp and realize her *whole body* is pressed against my own. I was expecting a fight or...or something! *Anything* but this. I stutter out uh, y-yeah okay. Yeah, I like you too!

She laughs then hugs me and says good, now you're my boyfriend! If you look at any other girls I'm going beat your ass for that *too*, okay? She laughs again like it's a really funny joke. I don't get it. I hug her back, terrified, force a smile then nod and say okay.

I just wanted to play in the park this summer and go swimming! What does a boyfriend even *do*? What does Rowdy do? Sit on the couch all day, complain about his job, then smoke weed and drink beer? I can't buy *any* of that stuff! I'm only *ten*! Jessica is already twelve and going on thirteen, and she's at *least* a foot taller than me! Oh man, I'm so screwed...I just *know* she's going to kick my ass...I don't want this kind of pressure!

And I look at other girls *all the time*! Most of the time I *don't even know* I'm looking, I just do it!

And what about her and Tyler's dad, Hank? He's *huge*! If I hurt Jessica's feelings when I look at another girl, he's gonna *kill* me!

I ask Jessica if we can keep this secret from Hank so he doesn't squish me.

She smiles then presses her forehead against my own before giving it a little kiss and says okay.

Over the next few days I only look at Jessica when we're around each other. I realize that, even though she was real scary at first, she's actually *real* pretty, too! We're walking around the park together when I think to myself why does she want *me* to be her boyfriend? All the girls at school say I'm ugly *and* gross

...*and* stupid.

I relax under a tree in the shade while Jessica stretches in the afternoon sun, a pleasant breeze cools us both. I take a moment to admire her. She reminds me of a cross between Mrs. Brookes and Michelle with long, dirty-blonde hair that extends past her waist, a swimmer's tan, blue eyes, freckles across the bridge of her nose, and long lanky arms and legs.

She's got a pretty smile and a nice laugh too. She even has boobs! They're real small, but they're there! Though when I think about it, Logan has bigger boobs but I don't think he's supposed to.

Roland Amariah Gonzales

I join Logan's family for dinner and I'm horrified when Jessica announces in front of *everyone* that she likes me, I like her, and now we're boyfriend and girlfriend.

Everyone stops eating pizza, looks at her, looks at Hank, and then me. I look at Jessica with a face that screams *why?!*

Hank is a *huge* hairy guy with *bulging* muscles and a receding hairline. He stares at me while meticulously chewing his pizza, then slowly lowers it to his plate and wipes his hands on a paper towel. He slowly stands and trudges around the table to where I'm sitting, the floorboards creaking under his weight. Everyone is *dead silent.* He stops and looms over me while I'm sitting with a wide-eyed, mouth-agape look on my face and a pizza slice in my hand.

Hank shoves his finger in my face and says he'd better not catch me doing *anything* with his baby girl or he's gonna give me...one of *these!*

He flexes his massive arms and says or one of *these!*

He turns around, flexes his massive back muscles then says or one of *these!*

Then he turns away from me, puts his hands on his hips, sticks out his butt and farts. *Loudly.*

We all yell ew!, then scream and run out of the house onto the front lawn, but now we're laughing.

Hank yells out hey, Jess! You be nice to that boy, okay? He's tiny. Don't break him.

Jessica laughs and leans down to wrap her arm around mine, then yells back don't worry Daddy, I won't!

I laugh nervously and stare at the ground then gulp because now I have *two* people who are definitely going to beat me up.

Jessica and I spend the next few weeks running around the park, because there's not much else I can offer. I'm not having fun because I'm too busy worrying about whether or not I'm being a good boyfriend. I pick flowers for her if I see really nice ones, and when I catch a butterfly I bring it to Jessica and we let it go together.

I'm worried that Logan and Tyler are gonna be sore that I'm spending so much time with Jessica. I ask them about it and Tyler says he's just stoked that she's not smacking him around because she's always with me. Logan doesn't care either so that's good...I guess. I wish I could play with my friends and not spend the whole summer with Jessica though.

Amariah The Boy

I don't even have a job or anything, and though I *do* have an allowance, it's *nowhere* near enough to take her to the movies or anything like that. I worry that by the time I save up enough money to take her to dinner or whatever the hell I'm *supposed* to do, summer'll be over and she'll be gone! I won't even get a kiss or anything, so what the hell is the point of this!

It's around mid-summer when I see that Jessica is no longer entertained by my catching lightning bugs or showing her a really big frog, or doing whatever else I can do for free. She gets more and *more* aggressive about what she wants. We have a sleepover at Logan's, and Renee says under *no* circumstance is Jessica allowed to sleep in the same room as the boys.

I laugh and say I don't see what the big deal is.

Renee looks at me for a moment then raises her eyebrows and says well, just don't you do it or Hank will use you as a chair.

We all sit down to fried chicken and mashed potatoes with gravy, then watch a movie. Jessica sits next to me and holds my hand after we finish eating and wash up. It's halfway through the movie when she whispers to me that she wants to get ready for bed. As she walks away she suddenly turns around, looks to see if anyone but me is watching, then smiles and whispers no peeking!

After ten minutes or so I notice that she still hasn't come back. I look toward the bathroom and the lights are off. I wonder where she went. I think to myself that I'll brush my teeth now while everyone is occupied with the movie, that way I don't have to wait in line later.

I head toward the boys' bedroom to get my toothbrush and stop when I hear light panting and whimpering from the other side of the closed door. The hell is that? I didn't see anyone go in there. I peek through a crack in the door and my jaw just about drops through the floor.

Jessica is in her underwear, or at least in her bra. I can't see her panties because they're hidden by a pillow she's sitting on. I think hey that's *my* pillow! I gaze at something I'm *sure* I'm not supposed to see. Her bra is pink with white trim and little yellow daisies. Jessica is *aggressively* humping my pillow. She even whispers my name while she furiously moves her hands below and out of sight.

Wonder fills my being. I'm seeing something I'm not supposed to. If I walked in right now would we...would we have sex? I mean, I *know* that we can't because all the other people are in the house.

207

Could I even do it? I know how it works from the videos I watched but I've never actually done, well, anything! I haven't even kissed a girl.

...except for Michelle and that was years ago. I think sex-kisses are different from I-love-you kisses though. An ice-cold bucket of fear and realization washes over me. Hank would *kill* me if he found out I did *anything* with his daughter. My God, I can't look away. I've never seen anything like this. Jessica is so...I swallow dryly and almost cough. I think for a moment about the only other naked lady I've ever seen, and that's Mom.

Mom walks around naked, sure, but she farts and burps all the time and even shits with the bathroom door open. Mom is as much a *lady* as a frog is a *bird*. Mom is ugly and *disgusting*. Oh man why the hell am I thinking about her? I shake my head and stare at Jessica.

Jessica is...well, *wow* she's beautiful. What if I do the sex *wrong*? What if I'm bad at it? I hear a loud thud down the hallway. I quietly step away from the door and go back to the sitting room.

Logan and his brothers are mimicking the fighting moves they saw in the movie and don't pay me any mind. Renee yells for them to stop being such lazy little shits and help her clean up.

Looks like the movie's over. Renee calls out Jessica's name and tells her to help clean up, too.

Lightning quick, Jessica slips out of the boys' bedroom without anyone noticing.

I walk to the kitchen with a bunch of plates in my hand when she sneaks up behind me and puts her hands over my eyes and says guess who!

I'm caught off-guard when I notice her right hand smells *weird*. I awkwardly laugh and say Logan?

She laughs and says nooo, guess again!

I shift the plates to one hand and pull her hand off my face, then turn to look at her. Her face is red and covered in a sheen of sweat. She's breathing like she just ran around the house for about an hour. I say oh I thought you were outside or something, I didn't see you in the bathroom. Hey, did you hear Renee? She needs help cleaning up everything.

Jessica leans in close and asks if I saw her in the *boys'* room doing *things* with my pillow.

I'm stunned. I thought she would *hide* what she was doing. I pretend I have no idea what she's talking about and laugh as I say no, I didn't

208

see you, what were you doing with my pillow? You didn't blow your nose on it, did you?

Jessica giggles and says you'll see!

She kisses my cheek before going to wash the dishes.

I smile and nod, then help the others gather up trash and take it outside.

After that, I go to the boys' room and look down at my pillow. Jessica's butt was on that. I don't want to put my face where her butt was, that's gross! I wonder if I can switch it with someone else. Would they notice? Jessica might get in trouble if someone finds out she was humping my pillow. What do I do?

I furrow my brow and stare at the ground and wonder what other kids are doing for summer break.

I pull the pillowcase off then stuff it into my backpack. I take my toothbrush out and stand in line outside the bathroom to brush my teeth. Dammit. I hate lines. I hate waiting. When it's my turn, I put the toothbrush in my mouth and notice that it smells *weird*. I stop brushing my teeth for a moment and bring the handle up to my nose. It smells like...it smells like Jessica's *hand*. Why does it smell like...wait...did she shove my toothbrush up her *butt*!?

I see myself in the mirror, toothpaste in my mouth, and am horrified. I gag and fight back a wave of nausea as I run out to the back yard and chuck my toothbrush into the trash can. What is *wrong* with girls!?

I make my way back inside, wash my hands, then put a bit of toothpaste on my finger. I need to get a new toothbrush. Great. What am I gonna tell Mom? I guess I can just use some of my allowance. Man, this boyfriend stuff is *bullshit*!

I try and sleep but can't because when I close my eyes, I see Jessica's writhing and almost naked body in my mind.

The next morning, Tyler notices I slept on my pillow minus the pillowcase and asks where it went.

I say oh man, I sneezed on it when you were asleep! I had to wipe my butt with it, too.

I reach into my backpack then pull it out and thrust it toward his face. I say here, ya want it?

Tyler screams and says ew, man! Hell no! Throw that thing in the dirty clothes!

Roland Amariah Gonzales

I laugh, then go and hide Jessica's adventures in the middle of the dirty clothes hamper.

After everyone wakes up, we all eat pancakes for breakfast. Afterward, I get ready to leave. I go outside and Jessica gives me a knowing smile then blows me a kiss. I smile, reach into the air to grab it, then put it in my pocket.

Jessica *slowly* runs her tongue over her upper teeth and I don't know *what* that means. I laugh nervously and because I don't know what else to say or do, shout I like your tongue before I ride my bike home at full speed.

Amariah The Boy

Logan and his brothers all have pool passes that cost something like ten dollars per person per month. Mom hasn't given me allowance the last couple of weeks because she says I've been out messing around and not doing *every* single thing I'm supposed to.

I catch her during a commercial break when she's watching TV and in a good mood. I ask if I can earn or have some money so I can go to the pool with Logan and the others, 'because they go practically *every* day and it's real hot outside!

Mom says hell no, we ain't got that kind of money! She says who do you think we are, rich folk who livin' up in them there mansions, with fancy butlers wearing fancy white gloves...and all that jazz?

I stare at her and she stares at me before returning to her regularly scheduled programming. I look at the TV and it's something about a Jamaican lady who can see the future. I don't know why I bothered asking, anyway.

I ask Rowdy if *he* has any spare money that I could earn. Without looking up from his computer he says nope! He says he *can* get me a summer job at his workplace so I can make my *own* money.

I say oh? But I don't know how to do anything, I'm just a kid. I'm only ten!

He laughs and says well you can push a broom, can't you? You got two arms and you got two hands and ya got two legs with two feet, so you can pick up and carry stuff, too.

I scratch my head and say uh, yeah, I suppose so.

He pauses whatever he's doing then looks at me with a smile and says well, will you look at that, you're *over*-qualified already!

Rowdy talks to the owner of the print shop where he works, the same guy he complained *more* than a few times was an absolute prick, and gets me a job working a few hours from Monday to Friday. His boss, also named Hank, is an old man with a head of gray and white hair, in contrast to Jessica's father, Huge Hank.

I don't know what Rowdy is always complaining about because Old Hank doesn't seem that bad to me. He agrees to pay me ten dollars per week to sweep around the massive basement warehouse under the print shop. He says I'll also have to move things that aren't too heavy as well as fetch coffee if anyone wants anything.

If I have that much money then I can get a pool pass *and* maybe I can take Jessica out to get ice cream or something, too! If I can do more boyfriend stuff, maybe she'll be less crazy and won't hump my pillow anymore! Man, that'd be great.

I show up to work on the following Monday and am given a thorough tour of the building as well as shown where the cleaning supplies are kept. The building itself is big and made of faded red brick. The ground floor has all the printing equipment. There's an acrid smell in the air. Chemicals and burning. The upper floor has offices, and the basement warehouse is for storage. I'm told that the ground floor isn't for kids and I'm shown the places to avoid, which includes all of the space around the printing machines.

I spend most if not all my time in the basement, unless Rowdy or Old Hank sends me to fetch coffee or donuts or some other thing. The basement keeps itself surprisingly clean, and I find that I'm often sweeping nothing at all. I try to keep busy and clean whatever or wherever I can but find more often than not that there's nothing to do. I ask Rowdy or the others if they need anything and they tell me no.

During election season the print shop becomes a beehive of activity. The *moment* I arrive at work, I'm told to fill a series of base stands with sand, screw a metal pole into the centers, then set the completed election contraption on top of a pallet. There's at *least* two hundred of these things, and clean-up afterward is going to take *forever*!

I labor doggedly for *hours* to get everything assembled and placed on the pallets with only ten minutes to spare before the end of my shift.

I have no problem going to Old Hank during election season and demanding my pay, but I struggle during the off-season because I don't feel like I've done anything. I mean, I should be doing *something*. I sweep the basement floor for the hundredth time and see no dust, dirt or anything. I sigh and look around for trash, but I took care of it the day before and the day before that, too. I'm so damn bored.

At the end of the week I quietly tell Rowdy that I didn't get paid, in hopes he'll ask for me.

Rowdy's at his printing press. He arches an eyebrow and says I need to go ask myself.

I nervously approach Old Hank's office door and hesitate just before I knock. What if he asks me what I've done to earn this week's pay? Am I supposed to lie? He *has* to know that the basement is spotless. That I haven't done *anything*. What if he calls me a liar and fires me?

Amariah The Boy

I can hear him talking on the phone so I wait until he hangs up because I don't want to bother him. I knock on the door and Old Hank tells me to come on in. He asks how I've been and why I'm there. I awkwardly tell Old Hank it's the end of the week.

He says Is that right? Yes, I suppose it is.

I say um...can I get paid?

Old Hank furrows his brow, like he's trying to remember who I am. I feel like I've got a banana growing out of my forehead. His eyes light up and he pulls out his wallet then thumbs through it. I see a *huge* wad of twenty- and fifty-dollar bills. Old Hank asks me if I have change for a twenty.

I say uh, no sir.

He frowns and says he'll try to get change during lunch but he's real busy right now.

I stand there for a moment, and then he says that's all, you can go now.

I leave his office before he picks up the phone and starts talking again. Old Hank must've had something *really* important come up after lunch, because he never finds me. I don't chase him either because I feel weird hounding him over a measly ten dollars. I also feel weird *asking* him if I can get paid.

I return to the basement and aimlessly sweep nothing, then turn off the radio jamming out classic rock tunes. The silence is deafening. I look around and sigh. I wish I was at the pool right now with everyone else. I go to the basement restroom and see a pad of paper and flip through the pages out of boredom.

I think to myself work sure does suck. No wonder everyone is always so pissed all the time! I continue to absentmindedly flip through the pages then notice that someone has drawn a series of pictures toward the back of the pad. My eyes are wide when I see, in *graphic* detail, a series of cartoons showing Rowdy out in the countryside having sex with sheep. There's dialogue and plot and everything!

Whoa. Someone must *really* hate Rowdy.

Eventually, I meet the cartoonist when I see a guy fresh out of high school. He's walking around and introduces himself as Hank's grandson. After a while, I hear him talk to a buddy of his, also here for a summer job, about how much he can't *stand* Rowdy. He makes some disparaging remarks and I don't say anything one way or another because I don't really care.

213

Roland Amariah Gonzales

It's not that I *hate* Rowdy or anything, I'm just not fond of the guy. He loves my mom and I *hate* that woman. Anything she says, he backs up, and I see him as little more than an extension of her. He's not all bad though and does try to introduce me to hobbies of his so we can have shared interests. He lets me come up on the ground floor sometimes and shows me his workspace.

It's all pretty mundane, but there *is* a thick iron container nearby that holds bubbling-hot molten metal. I look at it a little too long with too much interest, and he notices. He says hey, now, don't you even *think* about goin' nowhere *near* that. That right there is lead, tin, and some other stuff. He tells me we use it here to make the letters for printin' stuff out and it'll melt your hand clean off.

I say uh-huh and watch the silver- and chrome-colored liquid bubble quietly. It occasionally makes a POP which sends little bits of molten metal in every direction. Oh man, I *really* want to put stuff in it or cover stuff with it.

I'm always near that molten stuff any chance I get. I mess with it when no one's looking and dip a metal rod into it—or whatever else I can find. I never get burned or anything and I don't get caught, either. If anyone sees me there I say I'm looking for Rowdy.

After a few weeks of mind-numbing nothingness and not getting paid, I stop going to the print shop entirely. Rowdy asks me where I've been.

I say I don't wanna work there anymore because I haven't gotten paid in forever.

Rowdy says well you gotta talk to Hank about that! I ain't gonna pay you!

I say I *did* talk to Hank and he always tells me he doesn't have change. I'm *tired* of working for free and standing around in the basement all day! I wanna go to the swimming pool, not spend all summer *underground.*

Rowdy sighs and throws up his hands then shakes his head and says well alright, it's your money, do whatever you want.

I use what little saved-up money I have from the election season, about twenty dollars, to take Jessica to the Soda Fountain and she's real happy about that. I get some drink called a muddy river, a coke with chocolate syrup in it. It tastes awful. We go to another spot together and I buy her some dumb thing she wants... and just like that, I'm broke. A month of wages earned from being a mole person and

214

working underground, minus two weeks of not getting paid, is gone in about thirty minutes. I decide that work is *bullshit* and I don't like it.

You know what? Being a boyfriend is bullshit, too.

Now I don't have money for a pool pass and I'm real bummed about it. I'm hanging around Logan's place when Renee sees my look of frustration. She asks what's up and I say that I can't afford the pool pass for the summer.

Renee laughs and says I thought you were making all that big money working out at the print shop! What happened?

I say angrily they didn't pay me everything they owed me and what little I got I spent on Jessica...and now I'm broke.

Renee laughs and says well, life certainly does go that way sometimes. Sucks, don't it?

I nod, look at her and say it sure does.

A few days later, Renee surprises me by buying me a pool pass for the *whole summer*. I can't believe it. Kindness from people has been few and far between in my ten years. I look at her in sad and sweet disbelief when she hands it to me and simply say *why*?

She says the way they did me at work is dirty after I put in all that effort. And from the way I made it sound, I was stuck underground all by myself. She smiles kindly and says why not?

All I can do is thank her while I look at her then down at the floor. I feel conflicted, something between gratitude, shame, and stunned disbelief at this unexpected kindness.

Roland Amariah Gonzales

I now ride with the brothers to Artesian Park and spend practically every day there. I love the pool and I *love* swimming. It's not t quite the beach back in Cali, but it isn't bad, either.

Jessica goes with us sometimes but she's not as excited to swim as we are. She'd rather lay out on a towel and tan under the sun. I don't get it. It's *hot*. How can you come to the pool and *not* swim? Why not just lay out in the backyard and tan there? It's like going to Disneyland, paying to get in, and sitting on a bench all day.

When she *does* swim with us I splash her, then go underwater and open my eyes to look at her legs and butt. They're nice. The pool water burns my eyes and it hurts like hell, but I can *almost* make out a blurry butt so I'm pretty sure it's worth it.

Jessica eventually catches me looking and begins posing for me in *and* out of the water. I still don't have a clue what to do and am worried if I *do* touch her that she'll tell on me. What if it's all a big joke and she *does* think I'm ugly and stupid?

The doubt is always there.

Girls from my class come to the pool sometimes, but not many. I notice that a few of them stare at me and Jessica when we lay out or swim together. I don't know *why* they're staring, and I hope they don't come over and tell Jessica how gross or stupid I am. These girls whisper to one another from the other side of the pool then look in our direction and giggle. I'm relieved that they leave us alone. Girls are weird.

I like it when Jessica stays home because then I can look at all the beautiful *older* girls without fear of her beating the ever-loving hell out of me. It's not fair that I can't even *look* at other girls. I mean hell, it isn't like I'm gonna walk up and ask 'em out! Doesn't Jessica know that they'd laugh at me if I even tried?

The girl lifeguards are my favorite to look at because they're all juniors and seniors in high school. They're about six years or so older than I am and they're *real* pretty. *All* of the boys, myself included, try and do tricks off the high-dive to splash the blonde-haired lifeguard. She has really long legs, tanned skin, and a pretty smile. She laughs, smiles at us and sometimes screams in mock surprise if we get her wet.

Sometimes I bring my body board from my time in Redondo Beach and have fun swimming with it, though the pool doesn't come close to the waves back in Cali. A younger boy has swimming goggles and offers

216

to trade for the day. With goggles, my friends and I can take turns playing with diving sticks and diving rings, so it's a good trade.

I swim around for about thirty minutes until some kid roughly grabs the goggles and rips them off my head before punching me in the nose. He yells don't touch my stuff, you fuckin' shitskin!

My nose is screaming in pain as I go underwater. I open my eyes and see crimson clouds billowing in front of me. By the time I break the surface, he's gone. I didn't even see his face.

The small boy returns a moment later and quietly says here's your board back.

I'm confused. In shock. Did I do something wrong? I didn't steal anything. Why am I a shitskin? What does that even *mean*? I showered before I came into the pool – everyone did. You have to! *Fuck*, my nose hurts. I look around at people having a good time. Laughing. I feel bad. I feel dirty.

I don't want to be here anymore.

The pool owner approaches me as I'm showering in the locker room. He asks me if I could *act* like I'm getting kicked out for the day then stay away for the rest of the week. He says the other kid who punched me in the nose said *I* stole *his* swimming goggles!

I'm indignant and protest. Emotion threatens to overtake me and I fight back tears. I explain that I didn't steal anything, that *his* younger brother asked if we could trade for a while and I said okay! Did no one see the younger brother swimming around on my body board *forever*?

The pool owner says yeah everyone saw that, but look, the kids' parents are here to pick up *both* of those boys. The owner says if I could just *act* like I'm getting kicked out, that'd be great.

I don't understand. It feels like I'm being punished for getting punched in the fucking face! This isn't right. It's not fair!

The owner stares at me, waiting for my response and after I quietly mutter okay, he quickly replies hey that's great, gives me a thumbs up and nods, then exits.

As I leave the pool I see both boys with their parents. The mother is yelling at the pool staff about some *dirty* little thief stole his son's swimming goggles, albeit briefly. She holds them up and in disgust says now she'll have to *throw* them away and get *new* ones.

The younger kid is looking at the ground and the older boy is glaring at me like I'm a piece of dog shit...but I don't know why.

Roland Amariah Gonzales

The pool owner sees me walking and yells hey, you're banned from the pool for a week! He yells and don't you try to come back sooner!

I yell back everyone at this pool can go fuck themselves! And I peed in this pool every day!

I walk to my bike. As I leave, I hear the woman say *ugh*, what an *awful* child. *Obviously*, letting someone like that into this place should've seemed like a bad idea!

I feel *wrong* about all this. Something about it *isn't* right—beyond the kid lying about my stealing—but I don't know what.

When I get home. I don't talk to Mom or Rowdy or anyone about it because I don't want to get in trouble for getting kicked out of the pool.

I spend the week riding my bike around. Mom won't let me stay in the house after breakfast and *man,* I wish I could go to the pool. Out here, it's hotter than a dog dragging ass on pavement.

While I'm riding around from one shaded spot to the next, I discover the town library. I lock my bike up then go inside and discover that the library is *air conditioned*. It's like an igloo compared to outside! The library quickly becomes my second-favorite place after the pool.

I also discover that the town library has *way* more books than the school library and computers, too! I spend my time either playing this neat old western ghost town exploration game on the computer or perusing books. They've got a lot of fantasy, science fiction, and books about movies, too. I end up staying at the library even *after* my pool ban is up!

I don't go back to the pool for some time.

It's better here, alone with books in a cool room. Books don't punch you in the face or call you shitskin.

218

Amariah The Boy

As summer nears its end I spend what time I can with Jessica over at Logan's house. We still haven't kissed or *anything* like that, and more than anything I just want her to go back home so the pressure is gone. It's not that I don't like her...I just feel bad when I'm around her, like I'm not good enough.

It's only a matter of time before she sees how stupid and ugly I am, and everything else that people always about me. Hell, maybe she'll even call me a shitskin.

She introduces me to an older high school girl named Melissa who lives down the road. Jessica stops hanging out with Logan and everyone else then drags me with her to her new friend's place, because she says I need to be around more mature company.

I go with her because I...I *guess* she's right? I don't really know. I'm still just a kid!

Melissa always has a bunch of friends over, all high school kids, and all they do is smoke cigs or weed and talk about sex *all* the time. I don't have a clue where her parents are or if she even *has* parents!

It makes me uncomfortable because even though I know about it...I haven't really done anything. They talk about their favorite positions and swap stories of almost getting caught having sex out in the park or somewhere else. I sit on the couch and try to press myself into it so I can disappear.

This goes on for a week, each day worse than the last, until one of the older kids asks me how far I've gone with Jessica. The questions get more graphic and more detailed as they ask me about all the things I want to do with Jessica. Seeing how uncomfortable I am, one of Melissa's friends laughs and says have you even *kissed* Jessica yet?

I quietly mutter uh, no, only on the cheek. I don't think Hank would like it if he caught us smooching.

They all laugh and the girl says well, Jessica's daddy ain't here right now, is he? Why don't you give her a big ol' kiss?

My voice catches in my throat as I look at Jessica. She looks back at me and flutters her eyelashes, then grins.

This...doesn't feel right. It doesn't feel like how it did with Michelle. I look around at all the older kids who are watching both of us expectantly. This feels wrong. I just wanted to play outside for the summer. With my friends.

My heart pounds and time slows as a million thoughts blaze through my head. I brushed my teeth earlier in the morning, but it's almost six in the evening now! What if I have bad breath? What if I kiss her wrong and she gets mad and bites me? What if I mess up and bite *her*? Or sneeze? There's a lot of dust in this room. *And* smoke from the older kids smoking cigs and weed. What if Jessica sneezes in my mouth?

I fight down a wave of nausea as I work myself into an imaginary panic attack. A terrible thought slices through all the noise as my mouth suddenly becomes a desert. What if the kiss is actually *good* and it leads to other stuff? I don't think I'm ready to have sex yet. Especially in front of all these people! I'm only *ten*! I can't even get a boner!

I stand up then clench and unclench my fists as I nod and try to build confidence. A hushed silence falls across the room as the older kids watch with grins cocked and loaded, ready to explode into laughter at any moment. I nervously approach Jessica then slowly lean toward her, place my forehead against hers, and we look into one another's eyes. I press my lips against hers but she doesn't kiss back, she just grins, like it's a joke.

After I pull away, uncertain, the older kids clap their hands and yell wooo, good job!

The same older girl from before says hey, why don't you kiss her longer this time and maybe use your tongue? She says Jessica might even let me feel her boobs too, and if things get crazy there's a spare bedroom we can use.

Everyone is staring at us now, still grinning, clapping or smoking. Waiting. Jessica doesn't stand up or embrace me. She sits. I look around at all the faces, then down at Jessica, then the ground. I quietly say I think I, uh...I think I need to go home.

The older kids yell *booooo!*

The older girl says aww no you don't, you ain't a little baby, are you? Why don't you stay here? No one's gonna say nuthin'.

I say indignantly no, I'm not a little baby, but I need to go home. I don't feel right, right now. This don't feel right.

Jessica's smile quickly disappears and is replaced by a frown. She finally stands then shouts fine you fuckin' little baby! Go on! Get the hell out of here!

I pause, surprised at the sudden change.

She pushes me out the door and yells again go on! Go! Get the hell out!

I fall and my knee hits the ground. Everyone's laughing. That older girl laughs and says what a *loser*!

Amariah The Boy

I limp to my bike then pedal back home. At first, my cheeks burn with shame and are redder than the sun but then, gradually, I feel like all the weight of the world is *off* my shoulders. I breathe a deep sigh of relief as the cool evening air whips about and envelops me. I realize I'm happier now then I've been in a long time.

I go to Logan's place a few days later. Jessica's still there for another two weeks and refuses to speak to me. Eventually, she says she's got a *new* boyfriend and he's a *real* man.

I say oh already? Wow, that was fast! Cool!

Jessica fumes, walks away and flips me the bird over her shoulder. From then on she flips me off any chance she gets, and I don't understand why she's so angry at me now that she has a new boyfriend. Why isn't she *happy?*

I go into the other room and play Pogs with Logan and the others. I'm *so* happy to be with my friends again.

Her new boyfriend shows up and he's from the same grade as me. He spends all day impressing her by popping wheelies with his bike. I hear Jessica clapping her hands and cheering like this guy is the *coolest* thing she's ever seen. Jessica turns her head in my direction and I hear her loudly say how *cool* her new boyfriend is and how he's *so* much cooler than RJ, because RJ is just a stupid little baby!

When she comes inside, I flip *her* the bird this time. She gasps in surprise then angrily tells Renee.

Renee tells me don't do that or she's kicking me out.

I say indignantly that Jessica has done it to me eight times already *this day*! I say hell, it's practically how she says good morning, how are ya' doing, and have a nice day!

Renee looks from me to Jessica who is the *picture* of innocence. Renee seems to know better and points at us both, one at a time, then says *neither* of you do that or *you're* grounded and *you're* going home!

Jessica huffs then storms off after she says oh my God, okay! He's such a dang baby!

I go back to playing with Logan and the others. Logan tells me all *kinds* of weird stuff about Jessica, now that she and I aren't dating. I'm positively *mortified* when he says she spied on me through a hole in the wall whenever I had to use the bathroom. He says he even saw her *hump a pillow* a *bunch* of times and say my name.

I carry over the genuine surprise and disgust from the first bit of information to the second. I say what? No *wayyyyy*. Who *does* that, man? Who watches someone using the *bathroom*? Are *all* girls this gross?

Logan says *hell*, man I don't know, probably!

Amariah The Boy

After Jessica leaves, Renee takes us to a spot everyone calls The Beach, otherwise known as Lake of the Ozarks. When we get there, I see it's just a big-ass lake and am *very* disappointed. Renee and Huge Hank open up a couple of folding chairs and take some beer out of a cooler as Logan, Tyler, Ricky, and I run into the water.

The first thing to strike me as I reach the gently lapping waves is the feeling under my feet. I recall the soft and gritty feeling of sand between my toes in Redondo Beach but the sensation here is something else entirely.

There isn't any sand here, it's all mud! *Mud!* It squishes and glops and gloops underfoot. It feels fascinating *and* disgusting, but I can't quite place *why* it feels disgusting. Tyler yells out hey, how many fish you think done shit and *died* in this here water?

I look down in horror. I gag a bit as I become aware that this place smells like a great big fart. Huge Hank yells out from behind his sunglasses, boy, you better watch your mouth. Don't make me get up and lake-spank you!

Tyler yells back yessir, sorry.

I walk out of the water and make my way to Huge Hank and Renee, staring in morbid fascination at my feet covered in muck. I say hey uh, this lake isn't filled with *poop*, is it? 'Cause it sure *smells* like poop and I don't think I'm s'posed to *swim* in poop.

Huge-Hank says guess what, kid, *you're* poop. He smiles at his joke and says no, there ain't no poop in the lake, no *people* poop anyway. Well, maybe. Probably not. Then he drinks from his beer can, lets out a belch, then blows it in my direction and tells me to go away.

I flee back to the water. I watch Logan and the others play and I see they're not *that* bothered by swimming around in whatever this is. Maybe it's okay? I slowly make my way into the water and hear Huge Hank shout watch out for the gar, they bite!

I yell back a car? How's a car bite? In the *water*?

Huge Hank says no, d-d-d-dummy. G-g-g-gar. It's a fish. Big teeth. Likes eating RJs.

Renee laughs and tells Huge Hank to hush.

Now I'm worried about gar *and* poop. As I stand there pondering which way I'm gonna swim, a *giant* horsefly the size of a *baseball* buzzes around my head. I scream and yell bee!

Huge Hank doesn't even look up but says he can hear that thing from where he's sitting and that ain't no bee, RJ, it's a *horsefly*. He laughs and says damn boy, *everything* is trying to eat you! You'd better run into that water!

I shout in panic, ahh, *fuck*!

Then the horsefly *bites* me and it *hurts*. Huge Hank and Renee are laughing now as they watch me frantically zip up and down the beach, trying to outrun the horsefly. I run toward Logan and the others out in the water and they yell at me to go away and don't bring it to them!

I dive under the water and swim in their direction after I yell back fuck that!

I hear screaming when I surface for a second and gulp down mostly air with a little bit of the nasty water. Everyone is panicking and swimming in different directions while they try to splash the horsefly away.

I keep swimming underwater for a bit until I come to a safety net meant to keep out the gar, I imagine. Probably like the anti-shark nets back in Cali that my dad told me about. I laugh as I watch Logan and the others panic and splash around. I think to myself shit, better them than me!

Then I both hear and *see* the damn horsefly buzzing straight for me. I yell out oh shit! Before I take a deep breath and dive under. I hold my breath for as long as I can and when I come up, the damn thing bites me right on my head! I scream out in pain gahhh!

Logan and the others are laughing. I take a deep breath, dive under, and desperately thrust my hands up and out of the water as I stay submerged and try to splash the thing away. After holding my breath for what feels like an hour, I surface the horsefly is gone. I breathe a sigh of relief and swim back to the others.

Logan and I tread water and talk about a TV show called *Power Rangers*. We argue about which of the rangers is the best. I think it's the red ranger but he says nuh-uh, it's the *green* ranger. I start to think of a counterpoint when a thick glob of *something* splats the back of my head. I reach back to touch it. Dear Lord it's the mud poop that's on the floor of the lake.

Tyler is laughing like a hyena and just like that, a war is on!

Logan and I move to more shallow water where we can stand and lob piles of mud poop at Tyler. He yells no *fair* and calls out for someone to come join his side.

We tell Ricky to go.

Ricky says no way! I ain't goin' over there!

Amariah The Boy

Logan says you *best* go, or I'mma hold you under this here lake!

Ricky says a few choice words then angrily swims over to Tyler.

Now that our sides are even, we have a blast trying to nail each other with what we start to call moop until Ricky takes a glob of moop straight to his face.

He screams and covers his eyes and we say a collective oh shit! Before swimming to him.

Ricky got it right in his eye and I'm both real *proud* of my aiming ability...and real *worried* about the hell that's sure to come.

We pull Ricky with us into the deeper water and tell him to force his eyes open, then we duck his head underwater and try to flush out the moop.

Ricky is screaming and crying in pain and saying glub glub when we force his head underwater. We *have* to get this out before Renee notices or we're all *dead.*

It's not one minute before Renee sees Ricky, and we collectively clench our butt cheeks as she yells out hey, HEY! Just what in the *hell* is going on over there. C'mere... you better get your asses over here right *now!*

We're all quiet, except for Ricky who's still hollering as we help him get to the shore.

Logan quickly explains that we were all tossing moop at each other and Ricky didn't get out of the way quick enough!

Before he can go on, Renee smacks him across the face *hard* and yells look at what you did!

Logan hops up and down in pain and yelps while he grabs at his face.

Huge Hank is pissed and says oh great, now we gotta drive *all* the way back into town. He says that's an *hour* away and we have *one* goddamn afternoon to relax without y'all fuckin' it up? Then he says hurry the fuck up and help me get everything in the car before I beat *all* your asses.

We scramble to help as best we can. The drive back is quiet, no music or nothing, just the sound of Ricky crying and occasionally screaming when Renee tries to open his eye to see how much moop is in it.

Renee tells Huge Hank to head to the Casey's General Store, because we need water to flush it out.

Roland Amariah Gonzales

I'm real worried we'll go to the one my mom works at. I *know* she'll whip my ass if she catches wind of this. Somehow, by the grace of whatever is looking out for me that day, we go to a different one. We sit there for a good fifteen minutes and listen to Renee chew our asses while Ricky cries and shouts. Eventually, Renee cleans out Ricky's eye.

By the time everything is said and done, *everyone* but Ricky is grounded for the remainder of the summer. It's only like a week left, but still! Being grounded sucks.

No one says a thing to my mom which is great. I spend the rest of my summer break hiding in the library, reading the hours away.

Amariah The Boy
BIG BOY PANTS

Autumn 1996. The start of sixth grade. I'm headed to an entirely *new* school now, the middle school about one minute down the road from my grammar school. Everyone says sixth grade is *way* different from fifth grade because every subject has a different teacher. I'm worried that I'll have to scramble from class to class to get there on time! I learn after a few weeks that it's not as bad as that, though I *do* need to hustle after gym class.

Gym class is my favorite! At first. We play dodgeball, basketball, football or some other sport, and it's usually a lot of fun. What comes after gym class is downright *traumatizing*. That's *naked shower time*. In school! The gym teacher, Mr. James, bellows in the locker room that if we don't get naked and get in the shower then that's an F for the day. He says he won't *hesitate* to flunk us all if we don't wash our dirty nasty bodies!

I reckon he's right about dirty and nasty because the boys' locker room smells *awful,* like old moldy garbage and *unwiped butts.* I manage to avoid the showers the first few classes but eventually Mr. James catches me and yells hey, what do you think you're doin'? You get your skinny butt in there and wash up!

I say no, it's okay Mr. James, really! I didn't sweat that much at all!

Mr. James says no kiddin'? Hey, do me a favor. Take your socks and put 'em *right up* to your nose and tell me how they smell.

I don't move an inch and he says yeah, right, that's what I thought. Now, get in there!

I turn and face my locker to consider my options. I hear Mr. James call out a kid named Frankie. Mr. James tells Frankie he smells like a week-old unwashed butthole and he can be *damn* sure he's getting an F until he showers. I take a deep breath, face my locker, drop my shorts and underwear, then take off my shirt and socks. I cover my junk, a term I picked up from Dad years ago, with one hand and walk into the shower with a bar of soap in the other. A wave of revulsion hits me as the shower somehow smells *worse* than the rest of the locker room.

Roland Amariah Gonzales

I glance out the side of my eye and realize that not *only* is everyone *much* taller than me, their junk is *huge* compared to mine too. Grandma Dena told me because I skipped a grade I'd always be just a *little* bit smaller than everyone else. I never even *thought* to consider that this would apply to my junk as well, but now here I am and—good *Lord,* that dude's balls are the size of my *fist,* what in the *hell!*

I'm in a state of horror. I *desperately* need to get back to my locker before anyone notices how *tiny* my junk is and tells all the girls!

I haphazardly apply soap to myself then frantically wash it off. I exit the shower and scurry toward my locker, covering my junk with one hand and clutching my wet bar of soap with the other. I'm so nervous that I squeeze the bar of soap right out of my hand and it falls to the floor. My eyes go wide for only a moment before I kick it far out of sight. No one seems to notice.

I think to myself fuck it, I'll get another one. I yank my towel out of my locker and quickly cover my butt, then lean into the open locker, trying to hide my junk, as I think how to dry myself. *No one* can see how small my junk is or I'll never hear the end of it. I breathe a sigh of relief as I dry off my upper body, I'm *pretty* sure no one saw anything.

Mr. James steps out of his office and sees me with my hips thrust forward into the locker. He yells out hey, you, stop humping that damn locker!

I look over my shoulder in terror then release something between a laugh and cry and say sorry.

I *hate* naked shower time. After gym class it's a mad dash to the next class, and my hair is always wet. When I sit at my desk, I notice that girls from my gym class smell *great,* like flowers! I wonder what *I* smell like. I take a moment to pretend to scratch the back of my head and smell my underarm, then gag because I smell like the locker room. I wonder what the girls' locker room smells like? Probably flowers.

Amariah The Boy

There's a little blonde girl named Brittany who follows me around in one of my classes. I don't think much about it. Whenever I need to talk to the teacher, she's there, too. When I need to sharpen my pencil, she needs to sharpen hers. It's crazy how the timing works out!

Brittany is a little shorter than me which is odd because I'm *real* small. She's pretty though! She's got shoulder-length blonde hair, green eyes, a pretty smile, and she wears these little earrings of silver spheres. She never says anything to me, and I don't say a thing to her, recalling from the previous year how all the girls in this school think I'm ugly and they hate me.

I develop a crush on another girl named Kelsey, (the younger sister of Kristi, that high school girl who visited us in fifth grade). Kelsey is starting to look more like her older sister. Kelsey doesn't know how I feel, of course, because I'm a nobody.

The other kids in my grade never really look my way unless they're saying something mean or threatening me. I'm pretty lonely at school and don't have anyone to talk with.

However, admiring Kelsey from afar is free, and no one notices, so that's what I do. I always hope to hear or see her laugh or smile because it kind of makes me happy. We never really talk much, but when I say good morning she usually says it back and even smiles, too!

That's a lot better than hearing someone tell me to go fuck myself.

A girl in my social studies class named Helen tells me she's having her birthday party at Pizza Glen and that her mom said she can invite a bunch of people. I'm incredulous and ask if she's *really* having it at Pizza Glen, because that's my favorite pizza place and I didn't know that others knew about it!

Helen grins and says yeah Pizza Glen is the *best*. She says a lot of other kids in class are going too!

She tells me the party is at 4pm on a Saturday. I'm *stoked* to finally be a part of the pack! This is my first birthday party invitation since that one girl invited me back in second grade.

And that invitation only happened because her mom made her.

I think sixth grade is going to be different. Maybe things are going to change! A moment of panic hits me when I worry that boys might compare junk sizes at the party.

I use my saved-up allowance to buy a bunch of stickers because I see girls put stickers and shiny stuff on *everything* at school. Rowdy

Roland Amariah Gonzales

drives me to Pizza Glen and there's a bunch of cars out front. I excitedly tell Rowdy hurry up, hurry!

There's a great big smile on my face. My stomach is full of a hundred fireflies excitedly glowing and buzzing about. I wonder what kind of friends I'll make. Will this lead to other parties, too? Maybe I'll be able to hang out with more kids my age! I get inside and see a bunch of people, but Helen isn't here. I look around and slowly realize I don't see *anyone* from my class.

Rowdy and I sit at a table and I carefully protect Helen's gift next to me. I wait for ages. At four-thirty, Rowdy orders us a pizza to share. Every time the door opens, my head almost flies clean off from jerking it in that direction, eager and with a smile on my face.

At five o'clock, Rowdy quietly says come on, let's go on home.

I protest and say maybe they're all late, maybe they took a bus and it got stuck in the mud or something?

He shakes his head no then says well, you can talk to 'em all about it on Monday and find out, but it's time to get back.

When we get back home Mom looks up from the TV for a moment and asks how the party went.

I say it was fine then go to my room.

I'm confused. Did I get the day right? I thought she said Saturday. I turn on the TV in my room. Mom and Rowdy got a new one for the sitting room. This old one's kind of busted so they can't sell it, especially with the big green line going down the front, so they gave it to me. Mom acts like it's a gift straight from heaven itself. I can't complain because I never thought *I'd* have my own TV.

I absentmindedly put that Final Fantasy 3 game into the Super Nintendo, erase one of the saved games, then start a new one. After about twenty minutes, I'm really into it and conclude that this game isn't so hard or confusing at all. I really like it!

I force myself to forget Helen's party and instead throw myself completely into the game. It's nothing like Sonic the Hedgehog *or* Mario or *any* other game I'd played before! I discover that, unlike the last time I played, there's a whole story and lots of reading, too. Before I know it, I hear Mom yell turn that thing off and get to bed!

I blink and look at the clock. It was *just* six o'clock...five hours ago. Oh, wow.

On Sunday, it's much the same. I play the game all day until Mom yells for me to go to bed.

Amariah The Boy

Monday rolls around and before class starts, Helen asks me if I went to Pizza Glen.

I say yup, I sure did. I thought you said four o'clock though. Did I get the time wrong?

Helen looks at me with a sad face and says ohhh, *sorry.* She says her mom changed the party to a different restaurant and she didn't have my phone number.

She shrugs her shoulders at me and says sooo, oh well!

I look down at the ground for a moment then look up and say oh...well, do you want me to write my number down? We've got an answering machine at my house and everything.

Helen laughs and waves away the suggestion. She says *no* that's okay. Then she gives me a perky little smile and in a baby voice says thanks anyways!

I stare at her. I'm confused. I notice the other kids are staring at me, waiting. They all burst out laughing. My face is a red balloon. I weakly laugh and say yeah, that was a good one, guys.

One of the boys laughs and says *man,* RJ. You are such a *loser!*

I try to laugh then look quietly down at my desk and say yeah, you're right.

I had the stickers in my backpack. I wanted to surprise Helen with them but kept them in there instead. I sit glumly through class then toss them into the trash, making sure that I'm the last person out so no one sees. I don't go to any birthday parties after that.

Roland Amariah Gonzales

Rowdy moves us to another part of town because Mom just mopes around the old place and cries a lot. I think she misses Grace. The new house is bigger and is a dark blue color that I really like! Much better than the faded gray of the last one...and who paints a house faded gray, anyway? There are *so* many colors to choose from and someone decides they want their place to look like a sad cloud.

The new place is more or less the same distance to school, just from a different part of town.

A few weeks have passed and the teachers are all *sick* of stinking kids who never shower after gym class, so they encourage us with little handouts of free shower gel samples. That doesn't work and everyone— well, mostly the boys—continue to either *not* shower or do so poorly.

We have sex-education classes soon after, and they tell us *why* we stink and inform us that we *do in fact stink.*

They split us into two groups, the boys and the girls. They tell us all about puberty and the changes we can expect. They stress that body odor is something new we'll all have to learn to deal with, then *strongly* recommend we all wear deodorant.

I keep my surprise to myself when I see diagrams showing giant mammoth dongs and balls the size of apples. I think to myself how I am *so* far behind and you know what? The vagina is *terrifying.* Why are they even *showing* us the vagina?

Sex-ed classes last for a week and focus primarily on how not only will sex lead to death by an STD, but in the odd instance we *don't* die, we'll likely get some girl pregnant.

The sex-ed teacher says after we get a girl pregnant, we'll have to drop out of school together then live on the railroad tracks with our new hobo family.

Mom, having signed the permission slip which okayed my taking sex-ed class, takes it upon herself to add *her* two cents by the end of the week. She calls me into the living room on a Saturday and says, sit down, Rol, I got somethin' *important* I need to talk to you about.

The smell of weed is as pungent in the room as is her sour, rancid beer breath. I grit my teeth then sit on the couch as far away as I can. I steel myself.

Mom launches into her story, and it goes something like this: So, there's this guy and this girl, right? They was partyin' and drinkin' right *here* in Clinton! I *just* heard about this a week ago, an' I'm real glad I did 'cause you need to hear it, Rol. And – hey! Are you payin' attention?

I nod and say yes, Mom.

Mom takes a deep breath and continues. So, they was havin' a good ol' time and decide to drive out to the country and enjoy each other in the backseat, *if ya know what I mean.*

I look at her, confused.

She snaps her fingers to get my attention then says I'm talkin' 'bout sex, *Rol.*

She spreads her hands in the air like she's separating a rainbow in half and says seeeeeex.

Now listen up, 'cause this here's important!

I nod again and stare at the wall, my hands folded in my lap.

Mom says this couple, now, they start *goin' at it.* The guy's makin' her feel *good.*

I wince.

She says, He's playin' with her tits, and fingerin' her, and all that.

Mom laughs and says this guy knows what he's *doin',* if you know what I mean?

She looks at me for a moment, laughing, then looks away and continues her story.

Before you know it, the girl's all *wet* and tells the guy to put on a condom and get to fuckin' her already! So, the guy puts on a condom and they start fuckin' in the backseat and the *Lord* sees this and he ain't at *all* happy, 'cause not only are they fuckin' before marriage, but the guy's wearin' a condom *too,* and *that ain't okay* with the Lord!

She stops for a moment then looks at me and says so the Lord – hey, you listenin'? Whaddid I just say?

I say the Lord ain't happy 'cause of condoms.

She nods and says aaand?

I say aaand he was't happy because they were...fuckin'.

Mom nods again and says good, right. So, the lord whips up a storm as a warnin', but the guy and the girl ain't payin' no heed 'cause they're too busy fuckin'. The Lord decides, you know what? Enough is *enough* and a *lesson* is needed in this here town, so he sends down a lightning bolt that hits the couple while they're goin' at it and...

She pauses for a moment for dramatic effect then yells POW and slams her hand against the coffee table, knocking over a half-filled beer bottle.

Roland Amariah Gonzales

Mom frowns and says goddamit...hey, don't you go nowhere!

She stumbles to her feet then lurch-waddle-thunders into the kitchen to get a towel. I hear her fart loudly in the kitchen, laugh, then lurch-waddle-thunder back into the sitting room holding *two* beer bottles and a towel. She tosses the towel onto the spilled beer, doesn't make an attempt to clean it past that, then falls back onto the couch down next to me.

I stare ahead at the wall filled with a mixture of concern, worry, and disgust.

Mom continues her story.

So the girl, she comes to after a bit and she's in a lot of pain 'cause lightning fuckin' hurts. She notices that her man is all passed out. The girl shakes him and realizes that this dude's fuckin' *dead!* The girl tries to pull away but she *can't.*

Mom turns to me and asks, you know why, Rol?

I shake my head.

Mom intertwines her fingers, then says the damn condom done *fused* the boy and girl together, 'cause of the lightning bolt, dummy! Don't they teach you *nothin'* in school, I swear to God!

I say ah, okay. Yeah, that makes sense, I guess.

Mom continues her story.

So the girl struggles and she's screamin' and hollerin' in pain because she's got a dead dude's *dick* stuck inside her *and* she realizes she's a whore!

I think to myself, man, I wish I was *anywhere* but here right now.

Mom snaps her fingers in my face to get my attention again and says hey lookit me, boy. The Lord's wrath is *real,* Rol.

Mom goes on about how the girl feels *real* bad but that ain't *enough* for the Lord, so he sends a *bear* from the woods to *eat* her dead boyfriend. This is a lesson for the town as much as it is for her.

Mom snaps her fingers again and asks ya see?

I stare at the ground and mutter yes.

Mom takes a break to open one of bottles of beer and drinks half, then belches and continues her story.

So eventually the police get a call from the Lord and they say yes, lord? And the Lord says there's a *whore* right outside your town and so sayeth I that she's learned the error of her whore ways. The police go to pick up the girl and shoo the bear away. They take some scissors and snip the dick off what's left of the whore's boyfriend and she goes

234

on and becomes a *nun*! *And,* 'cause she's got a dead dude's dick melted *way* up all inside her, she can't piss *to this day*. She has to use a special medical bag and *to this day* everyone calls her Pissnun!

Mom breaks into laughter at the last part, wipes away a tear, then calms down and slowly looks at me. She downs the rest of her bottle, belches, then rests her hand on my knee as she slowly nods and says do you understand, Rol?

I look down at the various beer stains in the carpet and think about her story, my mind abuzz. There's no way it could be true, but what if *parts* of it are? Hell, I don't want my dick to get cut off, and I sure as hell don't want a bear to eat me *or* get hit by lightning! Did everyone who's been struck by lightning have sex *before* they were married? Hell, I didn't even know the Lord threw down lightning bolts like Zeus!

I stop and think for a moment then say wait a minute, Mom. You and Rowdy ain't married and you have sex all the time!

Mom leers at me for a moment, blinks a few times, then says well, yeah, but we're married under *common law,* dummy, 'because we been together for so long. The Lord understands and *respects* common law!

A minute or two of silence passes when I say oh...alright then. Hey, can I go back to my room?

Mom's focus has turned to the TV. She's watching a commercial for some Jamaican psychic lady who goes by Miss Cleo. Mom picks up the phone before I speak again.

Hey mom, are we done talking?

She blinks for a moment, confused by my presence, then looks at me and says huh? Oh, yeah, sure.

She waves me away before reaching for the unopened beer bottle with her free hand, then sits back into her well-worn seat on the couch, satisfied with the lesson she imparted and the wisdom she's about to get from Miss Cleo.

I go back to my room and sit against the wall on my dirty, brown-colored carpet. I play Final Fantasy 3 for the rest of the day. I try not to think about anything Mom has said.

On Sunday, she decides we're all sorely lacking the word of God and, after piling us into her beat-up, pea-green 1967 Maverick, drives us to a random church.

I don't see any of the kids I know from school and wonder where they all go to hear the Lord's word.

Roland Amariah Gonzales

My time in the church is nothing special, just the pastor telling everyone how we're not worthy and talking about God's love and how we're all going to hell unless we accept Jesus into our hearts. Same ol', same ol'.

I spend a couple of weeks studying the Bible and Mom is real happy about that. She says it's important for me to *appreciate* the lessons in the bible, *especially* the parts about obeying thy mother and father.

After church is over one Sunday, I get the chance to ask the pastor a bunch of questions while Mom and Rowdy are off talking with some other adults and drinking coffee.

I ask the pastor *why* God would create an angel then punish that angel for rebelling...when God knew all along that the angel would rebel and become the devil. Why even create that angel if he only wanted to turn him into the devil and hurt him? That isn't fair. Hell, it's *wrong*!

The pastor says well, child, it's all part of the Lord's plan to save us from original sin. He needed the devil to *tempt* us into sin, you see.

I say oh, then why would God put Adam and Eve in the Garden of Eden with that magic tree and—

The pastor interrupts and says you mean the Tree of Knowledge of Good and Evil?

I say ah, right, sorry. So, why would he tell them not to eat from the Tree of Knowledge of Good and Evil *then* punish them and *everyone* forever after. God *knew* Adam and Eve were gonna eat from that tree. That isn't fair either. It's cruel!

The pastor pauses and considers my words then says it's all part of God's plan, too. If humans didn't have original sin, there wouldn't be a need for Jesus to be born and save us.

The pastor puts his hand on my shoulder and says you love Jesus, don't you? Jesus loves you and if you let Jesus into your heart, then you can be saved. And if you *don't* believe then you'll burn in a lake of eternal fire.

I nod and wait for the pastor to finish. I can tell he's not going to tell me anything I haven't heard before. After he turns to leave, satisfied, I think to myself that if Jesus loves us, why does he let people get hurt? Why doesn't he send an angel or a lightning bolt to stop people from hurting little kids or babies? Why does he only save lightning bolts for people who piss him off?

...what the fuck did little kids and *babies* ever do to the Lord?

Amariah The Boy

The pastor turns, and I realize I said this out loud. With an icy smile he tells me that it's all part of God's plan and that the Lord works in mysterious ways. He says look, all you need to worry about is coming to church, believing in Jesus, and that's it. And never swear in the house of the Lord or you'll go to hell.

I ask the pastor if he's heard of the Greek gods like Zeus, Athena, Ares or Aphrodite, and he laughs and says that's called *mythology,* and the Greek gods aren't *real.*

I ask the pastor well how do you know they're not real?

He sighs and tells me because the only God that is *real* is the God of Abraham.

I respond well, don't you think the Greeks thought the same thing about *their* gods?

The pastor gives me a polite smile and says I should read the Bible if I have more questions, then excuses himself.

I nod okay, then think to myself that this guy doesn't know anything. Hell, the pastor should read about the *Greek* gods. *They* had *actual* reasons for doing whatever the hell it was they did long ago. That is, based on the books I'd read.

As we drive home, Mom screams at me from the passenger seat. She says how *dare* you say those things to the pastor, he's a man of God! She shouts we can *never* go back to that church! She says I'd better look *real* deep and hard within myself so I can *save* myself because no one else can do it for me.

When we get home she throws a Bible at me and tells me she doesn't want to see me do nothin' but read until supper time. She takes my Super Nintendo and throws it in her closet and says it's rotting my mind and I can kiss it goodbye for a month.

I shake my head no and tell her I *have* already read the damn bible and I *know* what happens in it!

Mom says oh yeah? Well, what happens on page eight in the Book of Numbers, smart guy?

I look at her with a mixture of disbelief, anger and laughter. I shrug and say some guy begat goats to another guy, probably.

Mom says well, it sounds like you don't know it that well, do you? Get to it.

Roland Amariah Gonzales

A new week starts and I ride my bike to school. I'm pretty sure of the way to get there but leave a little early just in case.

I ride through The Square and see a bunch of kids who have set up a ramp near the Soda Fountain, a holdover from the 1950s where folks go to enjoy banana splits and soft drinks. I stand with my bike for a few minutes and watch, but I don't want to be late, so I continue on my way. I eventually get to school, lock up my bike and go inside.

I look at the clock. Twenty minutes until school starts. I should've played on the ramp.

I enter the gym where all the kids are supposed to wait for the morning bell and sit on the bleachers. I quietly do some of the homework I'd avoided all weekend. I like waiting until the last moment with math or science worksheets because it's more exciting to do everything when the clock is running against me. I can't do that with English, social studies or art worksheets, though. They require too much thinking and I always make mistakes.

I look down and concentrate on a long-division problem when I hear shouting near me. Someone yells out bitch, don't you *ever* fuckin' look at me that way, I'll stab yer fuckin' eye out! I done it before!

I see a kid with dark hair, squinty eyes and a *mean-looking* bulldog face glare down at Frankie, the nasty kid who never showers.

Frankie starts to climb the bleachers and yells back *motherfucker*, you and *what army?* Say that to my face, Rocky, you little fuckin' bitch!

I look on and think to myself both these boys are *twice* my size. It seems like *everyone* else has hit puberty but me.

...those two dudes must have finished *all* their homework to have this kind of free time!

I watch the spectacle along with others present.

Frankie climbs up the bleachers to get in Rocky's face but when he gets one row down from him, Rocky lashes out quickly with his leg and boots Frankie hard. Frankie falls backward and tumbles down the bleachers. Red in the face, he struggles to his feet and yells out that he's gonna *kill* Rocky.

The vice principal enters the gym at that moment and yells just what in the hell is going on?

Frankie and Rocky point their fingers at one another and start shouting. The vice principal shouts over them to get their asses down from the bleachers, then pulls them out of the room.

Amariah The Boy

Ten minutes later, the man returns and announces that fighting will *not* be tolerated on school grounds and that those two kids are suspended. He asks if we all understand and everyone drones yes, sir.

I'm *really* kicking myself for not playing on that bicycle ramp now. School hasn't even started and I'm already getting yelled at! I resolve *never* to come to school early again if I can help it.

The bell rings and it's time for class.

In the morning during announcements, we all pledge allegiance to the U.S. flag and I see a boy holding up two fingers as he salutes the flag instead of holding his right hand to his heart. I remember my dad saluting the flag with his whole hand, not just two fingers. I think maybe the two-finger-salute is something that soldier's kids do, so I do it, too.

After the pledge is recited, the boy angrily whispers to me that I'm not *allowed* to salute the flag with two fingers. He says *only Boy Scouts can do that*, and I'm *not* a Boy Scout.

I say oh, sorry, and ask him how I can be a Boy Scout so I can salute the flag like he does.

He looks at me in disgust and says that I *can't* be a Boy Scout because I'm poor, stupid, and dirty.

I look down and the floor and don't respond.

I never salute the flag with two fingers again.

A week later during gym class, we all line up and the Boy Scout starts talking with me about a movie that came out over the summer, Batman Forever. I'm surprised he's talking to me and a little nervous because I haven't seen it.

...I can't afford to go out and see every movie that comes out. Hell, I can't afford to see anything, really.

I get excited as he talks to me, though. If he becomes my friend, maybe he'll let me join the Boy Scouts!

While he's talking he suddenly shoves me and I fall backward over *his* friend who had snuck up behind me on all fours.

I slam against the floor *hard*. The wind is knocked out of me and the Boy Scout and his friend laugh. I gasp for air, panicking because I can't breathe. After a moment or two I try to get up but yelp as I feel a sharp stabbing pain in my lower back. The Boy Scout and his friend aren't laughing anymore and look scared shitless. They tell me to stop foolin'.

They try to help me up but the pain is unbearable and I can't stand. I collapse onto the floor again.

239

Roland Amariah Gonzales

The gym teacher Mr. James comes out and, seeing me lying on the ground, yells for me to get up. He yells nap time is over, sunshine.

After I fail to stand he jogs over, ready to give me an earful, and again tells me to get up. There's tears in my eyes as I say I can't.

He looks at me with uncertainty and attempts to pull me up, but I cry out in pain before I collapse back onto the floor.

The pain is an icy dagger tracing from my spine along my lower left back.

Mr. James looks *very* concerned and he yells out everyone, get in line!

All the kids in class get in their spots and Mr. James yells out what in the hell happened to me. He's *pissed* and shouts do you *see* what happens when you horse around and act stupid?

After a few moments of silence, the Boy Scout and his friend say that they were just messing around with me and I fell over.

Mr. James repeats loudly, you were *just messing around?*

The Boy Scout's friend says um...well, RJ got pushed over and he hit the ground, but we didn't mean to push him over!

Mr. James is *pissed.* He screams at everyone that *this* is why we're not supposed to mess around! He points at me and says my back might be broken!

He leaves and comes back with s the vice-principal. They carry me to the mats and lay me on one of them. Mr. James tells everyone to jog around the gym then goes into his office to call my house.

As the kids jog around and pass by me, some say thanks a lot, RJ, look what you did! And offer a slew of insults. A couple of girls stop and ask if I'm okay. I say I can't move but thank you for asking.

Mom arrives after a short while in her Casey's General Store uniform. Mom is more caring with me than she's *ever* been in my *entire* life. I'm suspicious because I know better, but I'm also in a lot of pain and fake caring feels better than none.

She puts her hand under the back of my head and asks if I'm okay. I tell her I can't move and it hurts when I try. She looks at me with a concerned face then starts yelling at Mr. James. She says she can't *believe* that I got hurt like this during class and demands to know what kind of teacher is he, what kind of *man* is he?

Mr. James's face turns red and he clenches his jaw.

Amariah The Boy

I don't blame him at all. I blame that prick who pushed me over and...you know what? I don't wanna be a Boy Scout anymore. *Fuck* the Boy Scouts.

Mom starts screaming about lawsuits against the school for negligence and while Mr. James eyeballs her with a face between apologetic and pissed, she subtly lifts the back of my head so my lower back lifts off the mat. I see stars as an explosion of pain rips through my body. I scream before Mom talks about how I might need surgery, and who's going to pay for it anyway? She can't afford it! Not something like this!

She pulls up on my head again. I grit my teeth and start to whimper then cry. I try real hard not to because I don't want any of the kids in my class to see me cry. You *can't* cry at school.

An ambulance arrives and I'm taken to the hospital. Mom drives behind the ambulance because they say she can't ride along.

When we get to the hospital they do x-rays on my back. A bit later, the doctor tells me I'm lucky because there's nothing broken, but my muscles *are* inflamed. He says I need to put ice on my lower back and there'll be no gym class for a while.

Mom looks at me and scowls but I don't know why, I didn't do anything! I just fell. She smiles warmly when the doctor looks at her and thanks him for everything he's done, then she takes me home for the rest of the day.

The next day, the vice-principal meets me with the kid who pushed me over, who says he's sorry and *really* didn't mean to do it.

I look at the kid distrustfully. I know he doesn't mean his apology. He couldn't care less if I got hit by a car or anything like that. Hell, if I did, it'd probably make his day.

None of them care, they all hate me...and I hate them, too. But I tell him don't worry about it and walk to my class.

Roland Amariah Gonzales

WHITE CHRISTMAS

Thanksgiving comes and goes uneventfully. It's lost the magic of the two previous years, though I can't figure out why. I don't eat much during Thanksgiving. Hell, I don't eat much in general anymore... and not entirely by choice. I get school breakfast and lunch during the weekdays but hardly eat anything at home. Mom cooks far less than she used to, now that Grace has gone back to California. My diet consists mainly of discount canned raviolis and budget-select sliced bread.

It takes up space in my belly but offers little in the way of nutrition.

I have a spark of hope when Mom lands a managerial position at the Casey's General Store nearby. I think maybe now we'll get *good* food, but she unexpectedly quits soon after. She files for disability and says that lifting all the boxes of candy, donuts and bags of chips has *permanently* injured her back. She repeats this a few times to me and when I ask why she says it's just in case anyone asks.

She's at home *all* the time now and as Christmas gets closer she sinks into depression. She drinks and gets *really* high then moans about how much she *misses* her little Gracie Bear. She weeps and says she never should have let Kenney take Gracie away from her, that Kenney *stole* Grace! She yells Kenney is a son of a bitch bastard and God will punish him some day!

I yell Dad isn't *any* of those things and you're wrong!

Mom offers a swift counterpoint to my argument in the form of an empty beer bottle hurled in my direction. It shatters against the wall. I close the door to my room while she screams from the couch how *I'm* a bastard, too.

Rowdy, who is sitting at his computer and trying to tune out the noise, stands up and starts yelling at Mom.

I open the door to see Mom chugging as much alcohol as she can before Rowdy wrenches the bottle out of her hand. She swings at him, trying to punch him in the face, but she's too drunk and falls onto the coffee table which breaks under her gargantuan weight.

Amariah The Boy

They start wrestling on the floor and screaming at each other. She bites him and he yells you stupid fuckin' bitch what is *wrong* with you? He shouts at her to knock it off and calm the fuck down!

I run outside, hop on my bike, then ride to the park. I stay there for a few hours and watch the happy families playing. Loving each other.

I ride home after the sun sets and Mom is cheery. She acts like nothing happened. I go into my room and shut the door, then try to make as little noise as possible so I don't attract her attention.

She knocks on my door just before I go to bed and tells me she's going to the hospital the next day to get help.

I say okay, and she quietly shuts the door. I try to fall asleep but mostly stare at the wall. A deep and gnawing pain attacks my stomach and my throat.

Mom gets pills from the hospital. She says she needs them to cheer her up.

Pretty soon, her initial pills require *other* pills to counteract their side effects. Soon thereafter, she's taking upward of ten different pills per *day.* When she's not popping pills, she drinks and smokes weed while watching TV or calls Miss Cleo and other psychic hotlines for life advice. She often gets angry and starts yelling at me for something that *never happened,* then takes away my Super Nintendo.

Sometimes she screams at me then tries to hit me. I'm thankful that one of the side effects of all her pills is that it turns her aim to shit. More often than anything, she falls over and I leave the house.

Mom preaches the word of the Lord when her mind is out there. There are also long pauses where she stares blankly ahead. She often bursts into laughter or just sits there and cries, then talks about how much she misses her baby girl.

Rowdy looks over with a frown and says it looks like the pills didn't do shit.

He sits at his computer and plays his games, seemingly numb to everything.

I try to stay away from home and find any excuse I can to invite myself over to a friend's house. Well, the one friend I have, Logan.

The mood at Logan's place is a bit brighter and they're getting ready for Christmas, with all the decorations and everything. I help where I can and it feels good to be a part of it all. I tell myself maybe Christmas won't be all that bad if I can hide out over here.

Roland Amariah Gonzales

A lice infestation sweeps through the school shortly before Christmas break like a plague of locusts *decimating* a wheat field. All the students have to submit to mandatory testing with the school nurse. If kids have lice, parents are called and they're taken home. I'm worried as *hell* because my head *has* been itching a lot recently. The nurse of course finds lice crawling around on my head and they call Mom to come get me, but she says she's sick, so they call Rowdy instead.

Rowdy drops me off at home and I'm not at all surprised to see that Mom is very drunk. She scowls at me and is pissed for my having lice, but I think it's more so for forcing her to sober up. When she says she's good enough to drive she tells me to hurry up and get in the car, then we head to the pharmacy.

Mom takes a look at all the anti-lice shampoos, salves and ointments, decides they're all *way* too expensive, then takes me home to shave my head. I *beg* her not to. I say Mom, Christmas break is *only* a few days away! More importantly, the music teacher Mrs. Carroll has put together a "Santa's Singing Christmas Elves" performance in the gym for the *tomorrow*. I'm almost in tears as I beg her to get some anti-lice shampoo for me, just this *once?* Or share some of the stuff she'll use for herself?

I know begging is pointless because Mom has *never* been keen on spending money on me unless she *absolutely* has to and, unfortunately for me, having lice doesn't make the absolutely list. She looks at me with a sneer before bringing out the hair clippers and says it's for the good of the school.

I'm absolutely *miserable* as she shaves my head. Now *everyone's* going to know. Mom has a broad smile and even laughs as she watches me struggle not to cry. She consoles me insincerely and says aww, don't be such a baby, it'll grow back. It's just hair, Rol! Are you really going to cry over *hair?* Who cries over fuckin' *hair?*

I think to myself I can't fuckin' *wait* to see Mom cry again. I'm going to bring up how *sad* Grace must be, missing Mom, and anything else I can just to make her hurt.

All the elves see my shaved head the next day and give me a wide berth. When Mrs. Carroll sees me, her eyes go wide and in exasperation throws up her hands and says great!

She makes me wear a lunch-lady plastic hair cover over my poorly-shaved bald head. She looks me in the eye and says *just* in case. She sees my glum face and says hey, don't worry! No one will even notice...the elf hat will cover it!

I go into the bathroom and look in the mirror and see that the elf hat doesn't cover the lunch-lady hat at *all*.

As we all walk to the gym I force a plastic smile and try to pretend I'm somewhere else.

Soon enough, the lights in the gym turn off and the spotlight focuses on us as we sing Christmas songs.

My classmates laugh from the bleachers the moment they notice my ridiculous appearance. I can't see anyone because of the spotlights blinding me though I hear someone shout eww, that dirty bald kid has lice!

The entire fucking audience breaks into laughter before the vice principal clears his throat and I can *hear* him smiling when he loudly says alright now, keep it down, everyone.

My face may as well be a damn *cherry tomato*, it's so red. I try to focus on singing but my voice cracks several times from stress and I blink back tears, a horrified expression on my face.

After the performance is over Mom, sitting next to Rowdy and high as hell, claps and laughs with everyone then shrilly whistles and shouts that's my boy!

I stare *hard* at the floor and take slow, deep breaths as my arms and hands shake. As soon as Mrs. Carroll finishes saying good job and merry Christmas, I rush outside to try and find our car in the parking lot. I can't find the damn thing and where the hell is it, it's the biggest eyesore in this entire town!

I stay low and hide behind someone else's car until I spot Mom. When she goes to the car, parked around the corner far away, I run after her then quickly open the door and jump in.

Christmas break starts the next day.

If Mom experienced peak happiness the day before at my expense, the following day is abject *misery* for her. She's either quiet or crying and won't shut the hell up about Grace, and I haven't even brought her up, yet! I can't *stand* all her moaning, so I spend the weekend hanging out with Logan and his brothers. It's Christmas break, so Renee and Hank don't care so much about me spending the weekend there, and everyone's in high spirits.

On Monday, Rowdy drives up to their house and says hey RJ, go grab your bike and get it in the car, we need to go visit your mom.

Roland Amariah Gonzales

I say what? She's at home. Why do I need to visit her at home?

Rowdy shakes his head, like he's really sad, and says no she ain't home, she's at the hospital. She tried to commit suicide on Friday, after you left.

I say nothing, get my bike and put it in the trunk. As we drive to the hospital, the first thing to strike me is *I don't really care.* I actually *hope* she succeeded or *will* succeed in the near future! If she dies, I can leave this fucking *awful* place and go live with Dad out in California! Oh man, that'd be great.

I pray to Jesus, the devil, or *whatever* god may be listening, to just go right ahead and strike that woman dead. I whisper to myself please kill that bitch, please kill that bitch...over and over.

Rowdy's got the radio turned up and doesn't hear me.

We pull up to the hospital and Rowdy checks in with a nurse, and then we're taken to the psychiatric ward.

I cross my fingers and hope I'll see her on a bed...in her last moments.

The first thing that hits me when we enter the Psych Ward is the *music.* James Taylor is squeezed through tiny gray speakers attached to the ceiling, and pretty much force fed into the ears of all the patients housed herein, these crazies kept away from the world. I also hear men and women mumbling, screaming and arguing with one another...or with unseen phantasms.

Next, I *see* white walls, white floors, white ceilings. *Everything* is white. Gleaming. Blinding. Suffocating. Both patients and orderlies wear white clothing: the patients, hospital gowns, the orderlies, white pants and white shirts.

The smiling faces on ID cards affixed to uniforms are a stark contrast to the faces of those wearing them. If not for the badges, one would be hard-pressed to tell the orderlies from the patients.

I hear the scrape of paper footwear shuffling against the concrete floor as *Deck the Halls* is now pumped through the speakers. A few patients have noticed me, since I'm the only child in the room. Some scowl at me, others offer a smile, and one man raises his arm to wave, a bandage covering his wrist. He says hey, Ted! Good to see you again!

I raise my hand and weakly wave back.

The last thing I notice before Mom sees me is the *smell.* It's a combination of bleach and ammonia, interspersed with body odor, urine, vomit and shit. I gag as this overwhelming sensory-heavy assault fist-slams my existence.

An unseen man bellows then I hear something banging. As an orderly leads Rowdy and I to a waiting spot I finally see him. He's hitting his head against something...repeatedly. The dull thump of his skull slams against concrete and repeats until seemingly lifeless orderlies spring to life and rush to sedate him.

All of this happens in the span of a couple minutes.

Mom is brought out and walks over to me, gives me a hug, then tells me how happy she is that I'm here. She's looking at me...but it *feels* like she's staring through me, like I'm not here.

Paul Simon starts playing over the speakers.

I force a smile. An orderly has Rowdy sign Mom out for a short time, and then we step outside and sit on a bench so she can light up a smoke.

Mom asks me how I'm doing and doesn't mention her suicide attempt. I nonchalantly look at her wrists. No bandages like that man. Hmm, maybe she tried pills? She mumbles some nonsense and spits a few loogies at a wall.

At the end of our meeting she hugs me then Rowdy and we say good-bye.

On the drive home, Rowdy says it's gonna be important to visit her during these hard times.

I look at him like *he* belongs in the Psych Ward. That visit wasn't worth a *damn*—Mom barely knew I was there!

In the coming days Rowdy drags me along and I *hate* going to the Psych Ward. *Everything* there feels *wrong*. I desperately want to stay away but he says if I don't go I can spend all of Christmas break at home in my room, grounded.

As usual, we arrive, sign Mom out, and go outside for her smoke break. She takes a few puffs then looks at me and with a snarl says it's your fault I'm here!

I don't know what to say but I'm not surprised. It's always my fault...or everyone's fault but hers. She says I'm a horrible son and if I weren't so worthless she'd have something to be happy about.

I stare through her, expressionless.

Rowdy says come on now, Kathleen, you don't mean that.

Mom rocks back and forth on the bench, as she hugs her knees and shakily brings a cigarette to her mouth. She says no, I do, I really do!

247

She takes a *long* drag from her cigarette then blows the smoke in my face.

I hold my breath and glare at her, my eyes burning.

I'm relieved when Rowdy drives me home.

We return for Christmas. Mom apologizes for how mean she was last time. She pulls me in for a hug and says it's just the meds and *of course* I love you!

She's giddy when we go outside for her cigarette break. She leans in close like she's got a great secret to tell me, and whispers that *I'll* end up in the Psych Ward someday, because crazy runs in the family.

I look down at the ground. I can hear the muffled sounds of James Taylor's *You've Got a Friend* through the shut door, and think to myself no, I'll never be like her. I'll *never* be in this kind of place. I'd rather die.

After Christmas, Mom leaves the Psych Ward with a whole *new* slew of meds. She says she's all better now.

NEW FRIENDS

School picks up after the New Year, 1997, which turned out to be another celebration where nothing is celebrated. I'm in class when the teacher tells us to quietly read a section of our textbooks and we'll be quizzed after. A boy in front of me won't stop coughing and I can't concentrate, so I subtly get his attention and whisper hey, *hey*!

When he turns around, I whisper *shut the hell up*!

He looks at me in anger, and the teacher announces, oh my *goodness* RJ, what is wrong with you? You apologize right now!

I guess I need to work on my whispering.

I say *what*? People tell me that *all* the time...and he won't stop making noise! I can't concentrate on reading!

She says just because other people are rude to you is no reason to be rude yourself!

She points at me both of us in turn and says *you* apologize right this instant and *you* go drink some water then come back.

I sigh then say I'm sorry.

The boy leaves to drink some water then returns and coughs for the rest of class. I bring some cough drops from home two days later and hand them to him, not so much to be nice, but because I can't do *any* reading if he's pulling my attention away with his coughing.

He says thanks and his name is Josh.

The teacher smiles and says see, *everything* is better when people are nice to each other!

Josh and I talk after class. It turns out he lives down the road from where I used to live, where Lady and Cyan died. Josh says he plays video games, too!

I say *no way*!

No one in school talks about video games *or* seems to play them.

He's my *first* same-grade friend, though he's a bit older. When I first visit his home a strong and pungent smell hits me, like old wet cat food and cardboard that's been left out in the rain for too long. I wonder what in the *hell* could be making that awful odor when I notice old wet cat food and cardboard that's been left out in the rain for too long. Then I see a *bunch* of kittens walking around his porch, not boxed up or anything!

He says most of the kittens are only a week or so old and a couple of them can't open their eyes for some reason. I look down and see a few of them have eyes that look *permanently* shut. I feel a wave of sadness hit me. I try to focus on something else. There's a fair amount of trash scattered around the front yard and back yards. I've learned that lots of people would vehemently argue that this is *not* trash. Typical for this town.

We go into his house. If I thought the outside was a bit messy, holy cow! The inside must've had a twister come through because stuff and garbage are strewn about *everywhere*. There's a *new* pungent smell in here that I can't quite place. After he introduces me to his parents and shows me his room, the realization hits me: this place smells a *lot* like the boy's locker room at school!

We go into the kitchen and I catch movement out of the corner of my eye. As Josh opens a cupboard to grab a bag of chips, about a hundred cockroaches scurry away, a few braver ones stand their ground and wave their antennae at him in challenge. I try to stifle my shock and revulsion, and see that Josh is comfortable with it.

Josh has an older sister. She's in high school and he *hates* her to such an extent that I wonder if every brother instinctively hates his sister. At first, I think she doesn't *seem* that bad, but then I remember that Grace doesn't seem that bad *either* to people who know nothing about her. I bet his sister is an absolute *prick, just* like Grace.

His parents offer me something to drink and I accept. When his dad goes to the kitchen, I see large painful-looking red sores covering his back on skin not covered by his filthy tank top. I try not to stare. Everyone here looks sticky and wet. I really don't like coming in here.

Josh's dad brings me back some water in a dirty-looking glass. I thank him then subtly dump it into the bathroom sink when no one's looking.

Me and Josh don't play together all that much. We only occasionally ride bikes together because he's busy with Boy Scouts, baseball, and other stuff.

I think briefly about asking him if he'd let me join Boy Scouts but decide against it. The part of me that wanted to join *died* when that kid knocked me over in gym class.

Amariah The Boy

For the most part, Josh and I get together only to trade computer games when one of us has something the other wants to play.

I don't necessarily *have* a computer but Rowdy does, and luckily for me he plays computer games, too. He doesn't really let me watch unless he calls me into the room to see something cool. He sits facing the couch ninety-nine percent of the time, with the computer screen opposite. If I go near him, he quickly clicks the mouse so whatever he's looking at disappears, then says yeah, what? Whaddya want? Go away. Go play outside.

Sometimes he lets me play on his computer but is *real* careful about it and keeps *everything* locked up with passwords. I can't even make it past the boot screen!

When he gets home, he says he can tell how many times I tried to log in, and then he yells at me. He'll accuse me of trying to break the password, say, forty-seven times, or some crazy-high ridiculous number, and gets really pissed.

I argue that at *most* I made a couple of guesses. There's *no way* I'd sit there for an *hour* to punch in a bunch of failed attempts, get locked out, then restart the system to do it all over again. That sounds like *work*, and I already learned over the summer that work *sucks*.

I think Mom is trying to log in with the wrong passwords even though she knows the right one, especially after Rowdy yells at me on days where I don't go anywhere *near* his computer.

She does *anything* to be an asshole and get me in trouble.

I have no clue how computers work outside of the games I play, so I stop making any attempt to get past the boot screen.

Valentine's Day rears its hideous head and *my* hideous head has regained a bit of hair in the two months that have passed...though I know it won't help much with receiving cards or candies.

By now I know better than to expect *anything*.

There's going to be a school dance at the community center, and it costs five dollars. I think about that girl I like, Kelsey. I wonder if she'll be there. Maybe I could dance with her?

I fantasize about an alternate reality where people like me. Where pretty girls want to dance with me and everyone wants to be my friend. I laugh bitterly then think to myself no way in hell...no way.

I joke with Mom about the school dance and how that's five dollars the school's *not* gonna get and she laughs, too.

Roland Amariah Gonzales

The day of the school dance comes around and Mom shoves five dollars in my hand and says to clear out so she and Rowdy can have some alone time.

I protest and say wait, what? No, no, I don't wanna go, it's gonna be awful!

Mom says look, I don't care *where* ya go but you can't stay here. Get out! Go!

I spend *maybe* three minutes picking out the nicest clothes I've got.

I don't have much to choose from. I put on a button-up shirt that I wear to church then ride my bike out to The Square. I probably ride around it eight times or so, hitting the bike ramp each time. I mull over possibilities. Potentially *good* outcomes. By the eighth trip, I've psyched myself up. I'm going to go to the dance. I'm going to do this! What's the worst that can happen?

I head to the community center, enjoying the cold evening breeze as I pedal. After I lock my bike up and pay admission to a smiling lady sitting at a table, I go inside. The main lights are off and *Cotton Eyed Joe* blasts from the speakers as a series of smaller lights shine down from the ceiling onto the makeshift dance floor (formerly the basketball court). A disco ball rotates slowly above the middle of the room, sending sparkling beams of light across everyone and everything.

I feel so nervous that my legs shake a bit as I make my way to the table with the punch bowl. I grab a red plastic cup, fill it, and bring it to my lips. I drink what *might* be water with orange-flavored powder. It's disgusting and stings my throat.

I look around the room then try to bob my head in time with the music but fail spectacularly. My entire body is completely tense.

Fuck *me*, this was a mistake.

I think to myself what in the *hell* am I doing here? when I hear a nearby voice call out over the music holy shit is that RJ? What is *he* doing here?!

A spear of laughter aimed directly at me lances my skull as I pretend not to notice. Some kids are making a game of jumping up and trying to hit decorations hanging from the ceiling. I join in. When they see me playing they quickly go to the other side of the room.

I grit my teeth then walk back to the punch bowl. I try to keep rhythm with my head to *Macarena*. I look around and see that *all* the popular kids are in exclusive little circles, talking and dancing together.

No one looks over at me and everyone avoids the punch bowl while I'm there. If they *do* know I'm there, they pretend not to.

I search the room, wondering if I can spot Kelsey, and eventually see she's with the popular crowd. That makes sense. She's real pretty and she's nice. I fantasize for a brief moment about walking up and asking her to dance but I definitely know better. I've already pushed my luck in coming here. *December* by Collective Soul starts playing.

I watch as fucking *Todd* walks up to Kelsey, puts his arm around her waist, then slips his hand down to her butt and gives it a good squeeze.

I think to myself oh man, she's *totally* gonna smack him. Only she *doesn't* smack him, or even move his hand! Kelsey looks at him and they share a kiss! What in the flying *fuck*!

Whatever fantasies I had are shattered...I can't believe that absolute *bastard* is getting Kelsey kisses! I'm stunned and make my way out of the building as quickly and quietly as I can, hoping that no one sees me.

I race home on my bike and try to open the door but it's locked. I bang on it a couple of times and Mom yells out through her bedroom window, GO AWAY!

I shout back wha!? – for how long?

I hear mom loudly say an hour.

I sigh. I feel like crap. I get on my bike and ride to Artesian Park. I sit under a tree and look out across all of the parking-lot lights. *Man,* I hate Valentine's Day. *And* school dances.

I resolve never to go to another, and I'm pretty sure this is the worst night of my life. I look at my watch. After an, I hour ride home and go to bed.

The rest of the school year is uneventful, and soon enough the summer of '97 kicks off.

Roland Amariah Gonzales

SUMMER VACATION

It's the first day of summer and cautious glee fills me as I look forward to swimming, hours spent in the library, Final Fantasy 3, and no school.

After a week or so Mom informs me that Grandma Margaret wants me to fly out to California and visit her. I remember Grandma mentioning this in the past but didn't think she was serious. The budding glee I held for summer is replaced by an explosive growth of elation. I'm getting the hell away from Missouri!

It's not that I don't *like* Missouri. It's great being the school pariah, getting punched in the face at the swimming pool, visiting my mom in psychiatric wards, being told I'm worthless by my classmates *and* my mother, or having the prospect of little-to-no food all summer, it's just that...hey, you know what?

I fucking *hate* Missouri.

Grandma Margaret buys me a ticket for a few days later. Flying, once *entirely* thrilling, is now only *vaguely* exciting. I still dream of living in the clouds someday, only now...the dream is tempered by reality.

I gaze out the window at the clouds below and ponder at what age dreams become untenable. I sleep away most of the flight and before I know it, I'm at the John Wayne Airport in Orange County.

After Grandma Margaret picks me up we get lunch at In-N-Out, then drive back to her house in Artesia. Grandma drives *sooo slowly*. She's all the way over in the slow lane and every driver *still* honks as they speed by. I try to sit as low as possible so they can't see me. Grandma laughs and says not to worry, these people will forget all about us by the time they get home, because someone else is sure to make them *even angrier*.

When we pull up to Grandma's house I realize I'd never truly appreciated how *huge* it is. Maybe I see it now because my house in Missouri, in comparison, is a shack.

Grandma's place is two stories tall, with five bedrooms and two bathrooms. She's an avid gardener and both her front and back yards reflect this. She's fond of planting small colorful flowers in the back and big yellow and red rose bushes in the front.

Mom never plants *any* flowers. We just have dirt, dying patches of grass, and gravel.

Grandma's got a tool shed off to the side of the backyard, and she tells me that it belonged to Grandpa Irish. She says to stay out of it because the whole thing is *filled* with black widows. She says one bite and I'll probably *die* or at least get very sick!

Houses in California are so *different* from Missouri! In Missouri you'd walk from one house's backyard to the next with nothing in-between to stop you. Some folks have small fences, like Mary (the lady who said I killed her dog), but for the most part it's all pretty open. Sometimes, I walk around in what I *think* is the woods, then hear someone holler to get the hell off their property before they sick their hounds on me.

That's always a lot of fun!

But here in California, the houses are sandwiched next to each other with hardly any space between them. Backyards are *tiny*, if folks have 'em at all. People in Cali usually put a *lot* of effort into making their patch of grass look as much like Nature as they can. I suppose it's because everything is paved over with concrete. You can hardly find a dirt road or trail *anywhere*, let alone the woods. Sure, there's parks and such, but they don't feel *wild* like the woods.

Grandma and I go out to parks, have a picnic or barbecue with her friends, or visit other family members. We *do* things together and I love it. Mom and Rowdy *rarely* do anything with me. Hell, they never even *ask* if I want to do anything with them. Rowdy took me fishing once but it was *awful*. All we did was sit out on a lake and fry in the sun while he enjoyed a few beers.

At first, Grandma doesn't feel comfortable leaving me at home by myself and takes me with her to her AA meetings. *Man,* are those god-awful. It's just a bunch of old people talking for two hours about that one time they had a beer *twenty years ago* and how *bad* they felt about it. When it's Grandma's turn to speak she says how bad she felt for having a drink over *thirty* years ago!

I think to myself that this has got to be at least if not *more* boring than church, and I don't see a difference between the two. They even pray at the end of the AA meetings! It's the same damn thing!

After one of the meetings ends, we drive home *just* before I die of boredom. I ask Grandma why she goes there? I'd think after thirty *years* she'd get the hang of *not* drinking.

Grandma Margaret purses her lips like she's drinking out of a straw then looks at me with a frown and says when did you get so smart? She laughs and says every *day* is a struggle and really, when you get as old as I am, well, AA is mostly just a meeting place for friends.

I nod in understanding and say oh, okay I get it. That's nice. But hey Grandma, can I not go with you next time? It's *really* boring for me.

She looks at me in annoyance then shakes her head from side to side. She says well, I can't leave you at the house all by yourself, RJ! You're just a boy!

I look at her indignantly then puff out my chest and stick out my chin. I launch into a tirade in thick Missouri twang: Hell, Grandma, I been home by myself before! *and* I been riding my bike *all over* Clinton by myself for over two years now! There ain't nothin' special 'bout bein' home by myself! I ride to the park an' spend just 'bout twelve hours there *every* dang *day* in the summer! I ain't no baby, Grandma! I'm almost a *man*!

I thump my chest for good measure.

Grandma looks at me in surprise, smiles, then breaks into laughter. She says you certainly have your mother's mouth, don't you?

I look at her in confusion before she laughs and says well, we'll see. Artesia's a small town, but it's not exactly *Taft*.

I say I...don't know what a taft is, Grandma.

Grandma says it's where she grew up as a little girl. It's a dusty little nowhere town somewhere up north. She says it's a lot like Clinton! ...or how she imagines Clinton looks, because she's never actually *been there*...and really, has no desire to go.

I tell her that I'm not a fan of Clinton, either.

When we get home, Grandma orders food. She isn't keen on kitchen work and prefers ordering food from restaurants or microwaving TV dinners. While we wait for the food, we sit down on two big and comfy recliner chairs then she puts on her favorite thing to watch: the news.

The food arrives and I enthusiastically eat my Chinese food while I stare at the TV.

Grandma says oh! Oh my! Oh, would you look at that! Oh, could you imagine?

Amariah The Boy

...And a bunch of other stuff that old people say when they watch the news.

I think to myself that this has *got* to be the most boring goddamn thing I've *ever* watched. I take in as much air as I can, then unleash it as a big sigh, like I'm some kinda sigh dragon.

Grandma takes a break from her oh-mys to frown, look over at me, then back at the TV. She mutes the volume then asks if I'd like to hear a story from when I was three years old. She says it was back when Grandpa Irish was still alive.

I look over at her then lower my fork onto my paper plate and say okay, Grandma, sure.

When I was three, I was a *hellion*, just like my mother. I walked around the house making all *kinds* of noise and when I wanted to go somewhere, or if I got bored, then I was even *more insufferable*. One day, having had enough of my nonsense, Grandma told me to be quiet. I started making loud gibberish noises *just* to be obnoxious, so she smacked me across the face.

I stared at her in shock then started to cry. At first, she felt satisfied, but then seeing me cry made her feel *awful*. She tried to console me but nothing she said worked. That is, until she asked if I wanted to go see a movie. That broke me out of my hysterics and, after rubbing my eyes, I asked what movie?

She told me if I was good and stayed quiet, she'd take me to see a movie about bears, and I loved that because I was really into bears at the time.

At this point, I interrupt Grandma's story and ask what the name of the movie was.

Grandma looks at me, pauses then says *The Bear.* When she sees that I have no recollection she says it was a movie about bears, alright?

I say oh, okay.

Grandma continues her story.

The movie was really *sad* and when the momma bear died, I started crying again. She asked why I was crying and I told her now that the momma bear is dead, the baby bear is all alone and he's gonna die too!

Grandma pauses again to tell me it was absolutely adorable but I just scratch my head in confusion. I don't understand what the hell is absolutely adorable about that.

Grandma continues her story.

Roland Amariah Gonzales

Just then, another boy about my age stood up in the movie theater and yelled out good! I'm *glad* the bear is dead because bears eat people and they're bad!

Grandma says well, you weren't having *any* of that, so you stood up on *your* seat and yelled that bears aren't bad, *he's* bad!

The boy called me all *kinds* of mean names. Every time she thought she had me calmed down, I'd jump right back up on my seat and yell at him again!

With this memory, Grandma laughs heartily, and I chuckle a bit.

Grandma continues her story.

So, the two of you yelled at each other in that theater for a good *twenty* minutes! It was so entertaining that the audience watched you *both,* instead of the movie! No one told you to sit down or anything! It was *very* peculiar!

Grandma Margaret stops reminiscing then pauses for a moment, then smiles and says you're very peculiar, RJ. She asks if I remember anything about that whole experience.

I tell her I can see myself in a movie theater yelling at some boy, but I can't picture the movie.

Grandma says ah, well maybe that's for the best. That movie was awfully *sad,* anyway. She unmutes the TV and goes back to watching the news, saying oh! Oh my! every few minutes or so.

Amariah The Boy

Grandma says it'd be good for me to spend time with my Aunt Mary and she needs a break from me anyway, because little boys have too much energy.

Grandma drops me off the next day. Aunt Mary is one of my mom's older sisters and she's real excited to see me. She says oh RJ, you've grown so much, look how big you are!

...and a bunch of other stuff that I'm used to hearing from relatives. I know it isn't true. I'm about as short as a possum standing on its hind legs and I *still* haven't hit puberty.

Grandma leaves and Mary says she's dating some guy named Karim. He owns a jewelry shop and we're going to visit him, then get some dinner.

I remember Mom telling me about her three sisters and how Aunt Mary's been dating older guys since high school. Mom said Aunt Mary goes after guys who have things she wants. Clothes, makeup, jewelry, that sort of stuff. Mom also told me that Aunt Mary gets what she wants and when she's done with the guy, she dumps his ass.

As Aunt Mary drives, I wonder how long she'll date this guy before she dumps his ass. As we near Little India in Artesia, I begin to see women dressed in flowing colorful robes who dart into traffic with small children dragged behind them. The drivers for the most part slow their cars and let the mothers pass, though a few honk angrily. The kids look *terrified,* and I wonder why in the hell these ladies are doing this.

Aunt Mary pulls up to Karim Jewelers and we're buzzed in through the security gate. It's a little cold inside, and a man behind the counter eyes me warily before he says in a thick accent no beggars are allowed in the store! He says you must leave this place now and return to wherever you came from!

I stop in my tracks, startled, and look up at Aunt Mary who laughs. I look from her to the man, who continues to look at me in complete seriousness. I'm unsure of what to do when another guy with a *huge* black bushy mustache comes out of the backroom with a broad smile. He hugs Aunt Mary warmly and she introduces me to him.

I say hello, my name is RJ.

He says in a thick accent that I can't place hello, Arrre-Jaaay. He throws his arms back like he's showing me a castle and says I am Karim and *this* is my jewelry shop.

Karim gestures to a fold-out chair next to a table and says why don't you have a seat here while I talk to your beautiful aunt?

Roland Amariah Gonzales

I sit down and, after their short conversation, Aunt Mary says we're going to go eat.

I think oh? Cool, I like food. I start to get up, when Karim puts a hand on my shoulder and says ah, wait a moment, Arrre-Jaaay. How would you like to make *ten dollars?*

I say uh, sure, okay. What do I have to do?

He explains that all I have to do is look down at the table in front of me and separate the tiny gemstones into different piles, based on their color.

I'm not at all excited and this sounds boring as *hell.* Seeing the frown on my mouth, he quickly interjects ah, you *do know* your colors, yes? Red is red, blue is blue and so on?

I look at him like I just caught him sniffing a dog's butt and say well yeah, I know what blue looks like, I—

He interrupts me and says and red? You are knowing what red looks like as well?

I nod and force a smile and say of course I know red too, I -

Karim claps his hands together and says splendid! It is so very good to hear that the public educational institutions are working so effectively in this country. Then he tells me to sit there and separate *all* those little beautiful gems - and you are being sure to not drop any, yes? You divide those by color into separate piles and I will pay you the amount of *ten dollars,* yes?

The way he says ten dollars makes it sound like a fortune. I think to myself well I guess I normally make that much in like...a *week.* Sometimes.

I look down at the table, frown, then look up and say what about food?

Aunt Mary and Karim are already walking out the door. She turns and says we'll bring you something back RJ, have fun!

They both exit before I can protest further. I'm left alone with a small table full of gems, and the angry man from earlier who told me to leave. I look up at him and he says with all seriousness do not even think for one moment about stealing any of those gems or your hands will be chopped off!

I look at him with wide eyes.

I spend the next ninety minutes carefully separating the gems. I nearly have to start over after I get up to get some water and bump the table. I look for the angry man and, not seeing him, call out hey, how much is all this worth, anyway? Shouldn't someone more qualified be doing this?

The man shouts from the backroom do not steal any with your grubby little hands...there are cameras all over the store and some of them are so secret that not even *I* am aware of their locations!

He then tells me that the gems are worth ten dollars each.

I look down at the table. There's got to be at least 500 of them. They're so *tiny*. They're not even pebbles. They're grains of salt. *How* are they worth this much? I think about how it'd be great if Karim surprised me and said go ahead. Take twenty of them, but I don't think *that's* gonna happen. I fantasize for a moment about pocketing all of them, all the *other* shiny stuff, then selling it and running away.

Eventually Aunt Mary and Karim return and they've got a to-go box from some restaurant. I open it up, starving, and see some weird food that I've never had before. Karim sees me looking at it in confusion and asks do they not have that in your village? It is called shawarma and it is delicious.

I take a bite and it *is* pretty good. It's also *cold*. With a full mouth I complain but it's cold!

Karim says ah yes, I *do* apologize. He looks at Mary who smiles back at him, then says there was traffic on the road, you see. Very long. Very *difficult* traffic.

Karim claps his hands then re-directs the conversation and says how did you perform the task which I assigned to your person?

Before I can respond, he walks over and looks at the separate piles I've created. He points with his finger and looks like he's counting how many gems there are. He eyes me and says you did not think to steal anything, did you? In my country, stealing is punished with chopping–

I interrupt him and say no, I didn't steal anything. The guy in the back told me about your hidden cameras all over the place.

Karim smiles broadly and says yes, that is *most* correct! Cameras everywhere! He says very well then, you stay here and I will procure your payment.

He goes to the back room and I hear the men speaking in what I guess is their native tongue. It doesn't sound like Spanish and I don't know what it is. They sound angry.

After a couple of minutes Karim arrives and points wildly at the guy in the back room, unseen, says something else, then puts on his smile and walks toward me and hands me a ten-dollar bill.

Roland Amariah Gonzales

When I go to grab it he holds it firmly before releasing it and says perhaps you'd like to buy a gem? I'll sell you *two* for the price of one. That is a steal and you will not find a better deal anywhere, I can assure you!

I do the math and he's right, ten times two *is* twenty. I say but that's twenty dollars! I only have ten.

Karim says since you are the nephew of your beautiful aunt, I am prepared to make this sacrifice. But only this once, and you must decide quickly!

I quickly look down at all the gems and say, Ah, sure. Yeah, that's a deal!

I hand him back the money, then he smiles and says that was a very wise decision. He tells me to pick two of the gems, then laughs and says to make sure I tell my friends at home about his incredible generosity.

I grab the two biggest gems on the table, thinking maybe they're worth a bit more because of their size. Karim doesn't seem to care as he smiles and tells me that *I* should be the one running the jewelry shop, as my eyes are truly sharp.

With that, it's time to leave. Aunt Mary takes me home to Grandma's house and I think to myself man, Karim sure is a swell guy.

Aunt Mary stops in front of the house and I get out of the car. I ask if she's going to come in, but she says it's late and maybe some other time.

I wave as she drives away then ring the doorbell. Grandma shuffles to the front door in an old beige nightgown and a bunch of curlers in her hair. She tells me to come in quick because she's watching the news and doesn't want to miss anything.

We talk briefly before I head to bed. I say that Karim was gonna pay me ten dollars to separate gems worth ten dollars each, but paid me in two gems instead. That's twenty dollars, Grandma!

Grandma looks at the gems then looks at me bemused. She smiles and shuffles off to bed...after she says oh, that was nice of him.

Amariah The Boy

I get ready for bed. I get a *strange* feeling near every time I'm in my room. It's a tingling that starts up my arms and neck before heading up my ears, and then to the rest of my head, then fires down my whole body. It's kind of like the feeling I get when I think I'm alone but can *feel* someone watching me. The room is terrifying, but I feel compelled to sleep here. But sometimes it's hard to sleep.

I wake up the next morning, restless. When I get downstairs Grandma says Mom misses me and I need to call her.

I think to myself that can't be right, then eat some cereal and sink into one of the comfy chairs. I dial our home phone and Mom picks up. After talking for a few minutes I can tell she's high, probably hitting the bottle as well. She asks in a slurred voice what're you up to? Seen any of my sisters yet?

I tell her Aunt Mary is dating some guy named Karim who owns a jewelry store and she laughs knowingly. When I proudly tell her Karim paid me two gems worth ten dollars *each* when he was only going to give me a ten-dollar dollar bill, she laughs again and says that I got ripped off. She says the gems are probably only worth a *dollar*, *if* that.

Well, damn.

I tell her about the weird room over the garage, where I'm sleeping.

She says that when she was a kid she used to lock my Aunt Gail in that room. She says she told Gail that the ghost of *her* dead dad, my Grandpa Doug whom I never met, *hated* Gail and was going to kill her. Mom laughs a cruel laugh and says how Gail cried and *begged* to be let.

I laugh, but then I think to myself well, that's pretty fucked up.

We talk for a few minutes about nothing, then I hang up and I go back to my bedroom. I wonder if Ghost Grandpa is hanging out in the closet, because that closet always feels *weirder* than the rest of the room, and sometimes I get real scared of it.

When Grandma goes to the store by herself, curiosity gets the best of me.

The house is *so* quiet when I'm here alone. There's no music or *anything*. It's a tomb. I sneak up the stairs and hope to catch off-guard whatever is in the closet. While the carpeting on the stairs may be relatively new, the stairs definitely aren't, and they creak noisily with each step. I wince, then my eyes dart upward, expecting to see some horror thrusting its appendage outward and grasping the doorway before launching itself at me.

Roland Amariah Gonzales

Nothing emerges.

I continue upward, take a deep breath, then step into the room and face the closet. It's pitch black. That *feeling*...that tingling sensation. I tentatively reach forward and feel about for the light switch, then flip it. Forty-year-old dusty clothes are illuminated. There's nothing here. I stare for a moment or two before I step into the closet, close the door, and turn off the light.

I stand there in darkness, my imagination my only companion. Terror washes over and then envelops me. I sit down and lean against the wall. I grit my teeth as my hearing kicks into overdrive, absent my sight. Every small scratching noise, house-settling sound, and who knows what else, lands on my ear like a space rocket returning to earth.

I spend an eternity on the shores of oblivion. When I've had my fill, I slowly stand up and spend a moment feeling for the light switch before flipping it on.

Nothing here.

The doorknob doesn't yield at first, and I experience a brief moment of *absolute* panic before the door bursts open. I breathe slowly, quietly, then make my way down the stairs.

Grandma gets back from the store and we eat some food. Afterward I ask her whose clothes are in the closet.

She smiles and says oh, they belong to your dead grandpa!

When I go back into the room for the night I notice that the creepy sensation coming from the closet hasn't left, though it feels a little more familiar.

Grandma asks me a couple of weeks later if I want to stay with her and go to school in California, but I know Mom won't let me. I can't be free as long as Mom is still alive.

At summer's end, when it's time to leave, I bid a tearful farewell and fly home.

MOVIE NIGHT

Upon my return to Missouri I find that not much has changed, except that Logan's Mom and Hank split up. Tyler and Hank are gone so it's just Logan, Ricky and their mom. They all live with Logan's grandma.

Logan broke his collarbone over the summer after he tried to race his bike up a seesaw at the park and fly off the other end, but instead fell off midway.

Ricky didn't get any moop in his eye this summer, because I wasn't there to chuck it at him.

Seventh grade starts and I, emboldened by newfound confidence, courtesy of a summer with Grandma, decide I can make new friends. I start with a kid named Brad. We were kind of friends in the second grade but haven't really talked much since. I know I'm real cool now, because I invite him over for a sleepover at my house that Friday and he says okay!

...it was more like yeah sure, I guess...but that's better than a hell no! and way better than a go fuck yourself!

Mom and Rowdy are okay with it now because our dark blue house is a *lot* bigger and also because I'm more mature, too.

I go over in my head what I'd done at Logan's place in the days before the sleepover. Let's see...we ate pizza. I wait until Mom is *really* high and lying in bed then I ask her if she wants to order a pizza. I know that a combination of pills and drugs will get me a yes. She tells me to take a twenty out of her purse and get one with sausage and cheese.

I keep my mouth shut about hating that exact pizza...I *know* she knows that's my least favorite. It doesn't matter, because I'm not ordering a damn pizza. Not now, anyway. When Mom wakes up three hours later she doesn't remember anything about the pizza and I pocket the money.

Alright! Pizza is taken care of.

Roland Amariah Gonzales

Next, I need some kind of movie. I look over the movies we've got and, hell, we really don't have anything worth watching that folks haven't seen a hundred times already. Damn.

I wait until Rowdy gets *really* high and is laughing at the stuff on his computer he never lets me see, then I ask for five dollars to rent a movie.

He waves me away. I annoy him and try to see the screen, until he angrily gets up and fishes his wallet out of a pair of blue jeans. He slaps a ten-dollar into my hand, then puts *his* hands on my shoulders, looks into my eyes and says *go away.*

It's Thursday afternoon when I pedal my bike to the nearest movie-rental place and look for a good horror movie. I don't get to watch those often and neither, I imagine, does Brad, my new buddy. I grab *Demon Knight,* a Tales from the Crypt movie, and walk to the register. The lady working behind the counter says I can't rent that movie because it's *way* too scary for kids.

I throw back my head and beg no, pleeeease! Can't you give me a break, lady? It's my *first* sleepover! If I don't make friends soon, I won't have any at all! I yell out it's already 7th grade and I ain't got but one friend my age and everyone else thinks I'm a total dork!

She looks at me and frowns, tells me to give her my address and everything, then has me pay her an *extra* five dollars. She says it's for insurance purposes to make sure I bring the damn movie back. Then she says I'd *better* bring it back, because now she knows where I live.

I give her the address of my old house. I'm not planning on stealing the movie, but I might want to keep it a bit longer is all.

I happily pay her and then race home. I call Brad and he says he can't come tomorrow because his mom doesn't have anyone to watch his little brother and she doesn't want to be stuck home alone with him.

I think to myself that his little brother is already in the fourth grade and I was by myself around then. What's the big deal!

Shit. Thinking quickly, I say hey man, that's *alright,* you and your little bro can come, it's not a problem dude, honest!

Brad says blandly oh, alright. Uh, gimme a sec.

A few moments later he comes back on the line, sighs, and says his mom says it's alright.

I try not to sound *too* excited and tell him oh cool, yeah man, that's great. Before the call ends, I shout oh man, we're gonna have *so much fun!* See you tomorrow!

Amariah The Boy

Mom and Rowdy head out for the evening, so they can enjoy a date night then go drinking at the Newsroom. They tell me *not* to start any fires, to stay off the computer and *don't* leave the house unless *it's* on fire.

I agree and happily watch them leave. I'm stoked! If I do the sleepover right I might get invited over to Brad's place *or* to go camping or something awesome like that. This could be the start of a totally awesome year and I feel like I've got nowhere to go but up!

Brad and his little brother Chris show up and I don't know Chris so well...but I guess I don't know Brad that well either...whatever.

The three of us go to the living room and sit on the couch. I order some pizza by phone, pepperoni with extra cheese, then we kill time until the pizza arrives. Brad and Chris talk about their adventures in Boy Scouts and baseball, while I nod as if *deeply* interested.

The food arrives and after we're fat on pizza and Royal Crown Cola, I start the Demon Knight movie.

After about thirty minutes, Chris says he doesn't like the movie because it's too scary. I roll my eyes and try to talk him into watching it but he's not budging.

If Chris wants to leave, then Brad will too!

This whole night is heading for the *garbage*!

Brad slaps his knees with both hands, says welp! and stands up.

I move to shut off the movie then rack my brain to come up with a solution, and then one is staring me right in the face!

I motion to Brad and Chris who are at the door about to leave and say whoa whoa, wait a sec. That movie was too scary? That's alright. That's cool, I get it...whatever. How about *this*?

Like a magician, I grab one of Rowdy's secret movies that's hidden behind all the rest in our home collection. I can tell *his* apart from the others because his lack *any* label whatsoever. Instead, they're marked with **XXX**, a symbol that is *very* familiar to me. I pop in the movie, hit **PLAY**, then sit back on the couch with a broad smile. I'm about to impress the *hell* out of everyone here.

After some initial static, the movie is in full swing. There's a lady with curly blonde hair and *huge* fake boobies bouncing on top of some guy. For some reason, they're both on a rooftop. I look over at Brad and Chris and both are in *complete* shock, eyes wide and mouths agape. I throw a thumbs up and say pretty cool, yeah? They're *doin'* it! It's a *porno* movie! With sex! I clap my hands and laugh.

Brad's eyes are as big as saucers as he says uh, oh. Wow, I don't think we're supposed to be watchin' this.

If my grin gets any bigger I'd be more teeth than boy. I *knew* this was the coolest thing I could possibly show them. I nod my head in agreement with Brad and say yeah, I know, right?

Chris is in a state of shock, covering his face with his hands and peeking through his fingers. He looks over at us and says uh...hey guys, I feel weird.

I flash him a thumbs up say, I know it's great, right?

We watch another ten minutes or so, then I turn it off. Can't show them *everything* the first time or they'll never come back! I hide the VHS tape back where I found it and plug in the Super Nintendo. We play games for a while then go to sleep.

Chris says he can't sleep and keeps thinking about the movie.

I say hey man, knock yourself out! Make sure you put it back, though.

There's a long silence before he says no, thank you. I'm just gonna go to sleep.

They both go home the next morning and I give them each a high five and tell Brad to tell all his friends.

Brad gives me an awkward laugh, then weakly waves as his mom drives them away. I notice that he and Chris are staring at the car floor.

Monday rolls around and I'm surprised that nothing new happens. I thought that I'd be really popular but Brad says he's not allowed to hang out with me anymore.

...maybe Brad got in trouble because his little brother told their folks that I showed them a porno? I don't get it because *I* don't think it's a big deal. I mean, people have sex *all* the time. Well...most people. I sure don't. Hell, I can't even jerk off. Not yet anyway, but I'm sure I'll be able to real soon! That sex-ed teacher assured us all we'd all be able to at some point in the near future, so that's something I've got going for me, I guess.

SASHA

Mom, Rowdy and I move to another house. Again. I ask why but they don't provide any explanation. It's located next to an abandoned graveyard across the street. The gnarled, skeletal limbs of dead trees, reminders of their cousins interred in the earth underneath, cast their menacing shadows on my window every night.

I keep my blinds closed. The only view I have is of the dead. Dead people. Dead things.

Our other house was *way* closer to my school and I'm bummed that I have to ride roughly *three times* the distance in the morning. On the flipside, I'm a lot closer to Logan's place, and hell, I guess the town isn't so big anyway.

I ride my bike to school and now that Logan and his brother are old enough, they usually join me. We always leave our houses early so we can stop at the bike ramp near The Square. There are worse ways to wake up than spending fifteen minutes or so racing up and down the ramp.

I love the feel of wind rushing against my face and hair as I fly down the ramp, though I don't try flips or tricks or anything like that. Not after that handlebar-to-the-throat experience. Logan's broken collarbone is also a reminder of the consequences when we get too big for our britches.

Seventh grade is more or less the same as sixth, and I immediately find myself bored. How many more years of this do I have to put up with? Same classmates, same school. A lot of the *same* teachers...teaching the *same* subjects, just at higher levels.

I sign up for a music class again because I love to sing and I love music in general. Mrs. Carroll, the music teacher, has us buy recorders and I have to beg Mom for the money because she's not at *all* interested in hearing me practice at home. She finally gives me the money, but only on the condition that I take the recorder to the park and practice there. I agree.

Roland Amariah Gonzales

It's fun learning how to play this instrument, and after a few weeks Mrs. Carroll decides that it'd be good for us all to practice outside... in the sunlight. I think it's too cold for that, being early October, and I say so.

Mrs. Carroll says nonsense, all the best musicians practice in adverse weather...it develops their *focus*!

I think to myself well, I *guess* that makes sense and if anyone would know it would be the music teacher.

We all put on our coats and trudge outside onto the football field. We break into groups and since I'm the *only* boy in music class, I end up in a group of girls. The teacher tells the groups to separate from one another and scatter across the field.

After practicing for about five minutes one of the girls in my group says hey, umm RJ?

I pull the recorder out of my mouth, a string of saliva connecting the two, and say yeah? What?

The girl hesitates a moment then blurts out, do-you-like-Whitney-do-you-think-she's-pretty?

I blink for a moment and struggle to process this word assault, as the girl giddily hops from one foot to another, giggling. I translate the girl-speak and wonder why she would she ask me this.

"Do I like Whitney and do I think she's pretty?"

Whitney is one of the girls I saw at the pool when I was with Jessica. Did Whitney tell her friends and now *those* girls want to invite me to *another* fake birthday party? I'm not falling for that shit again.

I say who? Whitney? No *way*, she looks like a horse!

The girls all gasp with hurt looks on their faces then pounce on me and pull my hair. Some even hit me or stab at me with their recorders. As they kick the crap out of me I think to myself I bet they thought I said *whore* and are pissed because of it!

I yell out horse! I said HORSE!

The beatings continue for about a minute or two before they come to an end. I try to laugh off the fact that I just got my ass handed to me by six girls. Mrs. Carroll had her back to us the whole time and either didn't see or didn't care or...hell, maybe she thought I deserved it!

The girls tell me I'm just a disgusting *loser* and no one will ever like me.

I mutter to myself hell, that ain't nothin' new.

Amariah The Boy

They don't ask me if I like anyone after that and I'm glad because to me it's a lose-lose situation. Either I say no and get slapped around, or I say yes and they invite me to a fake party and laugh at me in front of everyone. I'd rather get beaten than have everyone laugh at me, though they do that too, I guess, so it's better not to have either.

Hell, I know better. I'm not falling for *any* of their tricks anymore.

When I get home I don't say a *thing* to Mom or Rowdy about getting my ass kicked in music class by the girls. Rowdy sees the red marks and scuffed-up appearance on my face, frowns and stares for a moment, then looks away and turns back to his computer.

Mom doesn't notice my face and is high as hell. She says she has a surprise for me. She says she got a new puppy.

I'm hit with a wave of anxiety after what happened to Cyan. I don't really want another dog. I don't say anything, though. I just kind of go with it.

The dog is a female foxhound mix with a light brown coat and black eyebrows. I name her Sasha because it feels like a soft word and she's real soft.

Against my better judgement, I end up falling in love with Sasha. She's so great. She's my first pup and she's all for me. I put her in my backpack and leave enough space so she can poke her little head out when we ride around town on my bike. We go to the park as often as I can take us, which is pretty much every afternoon. I love to race downhill on my bike while Sasha barks excitedly in my ear. When I get to the bottom and stop, she licks the back of neck and my face and it makes me laugh.

We race all over the woods together, though sometimes she gets bitten by ticks and I do, too. I'm always careful when I remove them at home, making sure to kill them so they can't bite us again.

Sasha loves belly rubs and lies on her back then scoots her little body from side to side to move my hand to where she wants it.

I love my dog.

Sasha has to stay outside, just like any dog we've had before. She's got a little doghouse that I fill with spare blankets to stave off the winter chill. I *hate* leaving her outside, especially after what happened to Cyan. I'm real glad there are no storm shelters around for her to fall in and hang herself...though I'm pretty sure my ass will be grass if a tornado sucks me up into the sky.

Roland Amariah Gonzales

Mom spends her free time calling psychic hotlines, doing drugs and now she works on her garden, which she says to keep Sasha away from.

Mom's garden is *nothing* like Grandma Margaret's garden. There are no flowers here. Nothing beautiful. Only some cucumbers, tomatoes and a corn stalk or two. I don't think she really knows what she's doing. All she did was buy a bunch of seeds and sort of toss them in the dirt then spray them with a hose. Not that I know much about gardening one way or another...it just seems like it should be *harder* to do than that.

There's a three-day holiday weekend and Rowdy decides to go into work anyway, to make overtime money. Mom says she's gonna have friends come over and I'll need to make myself scarce.

The weekend comes and I'm a little late clearing out of the house. On my exit, I run into a guy as he pulls up onto our gravel driveway. He looks kind of like Randy...though I have to admit, they all kind of look the same to me. Fair-skinned men with trucker hats and mustaches. The guy doesn't introduce himself. I hang around for a couple, curious, and soon hear *Sadeness* by Enigma blasting from Mom's radio. I shrug, then head to the park with Sasha.

Sometime later, I find the guy hanging around our house when I get home from school. When he's there, Mom always tells me to go to the park or somewhere else, and then she usually gives me a couple of dollars, which is pretty cool.

I save up the get-out money for a couple of weeks until I have around thirty dollars, then I ride my bike to Pat's pawn shop. I hope I can get a cheap game, then I'll go to the Soda Fountain and get a Roy Rogers! Today's gonna be a kickass day!

I get about halfway across town before I realize I forgot my damn wallet. I pedal home, down my bike next to Sasha's doghouse, then make my way through the back door. That *Sadeness* song is practically *shaking* the house. It's a pretty cool song, but I don't know why Mom listens to it so much.

I unlock the back door then quietly make my way to my room. The last thing I want is to have Mom discover how much money I have because she'd *definitely* take it all back. This house isn't that big and the damn song is so loud that I can't hear *anything* until I try to sneak by Mom's door. As I pass her door I hear the unmistakable noises of *meat* slapping on *meat* and my mother moaning.

Amariah The Boy

I stop, stunned. My thoughts cascade off a cliff into the abyss. I'm hurt, angry, confused. Did this *stupid bitch* learn *nothing* from screwing over Dad? Wasn't ruining one man's life enough? How is Rowdy gonna feel when he finds out? That'll break him...does he have to know? Dad would've never found out if I hadn't told him. Rowdy would probably be better off without her. Is it okay for me to decide?

No...no, this is none of my business.

Fuck that. Burn her! She deserves it!

No...I should go.

Let him find out on his own.

I'm witness to her act of infidelity. *Again.* I consider my options for another few seconds, fists clenched. The sound of my mom fucking some guy in the next room makes me nauseous and I can't be here anymore. I go to my room, retrieve my wallet, then quietly leave through the back door, careful to lock it on my way out.

I don't ride to Pat's pawn shop or the Soda Fountain. I just ride out to the park by myself, find my tree, and sit under it. I feel the crunch of fallen leaves, then pick up a few and crush them in my hands. I watch the bits fall to the earth. Like sand on a beach.

Do fallen leaves remember their trees? Do they ever want to go home?

I watch happy families in the distance, idly crushing leaves as I do. My face registers no emotion. I feel no emotion. I'm blank.

Empty.

Roland Amariah Gonzales

I eventually find out the guy's name is Mitch. He's gone for a while, at *least* a month, then suddenly reappears sometime after my birthday. I get ready to leave when Mom says whoa there, Rol you ain't gotta go nowhere, me n' Mitch're goin' out for a country drive.

I say oh, then go back in my room.

Mitch's arrival makes Sasha bark angrily before she starts yelping. I run outside to see what's going on and to make sure she's okay. Mitch has brought his dog with him and it's a big ol' German Shephard. The thing is jumping all over Sasha before I chase it away. I guess it's sick as hell too, because it starts to throw up and poop everywhere.

Mitch laughs and says looks like Brock done got the shits!

I laugh. That's the most Mitch has *ever* said to me, and I sure didn't expect it.

Mitch's dog whimpers a bunch, then limps around after getting sick everywhere. Mitch frowns and puts his dog in the back of his truck, then shakes his head then gets ready to leave. He calls out to my mom and says he's gotta take Brock home because the dog is sick.

Mom calls out through the window aw hell, so some other time?

Mitch says yeah, sure thing! Then he climbs into his truck and heads out.

A week goes by and Sasha suddenly gets real sick. She doesn't run up to me anymore when I get home from school. She lays in her doghouse all day and only comes out to throw up or poop, and for some reason her poops are never solid. She's acting like Mitch's dog, Brock.

I try to play with her but she can't play. She just walks around real slow. She shakes a bit like it's hard to stand. I pick her up and put her back in her doghouse, then I pat her head. She whimpers and slowly looks up at me, before weakly licking my hand. I try to give her some food, but she *won't* eat. I'm really scared.

I ask Mom what's wrong with Sasha, and if we can take her to the vet.

Mom says hell no boy, we ain't got that kind of money.

I say oh, I've got about twenty, so can I take her to the vet?

Mom says it's at *least* a hundred, then packs her bong and takes a hit.

I ask if I can bring her in for the night, but Mom looks at me like I just smashed her bong with a turtle.

274

She says can we...? – hell no! You done seen her! She's poopin' and throwin' up all over the place! Nuh-uh, she can stay out *there* tonight. She'll be *fine*, dogs get sick all the time. She probably just ate something nasty.

I quietly say alright then head to my room. I don't get any sleep that night. I think I hear Sasha whimper a couple of times.

...maybe it's just the wind.

The next day starts as any other. I brush my teeth, eat some discount cereal, then get ready for school. Rowdy leaves for work and doesn't say a thing one way or another. Mom is sitting on the couch with a vacant look on her face as she watches talk shows and smokes a cigarette, beer in hand. I feel a weight on my chest but I don't know what from.

I pull my bike out of the washroom and head outside. The sting of the morning chill immediately bites at my fingertips. I put on my gloves, push my bike forward through the frozen grass and feel it crunch underfoot. I near Sasha's doghouse but don't expect her to run out. I hope she's okay like Mom said she would be. As I get closer, I see that she's not inside, and her chain is leading out of the doghouse and around the corner.

Oh? Maybe she's up and digging up something? Maybe she *did* get better?

Cyan's lifeless body, dangling in the inky-black darkness, flashes through my mind.

I stop breathing and lower my bike to the ground. I tread the frozen grass and turn the corner of her doghouse. On the ground is a pink bath towel. I whisper puppy's name, then fall to my knees.

My voice breaks as I croak out Sasha?

I reach out, sobbing, and slowly lift the towel.

Sasha lies before me, her soft brown eyes wide open, staring at me. At the world. At everything.

At nothing.

My mind races as sobs rack my body. We ran in the woods just a week ago. I was laughing and she was barking and chasing me. She was licking my face and she was happy. I delicately lift her cold lifeless body up into my arms and hold her tight as I weep into her fur. I rock back and forth as I sob into Sasha's corpse. My ears are burning, exposed to the cold.

I'm so alone.

Roland Amariah Gonzales

I struggle to speak and choke I'm sorry Sasha, I wish I had the money, girl. I wish I could've taken you to the vet, and they would've given you medicine.

Then you'd be okay.

You'd be okay.

You'd be okay. We'd run in the park and we'd chase squirrels and do all the stuff you like. I'm real sorry, girl. I'm so sorry. I'm so sorry. I love you, Sasha. I love you, girl.

I sit there on the frozen grass, weeping until my head is pounding. I weep until I run out of tears and I can hardly breathe.

I put Sasha in her doghouse. I bundle up all her blankets and then wrap them around her, tucking her in so she stays warm. I walk back toward the house, look over my shoulder, and find tears anew.

Inside, I glance at the clock. School started five minutes ago. Mom doesn't say anything or ask why I'm still here. After cleaning up a bit I head back outside, get on my bike, and pedal to school. I don't look at Sasha's doghouse again.

The teacher says I'm tardy, so she has to write a notice that my mother has to sign and I have to return.

I stare ahead. There's nothing. I mumble wha....? yeah, sure. Have a great time.

She regards me for a few seconds then heads out of the room. No one in class says anything. I'm barely aware of their existence let alone my own, but they're uneasy. Tense. Somewhere in the back of my head, I can *feel* it.

The teacher returns with the paper and begins to read the paragraph detailing *why* I'm receiving this notice. She reads the parameters describing how I need to return it at a given point, or further steps will be taken, something about permanent record and blah blah blah. The sounds coming out of her face lose cohesion. They are nothing more than noise.

I turn my head from side to side, and think, what is the *point?* Of *any* of this? Who cares? Who fucking cares? I look into the teacher's eyes, my expression somewhere between pleading and accusation. I regard her as one might a raving lunatic dropkicking babies into oncoming traffic. I whisper who the fuck *cares* about *any* of this?

I throw my head back and yell who fucking *cares!?*

Amariah The Boy

She's taken aback, startled even, as am I. Has she never truly considered the question herself? How can she *live* like that? How can *anyone*?

She stutters something about my permanent record, and I find myself incapable of even *beginning* to care about whatever the hell that's supposed to mean. I'm sick of her face. This place. Everyone.

I snatch the paper out of her hand and shout okay, *fine,* yeah! I'll take care of it. Thanks!

I can see that I've upset her. She says I need to go talk to someone and take my attitude elsewhere.

I say no, talking never does anyone any good. What can talking do? Then I say hey, I need to go to the restroom.

She studies me for a moment, then she says to make sure I come right back.

I put my wallet on my desk before heading out of the classroom. The pants I'm wearing don't have pockets, for some reason. After I enter the bathroom, I take a few deep breaths and look into the sink. Sasha's lifeless form *burns* in my brain. I sob.

A few minutes pass. I clean up, then return to class. The teacher is gone. I don't ask where she is, I just sit down and stare at my desk and...wait a minute.

Where's my wallet?

I look over the classroom, an amalgamation of shock, anger, amazement and confusion on my face. The classmates who dare to look at me shake their heads, then quickly look away. One kid is looking away with a faux-bored expression on his face. I stand up then say through clenched teeth give. It. Back.

He quickly says I didn't take your wallet.

I respond I never said a thing about my wallet, asshole.

My hand shoots out to grab him. I rip him out of his seat and throw him against the ground. He and the class are in a state of shock. Some girls yell out no, stop! Stop fighting!

I can hear one crying, somewhere far away. None of the boys say a word. Not one is cheering, hooting or hollering as is the norm. No one tries to separate us. They sit in their seats, terrified.

I grab the boy by his hair then strike him repeatedly in the face with my closed fist. I scream WHERE'S MY FUCKING WALLET? He grabs at my hair, swipes at my face with his fingernails a few times, and

I don't care. I don't register the pain as he claws at me. I have only the strong desire to *wreck* this bastard. This nothing.

He's gonna go home to his loving family. He's gonna eat a good dinner. His mom and dad will ask him how his day was. They'll give a fuck. They'll tell him how *special* he is and I'm sure he and his dad'll throw a baseball out in the front yard, while his mom bakes him a goddamn apple pie.

He'll get to play with his dog, still alive.

This *nothing* is stealing from me and I have *nothing*. I slam his head into the floor a few times while he desperately tries to claw at my eyes.

I hear a woman scream oh God, no! What are you doing?! She has returned with the school counselor. The vision of the kind and caring (and gorgeous) Mrs. Brookes is a thing of the past... she's been replaced by some middle-aged guy dying to retire who seems to hate kids in general. He quickly yanks us apart and I scream NOOOO!

The kids in class quickly shout to the teacher that the other kid started it when he stole my wallet, and I was only trying to get my wallet back. I'm still enraged and straining against the school counselor who is struggling to restrain me, a half-starved child.

The counselor shouts alright, ENOUGH!

The counselor shouts do you have RJ's wallet?

The other kid, battered, bruised and beaten, says I was just joking!

The counselor orders the kid to hand it over. Now!

I start to calm down.

The kid takes it out of his pocket and chucks it angrily at the floor. I surge against the counselor's grip, as if this kid has tossed a tank of gas on my fire.

The counselor holds me, *painfully,* digging his fingers against my ribcage and shouting, I SAID ENOUGH!

He picks up my wallet. When I reach for it he jerks it away and says hold on, what's *in* the wallet?

Confused, I say what?

He says if this is your wallet then you'd better tell me what's in it.

I'm absolutely bewildered that he'd even *think* to demand that from me right now. I try to say as quietly as I can that I've only got my meal card and nothing else.

He pretends not to hear and says speak up boy, I can't hear you!

I yell I only have a meal card and nothin' else, God *dammit*!

He digs his fingers into my ribcage. I grit my teeth and hiss in pain.

278

Amariah The Boy

The counselor opens my wallet, looks inside, then hands it over.

My face is on fire, but not from the boy's clawing. It's *shameful* to be so poor you can't even afford school food. I mean, it's only a couple of *dollars* per day...but I can't afford it.

I'm living on welfare. Food stamps, too.

I think for a moment to tell this man about my life. That I hardly get any food at home since Mom lost her fucking *mind*. That she hardly cooks much anymore *or* goes grocery shopping. That Rowdy hardly eats anything and tells me I can do the same. Or that my only regular meals are breakfast and school at lunch. Or how, sometimes if I'm lucky I get dinner at Logan's house. I don't tell him this. I don't tell him about the drugs, alcohol, or cruelty.

The counselor yanks me back to reality and says alright you two, you're coming with me.

He leads us out of the classroom, his hands gripping the back of our necks, then takes us into the main office. After interrogating us separately, he starts preaching about how violence is never the answer and I should've *told* someone and blah blah blah.

I'm tempted to ask if anyone's ever stolen anything from him and said to him bitch, *try* to get it back. But I know it'd be a waste of time.

It *always* is. I relax my eye muscles and blur my vision so I don't see him standing in front of me.

I'm given a three-day, in-school-suspension. When I tell Mom and Rowdy that I was trying to get my meal card back, Rowdy nods in approval. When I tell them *how* I beat the kid, Rowdy arches his eyebrows.

The next day, Rowdy tells me to go talk to Pat. Rowdy says to tell him that I need help controlling my anger, 'cause what I did ain't right.

I say Pat? The guy who owns the pawn shop? That Pat?

Rowdy says well yeah, Pat's a sixth-degree black belt in karate.

I say holy shit, I never knew!

Rowdy gives me a little smile, then goes back to looking at whatever is on his computer screen. He says yup, Pat probably likes to keep it that way.

In-school-suspension is actually a *lot* better than being in class. They put me in a tiny closet-sized room and I don't mind at all. I don't miss the kids in my class one bit! There's no one else here so I don't have to *smell* any of the kids who don't shower, and there's no one to cough on me. I don't have to deal with snickering kids making jokes about me, either.

They bring my lunch to the suspension room because I'm not allowed to go into the cafeteria. I think the idea is that I'm deprived of contact with other kids as punishment, but I mean...*fuck* those kids. The only time I leave the room is to go to the bathroom, or when it's time to go home.

After a few days it's over, and I think to myself that if this is what solitary confinement in prison is like, it's not all that bad.

I ask the counselor if I can just stay in that room instead of going back to my classes and he tells me no.

I ask well, how do I get back in here?

He says you're not supposed to *want* to be in-school-suspended. Don't you miss your friends in class?

I say hell, I don't *have* friends in class. I like it better here.

He gets annoyed and says well you can't come back here, and if you get into another fight you'll be expelled...and that's that.

I look at the ground and quietly say oh...that's a shame.

I head home.

KICKED IN THE HEAD

I ride my bike out to Pat's pawn shop the next day and when he sees me he breaks into a broad grin, pulls out games from the display case, and puts 'em on the counter. I hesitate and he says what? You're not excited about these games? Well, this is all I've got for now, so tough!

I laugh nervously then say Rowdy told me to come tell you I've got anger problems.

Pat looks at me quizzically for a moment then smiles. He says what happened RJ, your folks tell you to do the dishes and you said no?

I say ah...no not exactly. I tentatively tell him what happened in school with the kid who stole my wallet. He listens quietly while I relay the tale. When I'm done, my shoulders drop and I feel exhausted.

Pat considers my words then says look, I'm not going to tell you that what you did was the *right* thing to do...but standing up for yourself is never *wrong*, either. I remember being your age. Most adults tend to forget that if you don't stand and plant your feet firmly, well, *every* kid is looking to knock you down. There are, however, better ways to go about it. Not the way you did it – that would be the wrong way.

I wince and say I'm sorry.

Pat laughs and says hey now, don't apologize to me, you didn't ram my head into the floor!

I laugh then wince again before I say yeah, you're right.

I don't tell Pat about how I go hungry most nights or *why* I acted the way I did. Nothing good will come of that, just Mom trying to hit me for bringing trouble to the house and making her look bad.

While I'm lost in thought Pat tells me that he owns a dojo across the street and his classes are after school, Monday to Friday. He says he can talk to my mom and Rowdy about payment, and he'll get me set up with a uniform and all that jazz.

I thank him and head home. I'm a little surprised that Mom would willingly spend any money on me outside the bare necessity needed to keep me alive.

...though I suppose she *does* hate all outside attention. An investment for the future, perhaps.

School is awkward, come Monday. Kids from my class and those they tell give about my episode give me a wide berth. I don't get it. I'm tiny, what the hell am I gonna do to *them*?

The thief from my class is transferred to a different period so we're not in the same room. Similarly, I'm told by my teacher to avoid him best as I can, and not to get into any more trouble.

I sit glumly in class. At least no one is making fun of me.

I go to Pat's dojo after school and he hands me a plain white karate uniform. He says it's called a *gi* and tells me to hurry up and try it on because class is in fifteen minutes. I'm *real* nervous and wonder if any kids from school will be here, but *none* of them are! I think to myself where the hell does everyone always disappear to?

A couple of other people arrive. All are *giants* compared to me and I'm told that I'm the only kid. There's Terry, some guy with a brown belt who is covered in enough hair for it to be considered fur, and Howard, a kid in high school with a blue belt.

I'm told there are a couple of others who don't show up too often. There's also Pat's assistant teacher, a small and seemingly frail-looking older Asian woman with tanned skin who's named Miss Butt.

I'm in Pat's office when he tells me her name. I blink a couple of times and ask if I heard that right. I stifle laughter and ask if her name is *really* Miss *Butt*? B-U-T-T?

Sensei Pat looks away from his computer toward me, arches his eyebrows, holds out an arm to the side and says what, is there something wrong with Miss Butt's name? He calls her into his office and says there's something important that I'd like to tell her about her name.

Miss Butt comes into the office, seemingly *pissed*. Before I have a chance to speak, she gets in my face and says what, you no think Miss Butt is pretty name? I think is *very* pretty name. What *yo* name?

Oh, hell. I shouldn't have said a damn word.

I look off to the side toward the ground, embarrassed, and think of how to answer when Miss Butt throws a quick jab to my chest. I gasp and stumble back, eyes wide as I choke for air.

Miss Butt wags a finger in my face and barks do not judge by name!

Amariah The Boy

She laughs as I struggle to regain my breath and says also, do not drop guard! You stay alert and – she throws another jab at my chest and I stumble out of the way. Miss Butt smiles and says oh hey, *very* good. She yells you go get in line now! Go warm up!

I say sure thing Miss Butt then run into the dojo and start doing whatever I see everyone else doing. Mostly stretches. Terry laughs as he sees my strained face and says you asked Miss Butt about her name, eh? She doesn't like that.

I nod emphatically and say yeah. I can see that!

I learn all the warm-up routines over the coming weeks. Lots of push-ups. I learn that calling Pat by his name and not *Sensei* Pat gets me thrown to the floor. We practice punches and kicks against pads and I learn that I usually get knocked back when it's my turn to hold them.

Tuesdays and Thursdays are sparring days. I know it's important to practice what we've learned, but I *hate* sparring days. Terry becomes my coach when Sensei Pat is busy. He teaches me when to block and when to take advantage of an opening.

I *hate* fighting against Miss Butt. She's only a little bit bigger than me yet kicks the *crap* out of me. I mostly try to dance out of the way as any time I throw a punch or whatever, she counters it and I get *nailed.*

I take my hits and after a while learn the importance of being nimble.

Howard the high school kid is an absolute *prick.* He's got to be at least *three* times my size and must weigh about *three* times my weight. When we spar he punches and kicks me as *hard* as he can and it fucking *hurts.* My only solace is when he spars with Terry who does not hold back.

When Howard gets punched in the face too many times he starts crying and I look away because I've got a grin on my face.

Sensei Pat tells Terry to ease up a bit on Howard and that we're here not to *destroy* one another...but to *learn.*

Terry stops sparring then turns and says yes sensei and bows, *just* before Howard tries to nail him with a thrust kick. Terry smacks the kick out of the way with his arm and throws a snap kick to Howard's junk.

Howard collapses against the floor and I bark out a laugh. Sensei Pat looks over at me and shakes his head. I quickly sober up. Sensei Pat says that's enough for today and we all go home.

Roland Amariah Gonzales

One day I'm in Sensei Pat's office after class, just kind of hanging out. I ask him why he tells Terry to ease up on Howard, but doesn't tell Howard to go easy on *me*?

Sensei Pat says that my getting hit *really* hard is good for building my character.

I'm confused as hell and don't understand that one bit because getting kicked clear across the room into the fuckin' *wall* doesn't build a damn thing...or at least *I* don't think so.

I don't *say* that of course – I only think it.

I *do* however ask why Howard can't get some character-building as well.

Sensei Pat looks away from his computer then regards me with a frown and says Howard's character is already built. He is not likely to change one way or another. He asks if there's anything else.

I try to think on his words, to understand them. I say no Sensei Pat, bow, and leave.

PRESENTS FOR ALL

My twelfth birthday comes and goes. Rowdy gets me something called a breadboard and I'm confused by it. It looks more like *work* than anything else. Grandma sends me a chemistry kit and it looks more fun. The box shows a few kids in a state of amazement, growing crystals in a laboratory and wearing what I figure scientists wear. I open it and find nothing but a few bags of chemicals and a bunch of glass beakers.

Unimpressed, I open the breadboard box. There's a big flat white board with a thousand little pinholes. The rows and columns are defined by letters and numbers. In little plastic baggies are groups of colored wires, little pills with wires coming out of them, and a host of other stuff I can't readily identify.

Rowdy is *really* into the breadboard and spends an unfortunate amount of time forcing me to memorize the color designations of what he says are "resistors." I learn the other components and their purpose as well. After a week, he begins to quiz me on what four-band and five-band resistors do as well as the function of capacitors, ceramic and otherwise, and transistors, too.

Some of the things I can make with it are neat, I guess. I make an alarm clock and a light-sensitive bird-chirp function. The breadboard seems like building things with Legos, but with *much* more work. Over time I get bored with it because I get frustrated by not knowing *how* it works. I can follow instructions on how to make something, but *why* does electricity make an alarm clock when I connect these wires and put a few capacitors, resistors, and transistors here and there?

I don't get it and Rowdy doesn't provide any kind of explanation that makes any sense. I also have trouble differentiating some colors. Dark green sometimes looks like dark blue or dark brown, and other times grey and green are so similar I can't tell them apart. I find it infuriating when I waste two hours or more trying to make something, only to find that a color I thought was, wasn't at all!

Roland Amariah Gonzales

I don't tell anyone about my difficulty with colors and hell, they wouldn't care anyway.

My difficulty in understanding apparently extends to my school life when my grades plummet. I mean, they were never *great,* but now they're downright *awful.* I don't understand why. I do my homework, same as everyone else. When I finish, I run my homework by Rowdy as he's more coherent and much smarter than Mom, who is usually on the couch or in her room screaming or crying about something.

I avoid Mom as much as I can.

Rowdy usually looks over my work for a minute before turning his attention back to his computer screen and says yeah, yeah, 's'all good, man.

After he says this, I *know* my homework is good because he's *real* particular about getting everything *just* right. I confidently turn in my homework to my math or science teacher, Rowdy's assurance in-mind, and end up getting a shitty grade.

I just don't get it.

I begin to think that maybe *I am* retarded, like the kids I see in school who are stuck in wheelchairs or drooling all the time. And my classmates *do* avoid me like they do the wheelchair kids. Hell, sometimes I can't even tell the difference between dark colors, and my math teacher, a *real* mean and *ugly* toad-creature, often pulls me out of class to tell me how stupid I am.

We all call the math teacher Miss Toad behind her back. She's a short, *mean,* fat creature with beady little eyes hiding behind glasses, and a face that says Smile is just a city in Kentucky. She's got short red hair that look like pubes generously donated to make a wig.

Miss Toad prefers to call on kids who aren't very good at math, especially after she writes an equation on the board. She makes them stand up to answer her question so the whole class is looking at them. When they get it right she says yes, sit down.

When they get it wrong, she says *no,* you're *wrong.* You *obviously* haven't been studying and your grades reflect this.

A new girl, a math prodigy, joins our class a couple of months after school starts and Miss Toad is even *more* of a bitch because there's finally someone who can swim through her equations like they're doggie paddling in the shallow end of a pool.

Miss Toad *hates* this.

Amariah The Boy

She's not here to teach, she's here to make us feel like *crap* for whatever reason. Probably because of the pubes on her head.

One day, Miss Toad has enough of the know-it-all girl and shouts for her to put her hand down. Miss Toad says she doesn't want to see the girl raise her hand for the rest of the *year*!

The girl lowers her hand then looks down at her desk and quietly says oh, I'm sorry.

At first, I think to myself *good*, serves her right for being a show-off. After a couple of minutes though, I feel bad. I imagine I'd be real sore if someone just up and came into the music room and said hey RJ, you stop your trash-sounding voice right now and I don't wanna hear it for the rest of the year!

Miss Toad goes back to making *everyone* feel like garbage. I struggle with converting decimals to fractions and vice versa. I can do the conversions on paper but that isn't good enough for Miss Toad. She wants me to do them out loud and my mind can't process any of it.

That's when I fall apart.

We *all* hate her but there's nothing we can do to teachers. We can't fight them, they're too big! Someone mentions slashing her tires with a knife or putting sugar in her gas tank to break her car, but everyone's worried about getting caught.

A stroke of genius hits me and I take matters into my own hands in the most awesome and disgusting way I can think of. Miss Toad makes me sit in the front row and *always* stands in front of my desk when she tells the class how awful we all are. She practically puts her fat belly meat on my desk *every time*. It's *disgusting* and makes me feel uncomfortable as hell. So, I decide to eat as many vegetables as I can on the days before I have her class. Vegetables *really* hurt my stomach and give me awful gas.

I hold it all in until I get to her class and my stomach hurts so much...but I *know* it's gonna be worth it.

Miss Toad walks up to the board after collecting our homework and tells us she looks forward to the next round of F's.

As she begins to write out the day's equations I adjust my body and slightly tilt my hips, then relax my butthole. I take in as much air as my lungs can hold then gently expel as much gas as I can while simultaneously blowing it all in her direction.

I got the idea from a movie called *Dune.*

287

Roland Amariah Gonzales

Miss Toad writes on the board and says *maybe* if she dumbs the equations down *again,* we might *finally* understand...but probably not, and it's a wonder how *any* of us can...then she stops talking.

A deep frown creases her forehead before she rapidly finishes her example on the blackboard and retreats to her desk. Other kids make awful, grossed-out faces. Some gag and choke. I try not to laugh, and I act equally disgusted. I love that everyone thinks she's the one farting...and no one figures out that it's me.

I do the same thing *every* time I'm in her class for the rest of the year until I finally push Miss Toad toward a near-psychotic breakdown. She throws down her little clipboard then storms out of class shrieking about disgusting children and how much she hates her job. We get a substitute teacher for a couple of weeks, and I don't know about the other kids, but my grade goes up for at least a little bit.

When Miss Toad returns she doesn't say a *thing* about her mental break. I quit eating all those awful vegetables because being in pain every day for nearly a year wasn't worth just two weeks of peace. I was *hoping* she might quit!

My science teacher Mr. Smith is a prick and similar in nature to Miss Toad. If I talk in class, something *every kid* does, he makes me stand in the hall. One of my classmates confides that Mr. Smith used to be in the Navy, then says the guy is pissed all the time because he was a *butt-pirate,* and not a very good one. I don't know much about the Navy other than Grandpa Kenney having served, but I'm pretty sure butt-pirate isn't a real job.

Whatever his real job *was,* and for a reason I don't understand, Mr. James took an immediate disliking to me. One day, a girl at my lab table quietly asks if I have the notes from a class she missed when she was sick. She smiles and says that I take *really* good notes, and that's why she's asking.

I don't know what makes my notes so great, but I reach into my backpack and pull them out. Then I lean in and whisper yeah, sure thing, here ya go.

Mr. James bellows MR. Gonzales, OUT of my classroom, NOW!

I protest and say but I was just handing her –

He snaps his fingers then jerks his thumb to the door. Without looking up again he shouts OUT!

I sigh then stand up and head out of the room, my head down.

Amariah The Boy

Rumor around school is Rocky, who everyone knows fights just about anything he looks at, tried to take a swing at Mr. James and Mr. James *floored* him. I'm like *half* Rocky's size. Maybe even a quarter! I don't wanna take any chances. I step out of the room just as Mr. James calls out and don't come back until I tell you to, understand?

I say yes sir and sit in the hallway, leaning against the wall.

The lunch bell rings and my classmates line up single-file to get escorted to the cafeteria. Everyone got in trouble for excessive talking during lunch a month ago, so now we have assigned seats...and *no one's* allowed to talk...only eat. Mr. James either doesn't notice me or pretends not to as he and the class walk by. The girl who asked for my notes looks down at me and then motions for me to get up, but I shake my head no and stay planted right where I am. If Mr. James wants me to get up, he'll say so. I'm not about to get thrown to the ground because I pissed him off!

My stomach groans in protest at the notion of missing one of my two guaranteed meals.

As my class rounds the corner I think *shit*, was I *supposed* to jump in line? To get up?

...but he told me to stay here. I'm *sure* he didn't mean "no lunch." Did he forget me?

I laugh and think oh man, he's gonna feel so *stupid* when he realizes I'm not there! I'll sit here so he can run back and apologize and then we'll be good again.

Other teachers walk by and see me sitting there next to the door but no one says anything. They all ignore me and escort their students.

Ten minutes goes by and, you know what, I think Mr. James *completely* forgot me. I think about walking into the cafeteria but so much time has passed and I'd definitely get in trouble.

Oh man, what do I do?

The bell rings again and I see my class walking back, Mr. James in the lead. He sees me still sitting against the wall. His eyes go wide for a moment before he scowls at me. He tells the class to go in the room, sit down and shut up, then turns to me and points a finger at me and asks whether or not I went to lunch.

I say no sir, I sat right here like you told me.

He nods, then says through gritted teeth wait right here.

I stay seated as he goes into the classroom and tells the class to read some chapter from our textbooks then steps into the hall and snaps at me to get up. He marches me to the lunchroom, all the time leaning in real close to me and hissing through his teeth listen *here,* you little fuckin' shit. I'm not *about* to play your *bullshit* games, you *understand* me?

I protest and say but I just did what you told me!

He shoves his finger in my face again and growls don't give me that *shit.* You're gonna go to the lunchroom, you're gonna *choke* down your food, and you're going to be *quick* about it, understand?

I say yes, sir.

As we walk into the lunchroom, the lunch ladies look up in surprise. Mr. James points at me and says he missed lunch.

The lunch ladies eye him for a moment, then eye me. The one who's always coughing and smells like cigarettes says fine, then she motions for me to grab a tray and come around to the food.

Another lunch-lady who looks like she's *always* sweating slops some food onto my tray. I hate making eye contact with her because her left eye *never* stops twitching and she *never* stops staring at me when I walk by. She never smiles or anything! She just stares.

She says in a hoarse voice there ya go, kid.

I nod, say thanks, then follow Mr. James to a table.

He tells me to sit down then says hurry up, you've got five minutes. Because you want to be a smart ass, that's *all* you get.

I feel awfully nervous, *sick* even as I force myself to choke down the food. Each swallow feels like there's a brick being forced down my throat.

After five minutes are up his watch beeps. He snaps at me and says time's up, let's go.

I throw away my untouched food and we head back to the classroom. I don't understand why Mr. James and Miss Toad *hate* my ass. I used to *like* math and science. Where did I screw up? When did I mess up everything...again?

My English teacher Mrs. Glass is a nice older lady, in contrast to my other teachers. I do well in her class whether it's spelling, grammar, or any kind of writing. I do so well, in fact, that she enters me into spelling bee competitions along with other students from our school! I make it to regionals and we eventually take a bus as a group to a big competition.

I end up getting fifth place after they ask me to spell words I've never even *heard* of. At first I'm pretty bummed and mope around the competition hall. I've never won *anything* in my life and it'd be nice to be great at something no one else is. My sadness fades when I see there's a *huge* buffet...and it's all *just* for us! They don't limit what you can eat based on how well you did or *anything* like that, which is great. I haven't eaten this much food since Thanksgiving last year!

Mrs. Glass takes us on another field trip a couple of weeks later, though it's not much of one. We go to a local church to learn about writing methods from the 1800s. The church has archives, and Mrs. Glass tells us to carefully peruse them before we pick a topic to write about.

From the moment they get on the bus, my classmates act like insane monkeys.

I love reading and writing *way* more than I like people, so I stay away from everyone else. They don't look at the archives at *all* and make *so* much noise that I try to tell them to be quiet a few times.

One of the kids tells me to go fuck myself.

I can see Mrs. Glass looking at us in irritation from across the room, because her conversation with a church lady is repeatedly interrupted by shouts. Eventually, she yells at everyone and tells us all to take a seat and shut up.

She *never* does this she never gets angry.

Then she says she's *so* embarrassed by our terrible behavior and regrets having taken us out of the school. She says we *obviously* aren't ready to be adults and, indeed, we all belong in a zoo.

I raise my hand and complain I didn't do anything other than sit quietly. I actually *looked* for an interesting topic!

She says her words only apply only to those of us who were *awful*.

I feel slightly better until Mrs. Glass announces that the field trip is *over* and we're all going to go back to school to practice cursive writing for the remainder of class.

I finish the cursive writing exercise, then spend the rest of my time drawing stick figures of people getting murdered in various ways. I draw them getting shot by soldiers, run over by tanks, blown up by airplanes, and a bunch of other stuff.

Mrs. Glass pulls me out of class the following day to talk about my drawings. I sense that I might be in *real* trouble, so I tell her I was just upset because we *all* got in trouble for what a few kids did. I say I didn't think it was fair so I drew all those kids getting killed in war because that's what they *deserve*.

291

I am satisfied with my explanation and think it is a good one.

Mrs. Glass pauses then looks at me with great concern. She eventually says well, when the class is bad as a whole then punishment must be administered in a like manner.

I think for a moment then scrunch up my face and say but then, what's the *point* of being good if everyone else is bad and I'm gonna get in trouble *anyway?* Everyone else had fun and I didn't have fun at all, because I was trying to find a topic! Why not just have a good time and do whatever I *want?*

Mrs. Glass regards me for a moment then tells me in order for a society to function, those who are good must inspire and provide a firm moral guide for those who act out of line. They must lead by example.

I think to myself that's not what happened though...that *never* happens!

I repeat myself and say if the rest of the class can't care about being quiet and I'm going to get in trouble anyway, why should I be the only one who sits quietly and tries to be good? No matter *what* I do I get in trouble in *every* class...and it isn't fair!

My country twang comes out as I get emotional and I say I didn't do *nothin'* wrong at the church! I got yelled at for being good 'cause everyone *else* was bad! I can't do a damn thing 'bout how other folk act! I can only look after myself and that's the best I can do! How'm I 'sposed to keep everyone else from actin' up when they don't give a frog's spit 'bout what I say! No one cares about what I hafta say, and no one listens to me!

Mrs. Glass stares at me throughout my display, puts her hand up, and then frowns and says no, no, no, that's not how any of this works. She says look, I don't have time explain this to you, so don't draw unpleasant things like that anymore or you'll have to talk to the counselor, understand?

I look down and put a great deal of effort into not crying. I quietly say yes, ma'am and we return to the classroom.

Mrs. Glass crumples up my drawings and throws them in the trash. I suppose it's the best possible outcome. The *last* thing I need is another reason for someone to call home. Nothing good *ever* comes from talking to someone about my problems, *especially* counselors. I mentally kick myself after school for being stupid enough to make those drawings in the first place.

Amariah The Boy

The bike ride home is refreshing. It feels *so good* to be outside, away from school. A strong gale embraces me and I feel invigorated as I race down the road. My worries are swept away as the wind carries me...the wind, ever my constant companion.

As I get near home I ponder how the wind is even kind enough that it blows my tears away on a bad day.

I smile.

When I get home, I see Mom sitting on the couch staring blankly ahead at the television. It's not on. I regard her for a moment, sigh, then enter my room.

Mom is gone now, mentally. She spends the day either drooling on the couch or screaming at me. Sometimes she likes to play disgusting jokes on me while I recoil in terror.

I don't know how or *why* but she starts lactating again and I thought only pregnant ladies did that. Mom thinks it's the funniest thing in the world to chase me around the house, squeezing her nipples to try and hit me with rancid breast milk from her fat, disgusting body.

I learn her moods. I learn what lies beneath her seemingly placid and incoherent surface. I avoid home when I can.

That Mitch guy still comes over occasionally. Mom says that Mitch lost his dog Brock shortly before I lost Sasha. Like that's supposed to make me feel something.

Mom is now *much* less concerned with my seeing her with Mitch. I see him on top of her a couple of times when they're wrestling in her room. She still tells me to go play for an hour but doesn't give me a couple of bucks anymore. She knows that *I* know what she's doing and doesn't particularly care one way or another.

I return early one day to see Mitch take fifty dollars out of his wallet and leave it on Mom's bedstand, and she says thank you and puts it in her purse. I think nothing of it. Maybe he owes her money or something?

A few weeks later she proudly shows erotic photos to Rowdy *and* me taken of her in lingerie. Mom says some old guy paid her to take a bunch of pictures, and she *swears* they didn't do anything when Rowdy asks...but I know better. At the same time, I gag as a flash of my disgusting mother riding some fat, sweaty, hairy old guy plays across my mind.

My mom is a hooker.

293

Roland Amariah Gonzales

I wonder where that money goes when it's time for dinner and there *is* no dinner.

Christmas nears and I see Mom's much happier this year. She's drinking more booze, popping *way* more pills. She's smoking weed and...something else. I don't quite recognize it though it smells similar to the stuff that her and Connie would smoke together. Mom *rarely* makes dinner now and when she does it usually makes me sick. I avoid her food when I can brave the late-night hunger pains.

I fight the hunger by going to the library and looking for magazines or books with pictures of food. I sit alone against the wall, and slowly flip through the pages as I trace my finger along the pictures. I imagine all the tastes and flavors and I'm pretty sure none of these would make me sick.

I go to bed earlier and earlier and sleep as long as I can. If I'm asleep I'm not hungry. I spend what *should* be dinnertime curled up in bed trying to ignore the growling and dull aching pain in my stomach. I look at the magazine I checked out from the library. It's filled with pictures of food.

As my eyelids grow heavy, I see pictures of happy families sitting together. They're smiling and eating together.

The food looks *so* good.

They look so happy.

Amariah The Boy

Christmas break arrives. I'm happy to be out of school because my grades are *terrible*. That place gives me nothing but stress.

...but at the same time I'm also sad to be out of school, because that's where I *eat*.

I don't know what I'm going to do for the next two weeks. I'm over at Logan's grandma's house jumping on the trampoline they got as an early Christmas present, when Rowdy shows up. He's red in the face, *furious*, and demands that I get my bike and ride my ass home lickety-split. He yells he ain't playin' around, *hurry* the hell *up!*

I look at Logan and the others, my face red in embarrassment. I hop on my bike and start to pedal home. I think about making a detour to Artesian Park until things cool down but Rowdy follows behind me in his car, probably to make sure I don't suddenly split.

I arrive in our backyard and lower my bike to the ground, just as Rowdy pulls into the driveway. He hollers to get my ass in the house and yells that he's so fuckin' pissed right now!

I don't know *what* the hell is going on. I go into the house, confused, and Mom starts screaming at me. I can't understand a thing she's saying until she holds up a paper and smacks me in the face with her free hand. I immediately recognize the paper.

A report card. My school grades. *Fuck*. The teachers said they weren't going to send the report cards until *after* Christmas break. I *always* made a habit of checking the mail and snatching the report card before Mom or Rowdy get a chance to see it. They'd ask about it, sure, but they also smoke a *bunch* of weed and can't remember shit.

Rowdy is *fuming*, pacing back and forth and staring at the ceiling so he doesn't have to look at me, while Mom screams at me. She says I'm a fuckin' retard and smacks my head and face a bunch of times. She yells why are you not doing your homework? She screams why the *fuck* are you not studying? What the fuck is *wrong* with you...and why are you *completely* fuckin' worthless?

She grabs my backpack then rips it open and demands to see all my homework. She screams all the homework you *never* fuckin' do! She says she's gonna throw my backpack in the fuckin' garbage because I don't use it anyway and that's where *I* belong, too. She says she's gonna throw my Nintendo in the trash too, because *that's* why I'm failing everything. It's those god-damned video games, and—

She stops mid-sentence. There are months of homework, all filled out, sitting in my backpack. There's no grade on any of the papers. I

295

never turned them in, not any of them. Mom looks at the papers then me and shrieks what is *wrong* with you!

I *try* to tell her that it doesn't *matter* if I turn them in or not, I get the same bad grades *regardless* and I don't know *why*!

...but she smacks my mouth before I get halfway through the sentence.

And then she starts ranting incoherently. She hits me while she's crying then yells at Rowdy to do *something* and not just fucking *sit there* all day. She tells him that *he* is completely worthless, too. A worthless, *useless* piece of shit.

Rowdy stands up to her with well, what the *hell* do you want me to do? He ain't my boy!

By this time, I'm in a daze from getting hit so many times. My head is pounding and my face is on fire and I hear someone tell me to go to my room.

Mom and Rowdy fight and holler for a long while. I hear glass shattering against my door or maybe the wall nearby. The fighting goes on for a good thirty minutes. I scream in frustration and rage, and cry into my pillow.

I try so hard, but I can't do *anything* right.

I hear Rowdy storm out of the house, slam the back door, and peel out of the gravel driveway while Mom shrieks at him for leaving.

I hear her thunderous hooves as she stomps back into the sitting room, sobbing. Then I hear her crack open a beer can. She drinks it fast and I hear three more cans being opened.

I don't have to be in the room to know that she's lighting up her bong. I soon hear the familiar bubbling of the bong's water, followed by choking and coughing noises for about ten minutes straight.

Then...silence.

I stare at the wall, broken. My head hurts.

I take out the food magazine again and look at my favorite pages. I close my eyes and try to block out my hunger pains.

Dinner isn't coming tonight.

I imagine the people in the magazine being my family. They welcome me home when I walk into the house and the dad messes up my hair lovingly and says hey, sport! How'd school go today? Did you ask that girl out that you like? Just show her the ol' Thompson charm! That's how I got your mother! Then the mom walks in wearing a sundress and carrying a large platter of roast beef with mashed potatoes

296

and roasted veggies, just like I saw in the picture. She says that's certainly how he did it! And then she looks at me and says, Hey sweetheart, I made your favorite: roast beef and mashed potatoes!

I say aw gee, thanks Mom! I love you!

The mom puts down the tray then gives me a warm hug and smiles at me before kissing me on my forehead and telling me how much she loves me, too. She smells like flowers and she's soft and beautiful. The dad is tall, handsome and strong. He's good at sports *and* he's a former Boy Scout, so he makes sure I get in right away. He's a soldier, too, just like Dad, and he shows me how to be a man.

They both love me and never even think to call me *a fuckin' retard*. They ask me about my day and we go out to places together like parks for picnics and other things. They take time to understand *why* something is happening. They go to my school and *demand* to know why my grades are bad no matter what I do. They don't hit me. They make dinner. They don't do drugs all day...and they care about me.

They care.

My bottom lip quivers as I take deep breaths. I hope I see my imaginary family in my dreams. This family is the best I've ever had...even if they live only in my head.

Merciful sleep takes me.

Mom wakes me from my sleep, calling my name from the other room.

There is no dream family.

I'm groggy and I look at a small alarm clock near my bed. An hour has passed by. I rub exhaustion from my eyes and hold my hand to my stomach—I wince in pain.

That dull, *aching* pain.

I climb out of bed and slowly open my door, peeking through the crack.

Mom is a fat, disgusting blob melted into the couch. There's nothing there that resembles femininity. She's *nothing* like my dream mom. She slurs her words as says hey Rol, sit...over...

Her hand gestures slowly toward the coffee table as she says sit here, on the couch.

A couple of minutes pass of my sitting in awkward silence before her words ooze out like a viscous blob of foul black ink. Hey Rol, tell me: am I...am I a bad mother?

I don't hesitate for a *moment* before emphatically nodding and saying *yes!*

Mom laughs at this and then, slurring her words a bit more, says she *never* wanted me. She says she wanted Grace but *sure as hell* didn't want me. Mom says I ruined her life, I ruined her body.

She lifts her shirt and points to her cesarean scars and stretch marks. She shows me my crime for the *thousandth* time and says my birth cost her everything.

Mom says she tried to give me away to my uncle Alex or my dad Kenney, but the government only gives her food stamps and money *if* she's got the kid with her. She looks up at me and says people come-a checkin', Rol, they really do!

She doesn't say anything for a while then suddenly slaps my knee. She laughs and says, that's why I keep you around, Rol! Then she breaks into laughter then sighs and wipes a tear from her eye. She mumbles alright fuck off back to your room now. You're grounded.

I mechanically stand up then walk to my room, quietly close the door, and sit on the bed. I lift the blinds and look out at the graveyard. I didn't think Mom could hurt me any more than she has but hearing her say what I'd already *known* for ages...I stare at the dead trees, the tombstones, the gray grass. I trace my finger on the window, following the faded and forgotten tombstones in the distance.

She was never my mother.

I wish I'd never been born.

I wait until late that night when Kathleen and Rowdy are asleep and take out my chemistry kit. Kathy may not love me but there is one thing she *does* love.

And I'm gonna kill it.

I remove all the chemicals, still their powder form, then dump them into a large plastic bowl. Then I sneak outside.

In the yard, I use the hose to add water to the concoction, stir the hell out of it until it starts to violently bubble, then pour it all over her bullshit garden.

Her garden isn't that big so I'm able to cover every last bit of upturned earth.

I smile wryly as I think hey, would you look at that? I'm a scientist!

I look up at the sky, at the moon and the stars. I wish I could be up there right now.

Anywhere but here.

Amariah The Boy

I wish I could leave this world for another.

I go back into the house and run water on the plastic bowl a bunch of times before I wash it, then dry it off and put it back.

A couple of days later I find Kathy crying in the sitting room. I say hey Mom, what's up?

Kathy says all her plants died and after she worked *so* hard on them.

I feign surprise and say what? No way! How? I see you out there *all the time* watering them and working on them. Plants don't just die. Do you think...maybe some weird animal peed on them or something?

Kathy looks at me and thinks for a second then says no, I don't think so. I just don't know.

I say gee I'm sorry, I know how much they meant to you. And then I say hey Mom, if it's okay with you, do you think I can get out of the house and go ride my bike around? I know I'm still technically grounded, but maybe I could ride to the store and get you a candy bar or something?

Kathy doesn't look up then says, Yeah, that's fine. She tells me to get her a candy bar then hands me money. I think to myself that's *my* money you fucking *swine.*

I head out after I say thanks, Mom.

I go outside, grab my bike, and walk it over to her garden. I look back at the open windows, confirm she isn't there, then spit on her garden and ride off.

When I return an hour later she's gone. No one's home. A few hours after that, Rowdy gets home and, looking exhausted, says my mom is back in the Psych Ward from another suicide attempt.

New Years is in a few days. I tell Rowdy I'm not going to the Psych Ward again, not after last time.

Rowdy says well you can't go out and ride around, 'cause you're *still* grounded.

I hold up the candy bar and say Mom *just* sent me out to get this for her.

He retorts well, that don't mean you ain't grounded!

I say look Rowdy, I've got *four* days left of winter break. If you *really* wanna chase me down *every* day, then that's on you. I'll bet Mom doesn't even *remember* grounding me. If you *really* wanna tell Mom I'm still grounded just to make her happy, shit, why not just lie to her? Hell, she lies to you *all* the time!

Rowdy looks at me with a flash of anger then suddenly looks more exhausted than earlier and his shoulders slump. He turns away and says fine, you do whatever the hell you want. I don't really care one way or another.

I say alright, have a good night.

New Year's Eve comes and goes and, true to our respective words, I don't visit Kathy and Rowdy doesn't try to keep tabs on me.

She comes home from the Psych Ward and says she's all better now because they gave her *new* meds.

I hug her, then smile and say I'm so glad to hear that, Mom!

She sits on the couch and starts talking with Rowdy about new friends she made in the hospital, which is my sign to leave the house and ride around for a while.

I wish she'd fully commit and just fucking *die* already.

Amariah The Boy

School picks up again and the teachers tell us with great enthusiasm that we're going to a place called Exchange City in Blue Springs. Exchange City is held in a large building, a mock city run by kids, where everyone interviews for job roles like police officer, banker, baker, mayor, and a bunch of other stuff, too.

My morals and respect for rules and authority have degraded since Kathy told me I'm little more than a piggy bank for her.

Fuck everyone. But...carefully.

When we arrive at Exchange City I'm assigned the role of banker. At first I'm surprised because I was told by Miss Toad at least a hundred times that I *suck* at math. However, I reach a greater understanding when the job requires little more than inputting names, knowing their job's pay per hour, then calculating what they're owed.

I'm just a nameless face and no one will *ever* acknowledge or interact with me. I'm invisible, as long as I calculate salaries and hit the print button to print out checks that someone else delivers to the city's faux employees.

I learn how to manipulate the system in my favor and pay myself *more* than anyone else, *including* the mayor! The popular kids who received all the *cool* jobs like police officer, mayor, and shopkeeper are more concerned that the laws *they* came up with are respected.

Keep off the grass. Make a hoot noise like an owl when you enter a shop. Other stupid things they think are funny. No one checks or would even *think* to check what I'm doing.

By the end of the week I'm the *richest person* in Exchange City...but no one will ever know. This wealth affords me limitless candy, colored pencils, and erasers!

It's not much but it's a start.

I consider whether I can do this professionally when I finish school. Is it *actually* this *easy*?

We're all forced to watch a series of videos on the dangers of drunk driving the next week as part of an anti-drug awareness program. They were produced in the '80s or sometimes in the late '70s and they're *awful.* I get in trouble a few times for laughing because the girls' sports coach, the lady presenting these horrible things, takes them *very* seriously.

The videos play out like some of the shittier movies I've watched with Logan or at home. In one of them, a guy goes to get in his car after stumbling out of a bar, drunk as hell. He waves his friends away after they tell him not to drive, then peels out of the parking lot. His girlfriend, also drunk, cheers him on as he speeds and gets into a horrible wreck. Depending on the video, either only he dies, or the girl dies or sometimes they both die. There's *always* some asshole though, a voiceover, who says something like *still think drunk driving is cool?*

I get kicked out of the classroom while laughing and am surprised because I can't be the *only* one who finds this hilarious, can I? The girls' coach comes out and hits her fist against the open palm of her other hand and says that I need to take this *seriously* because it is *serious.*

She tells me how she once saw a person *crash* because they were driving drunk and they couldn't get out of the car, so the fire department had to be called. Before the firemen arrived, the car burst into flames because the person was *so drunk* that they didn't think lighting a cigarette would cause an explosion. She says the fire department could only watch, because they *knew* the person was *already dead.*

She looks at me as if waiting for an apology or some kind of response.

I blink as I process what she said. I stifle laughter and can only point toward the room and ask if *she's* the one who made that video, too?

She looks at me for a moment, her face looking like she just stepped in dog poop, then tells me to get back in the room, sit down, and shut up.

BLIND

Spring arrives and all the flowers are in full bloom. One day, I'm out in the woods and see someone burning away the underbrush. I pay no mind to the smoke at the time but about a week later discover that I am *highly* susceptible to the effects of poison oak. My entire body and face have a *violent* reaction. Everything swells up to about *three times* its normal size. I look like a giant, red puffy balloon.

The itching is *gnarly*. My ears, face, arms and legs are covered in itchy red rashes that crack, bleed and *ooze* painfully. My eyebrows, cheeks, and eyelids swell completely shut and I'm blind. I have to place my hands above and below either side of a single eye in order to pull apart the swollen flesh and glimpse the world. It feels like I am either on fire or itching to the point of madness.

Kathy tries to send me to school and both the students and teachers issue a collective gasp before I'm whisked away to the school nurse who immediately calls home. Kathy arrives in a huff and is visibly irritated. The school nurse tells her to take me to the pharmacy and get calamine lotion as well as some special eye drops, then whispers to her, loud enough for me to hear, that I could lose my eyesight if I'm not treated.

I gasp in surprise and shout I might go fuckin' *blind!?* From poison oak!?

The nurse says ah, sorry, I didn't know you could hear. Then she tells me it's not a sure thing but it's better to be on the safe side, okay? And then she says she's sure I'll be fine.

I grunt and grimace in pain as I pry open my left eye and see the nurse look at Kathy with a serious face.

I think to myself blind. From fuckin' poison oak.

Kathy takes me to the pharmacy, then we head home after making a much-needed stop to get her another carton of cigarettes and a 12-pack of beer. I don't go inside, because I'm fucking *blind,* but I do get to enjoy hearing James Taylor sing *You've Got a Friend* while I sit in the car by myself. Kathy grew fond of his music during her time in the Psych Ward and now it's like I never left.

We get home. But only after she drives around a bit to cheer me up. She takes the time to describe trees and birds to me as if I've never seen them before. I'm in a state of abject *misery,* as my flesh is on fire, itching, and oozing all at once.

When we get home, Rowdy's there on his lunch break and says he needs to go to the bathroom.

Kathy lays me back on the couch then tells me to pry my left eye open. She squeezes the dropper to release the liquid and I shriek in agony as my eye *burns* and my body goes into spasms of a pain I didn't even know existed. My mind is completely empty of all thought, replaced only with internal screams which I vocalize.

Kathy yells oh, stop overreacting! You're being a baby! Then she tells me to pry open my other eye.

I swing wildly at her and the medicine, trying to smack it out of her hand.

Kathy says holy shit, Rol, *what?* and then calls out hey Rowdy, get in here and give me a hand!

Rowdy calls from the bathroom asking what the hell's going on out there?

Kathy says RJ's lost his damn mind! Come give me a hand already!

I try to get up and run but I can't see. I trip over the coffee table and slam into the wall. Kathy drags me back to the couch as I fight against her. I cry no! and growl in pain, clenching and unclenching my fists.

Rowdy yells Jesus H. Christ! then storms over to the sofa and holds down my arms with his body weight while prying open my eye with his fingers.

I scream no, NOOO! and thrash wildly against his weight, trying to break free again.

Kathy smacks my face, oozing and cracked. A cigarette hangs from her lips as she shouts knock it off already! At the same time she tries to empty the dropper's contents into my eye, but I see her squeeze it and jerk my head so only a little bit gets in.

She yells *Goddamit,* RJ, you're grounded if you keep actin' up, I swear!

I squeeze that eye shut as hard as I can but the liquid seeps in and sets it ablaze. My right eye joins with my left as they dance in a volcano. I struggle to tear my hands free from Rowdy's weight and dig my fingernails into his ribcage. He jumps back in pain and says what in the hell is wrong with you!?

Amariah The Boy

I can only buck in pain, praying for something, *anything* to end this agony.

Rowdy says to Kathy hey, gimme that medicine. After a moment he says holy shit, this – hey Kathy this says *ear wax solvent.*

Kathy grabs the dispenser, looks at it, and says oh, fuck.

She calls the pharmacy and starts screaming at them for *making* her pour acid in her boy's eye. She displays the same fury she possessed when I got hurt in gym class...but now I know better. She doesn't care about *me.* She cares only about my existence as a source of income...*minus* any unnecessary costs.

She threatens to sue the pharmacy and says I might be blind now.

I'm hearing all this and am terrified. I can't see, despite prying my eyelids apart, and I'm *still* in agony. What if I'm *permanently* blind? I panic as angry tears pour down my ravaged face.

I hate my life. I *hate* this world and I *hate* everyone in it.

I resolve to kill myself if I've lost my sight.

After about five minutes of shouting, Kathy slams the phone down and yells motherfuckers!

Rowdy says what, what is it?

Kathy says those fuckin' pharmacy pricks said that the customer is responsible for looking at meds before using them.

Rowdy says okay, but what do we do about RJ?

I imagine him pointing to me because I sure as shit can't see anything.

Kathy says the pharmacy told her to flush my eyes with water for fifteen minutes and that's about all they can do. Rowdy helps me to the bathroom and when I get to the sink I bring handfuls of cool water to my scorched eyes for an *hour.* I'm too scared to try to pry open my eyes, so I sit in my room, blind, then lie on my side and cry myself to sleep.

After what feels like an eternity of hell, the swelling goes down. When the pain is finally gone and my vision returns, I breathe a sigh of relief.

Kathy never apologizes for pouring acid in my eyes and insists that it's the pharmacy's fault.

Roland Amariah Gonzales

A NEW SPINE

I return to school a couple of weeks later and no one asks whether I'm alright or even mentions noticing my absence. The only person who notices my presence is the jackass that Jessica started dating after me, the guy who was popping wheelies all day in front of Logan and Tyler's old house.

We have a school-wide Olympics competition with various sports equipment and Wheelies thinks it's hilarious to swing a baseball bat at my head when no one is looking.

Fuckin' just *because*, I guess!

I nimbly dodge the bat, then make my way backward toward the bucket filled with baseballs, as he keeps swinging and laughing. I pick up a ball and throw it at his junk as hard as I can. Wheelies crumples to the ground then gags a couple of times before he throws up.

He cups his hands over his crotch and growls that he's gonna *kill me* and says yer fuckin' *dead*. He somehow struggles to his feet, now clutching the bat.

I grab another baseball and get ready to nail him right in his stupid face. Mr. James, the gym teacher, sees us from a distance and yells hey *come on* man, can't we have *one day* of peace!?

I call out yeah, sorry, Mr. James!

Wheelies looks at Mr. James then at me and also apologizes then throws the bat on the ground and walks away.

A few days later my bike is stolen. The next day, Wheelies sees me at an assembly and snickers. He asks me, with two of his friends present, what happened to your bike?

We're all sitting on the bleachers in the gym, same as always. I grit my teeth, turn away to look at the floor, then turn back to him and say, I don't know. Some faggot probably stole it, took off the seat, then shoved the metal part up his ass.

His grin dies in an instant. He stands up and puffs out his chest, his friends doing the same. Then Wheelies says we're gonna fuck you up, shitskin. I bet you forgot about hitting me in my fuckin' nuts with a baseball, something only a *total bitch* would do!

I think to myself...there's that word again. That's the *second* time I've heard that.

Shitskin. What the hell does it mean?

I glance at the three of them. Hell, *none* of these pricks are Howard's size and he kicks the shit out of me *every* sparring session in Sensei Pat's dojo. I feel calm and I think to myself you know what? You can *do* this.

I stand up and say I been hit by dudes *twice* your size and it hasn't stopped me yet. If you're feelin' fuckin' froggy, *leap.*

With my eyes wide open, I lock onto the turd who stole my bike but I'm not just watching him, I'm watching his jerkoff friends to see who makes the first move. I can't wait to see who the lucky winner is as I shift my left foot behind me, onto the edge of the bleacher seat. I'll twist my left side backward, then land my butt on the bleacher seat behind me when one of them swings at me or moves toward me, then I'll kick that first idiot down the bleachers with both of my legs. Maybe he'll break his neck! Then I'm going to drive my elbow straight into the sternum of the next asshole who will probably jump on top of me, using his weight to his advantage.

I cannot *wait* to ruin these absolute bastards.

Wheelies looks at me and sneers. He expects me to back down. No one should be this confident when facing three dudes twice their size.

I'm not shaking in fear and I'm not cowering. It's not that I'm overly confident...it's just that I'm ready. I *want* this. More than anything I really want to *hurt* someone right now. I want to make these people *bleed.*

I think to myself *please* throw a punch. Please, you stupid motherfuckers...*someone* do *something!*

No one moves. After a moment, the vice principal enters the gym to keep an eye on all us animals. I think for a moment then breathe deeply and yell oh, *you're* the one who stole my bike?

The vice principal looks up at us and yells hey up there, how about you have a seat!

Wheelies looks at the man and whispers how lucky I am that the old man showed up. He says I can find my bike in the river, in the mud, which is where shitskins belong.

Roland Amariah Gonzales

I grin and say hey, I'll be walking home, because I don't have a bike now. Feel free to come say hi *any* time.

They never fuckin' do though.

Cowards, all.

BLACK CHURCH

School is uneventful for the rest of the year. I finish seventh grade with a barely passing grade point average. My teachers are generous in that my grades are *just* good enough to ensure they won't have to see me any longer than is necessary.

Just before the year ends, Logan introduces me to a Black kid coincidentally named Tyler and I'm wary at first. The only Black kids *I* know are that crazy-as-hell family from second grade and that prick Jeremy from fourth.

Tyler's different though. He doesn't try to pick fights for no reason and he doesn't try to put *anyone* down to make himself feel better. He likes to laugh, he tells jokes, and he's really cool to hang out with. We start to hang out often and he lives *way* closer to me, which is nice, since I don't have a fuckin' bike anymore.

He's also got a PlayStation which is cool, too. I bring my Super Nintendo over and we have a blast playing each other's games. We spend *hours* in his basement, just burning through the day, and it's the most fun I've had in a *long* time.

We both *really* dig games where we can shoot zombies, like *Resident Evil 2*, and I develop a love for strategy games like *Command & Conquer*. I find out that Rowdy has some of those games on his computer and we actually bond over this, which is kind of awesome.

When Kathy sees me playing *DOOM* on Rowdy's computer she becomes hysterical. She shrieks about demons and how she doesn't want that satanic shit in *her* house.

She sounds *just* like Renee back in California.

I say Mom, you know that in this game you *shoot* demons, right? You don't like...you don't help them eat babies, or anything like that. You're the *good* guy. What do you have against shooting demons?

Kathy's eyes look wild as she looks from side to side, then says she just doesn't want that in *her* house and *she* pays the bills, not me, and that's that.

Roland Amariah Gonzales

I think to myself yeah, you pay the bills alright. With money delivered from the government to pay for my needs, you rotten bitch.

Instead, I say well, alright, but the game ain't mine, it's Rowdy's so...

Kathy cuts me off and says well, Rowdy can do whatever *he* wants, but as long as you live under my roof...blah blah blah.

I roll my eyes. I *hate* how this woman thinks she has *any* kind of moral high ground to stand on. I can't help myself and say well Mom, do you have a problem with shooting *zombies?* Because I've been doing that for the past, what, six weeks? Seven. Yeah, seven weeks...over at Tyler's place!

She opens her mouth and spittle flies as she says you are not allowed to play *any* violent games! Then she pulls out a Bible covered in cigarette ash and tells me to swear in the name of Jesus that I will never again play violent games.

I wonder what fucking meds she's on now as I put my hand on the Bible and swear some *meaningless* words to appease her authority.

After I'm done and she's happy, I go straight to Tyler's house and shoot some more zombies.

Fuck that lady.

I go to church with Tyler's family after his mom invites me and am amazed by what I experience. It's *way* different from what I'd known in the past. I stopped going to white-people church because it was always the *same thing* from *every* pastor with oh, none of us are worthy. Oh, we're all going to hell. Oh, throw some money in the collection plate and thank you and praise Jesus!

No one ever answered the questions I had about God and sin and all that. I only got in trouble, so Kathy told me to stop going with her.

But in Tyler's church everyone is *happy!* They *sing* and they *dance* and there's this...this *energy* in the air that feels so...alive! None of that doom and gloom bullshit. I feel *happy* when I'm there, when I'm with them. I don't see Jeremy or any of those crazy kids and wonder if the nice-church Black people make all the *mean* Black people live on a different side of town...far away.

An older Black man seems surprised to see me, because as I walk by I hear him say boy, are you lost?

Tyler scrunches up his face and says no, he ain't lost, this is my new friend RJ!

The older guy rubs Tyler's head and says with a smile well, all right then, hallelujah and praise Jesus! You done grew the flock, boy!

Amariah The Boy

Tyler laughs and bats the man's hand away, but in a nice way.

The man introduces himself as the pastor and says if I have any questions, don't hesitate to ask.

I do, indeed! I hesitate then say well...yes sir, I do have some questions, and then I ask him what I asked the other pastors at the other churches. He patiently listens to everything. He smiles a few times, furrows his brow others and nods in general as he listens. When I'm done he says well, boy, you are *sharp.*

He becomes very animated and says now, I can't tell you I have all the answers...I don't. This may surprise you to learn but I'm *just* a man, *just* like you'll be someday. He says do I know why the Lord does what He does...and did what He did? No, sir! Praise his *name*, I do not. Do I know why some folk gotta hurt while others feel good? No, *sir*! Praise his *name!* I most certainly do not!

A crowd has started to gather around us as he continues. He says do I know *WHY* little baby *boys* and *girls* are born *sick, crippled, mute,* or *dumb?* No *SAH!* But if there's one thing I *DO* know, my boy...*yes* there's a *whoooole* lotta pain and there's a *whoooole* lotta suffering in this here world!

Some ladies have started moving their heads from side to side and humming, then holding up their hands.

The pastor tells says there's *poverty* and *war* and a *whole* lotta *hurt!* But do you know what *else* there is, boy? Do you know what *else* this world has *got? Love!* There's a whole lotta *love,* too!

More than a few people shout Praise Jesus!

The pastor says there's *love* for your *father* and *mother!*

Praise Jesus!

He shouts there's *LOVE* for your *SISTER* and *BROTHER!*

PRAISE JESUS!

He shouts there's *LOVE* for your neighbor and your friends too!

PRAISE JESUS!

He shouts there's *LOVE* for every animal and everyt*hing* on this *great big green beautiful earth*!

PRAISE JESUS!

And then he looks at me and says and do you know where that love comes from, boy?

All eyes are on me. I sheepishly look around and say...the Lord?

The pastor grins at me and says say it again boy, say it so the sweet little ol' ladies in the back can hear!

311

I laugh and shout The Lord!

The pastor declares in Jesus *NAME! Hall*elujah*!* He says can you feel the love in this room right now?

I laugh and shout yes!

The crowd shouts HALLELUJAH!

Before I know what's happening everyone is singing and dancing and clapping. I'm laughing and clapping too, and there are tears running down my face, but I don't know why.

I think about the pastor's words later and...I guess he didn't answer *every*thing I asked.

...but I really liked his answers just the same.

PARADISE LOST

I enjoy my summer break and go to the pool a few times but I'm mostly alone. Logan and Ricky are gone visiting some relative or another so it's just me by my lonesome. Tyler doesn't go to the pool and says he doesn't like it there.

I ask why one day and he kind of looks off toward a tree and says I don't know. It just ain't my thing. It ain't that I can't swim. That place just doesn't feel *right*, ya know?

I don't really know what he means...though I *did* get punched in the face and called a shitskin. Maybe that same kid punched Tyler, too? *Man*, I hate that kid. Never got to hit him back. Tyler and I still hang out outside of the pool and play games and whatnot.

I swim about lazily one afternoon and as chance has it, that little blonde girl who used to follow me around at school, Britney, happens to be there, too. She's with another girl from my class and as I swim around in the deep end, the other girl suddenly shouts hey RJ!

I turn my head and say yeah, what's up?

She grins then calls out Britney likes you!

Britney's jaw drops and she starts splashing water at her friend, at the same time laughing hysterically. She shouts no that's not true, don't believe her!

Britney and I have never said a word to one another. Of course I don't believe her friend. I've been down this humiliating road before. I look at them both then offer a sad smile before I turn and swim away. I say don't worry, I don't.

A few days later, Kathy tells me I need to pack all my things because we're driving out to California the following morning. She says while crying that she can *hear* her baby girl calling out to her, and her baby girl *needs* her momma.

I'm *furious*. It's late afternoon and this...this *creature*...I push aside my rage and say I *just* made some new friends and found a church I like! I *finally* found somewhere I belong! I start shouting. How come we have to move all the *fucking time* whenever you fucking *feel* like it?!

313

Roland Amariah Gonzales

Her jaw drops before she finds it again and says with a clenched jaw how *dare* you speak to me that way. I'm your *mother,* you son of a *bitch!*

She stands up, her expression livid, and screams *YOU* don't *ever* speak to me that way, you—

I interrupt her and give her a crooked smile then yell who the *fuck* cares? What are you going to do, *ground me!?* Take away my friends!? I'm losing *everything* again and all because you're *stupid* as *hell!*

I don't know *what* is going through what's left of Kathy's mind that led her to this life-altering decision for me but I'm sure as hell this wasn't the reaction she was expecting. She looks at me with a stunned face that twists into an animalistic snarl, and then she lurches forward and tries to grab me.

But I'm faster.

She begins to chase me, and I push over a shelf holding a bunch of vinyl records. She runs into it and falls over. Her fat and disgusting body makes the house rumble as she hits the floor.

It's time to say good-bye...again.

I bolt for my bike and pedal to Tyler's house. I know that Logan's out of town, and Josh isn't around, either. I'll only get to say goodbye to one person, Tyler, my new best friend.

I spend as much time as I can with him and then pedal home around ten o'clock. It's dark outside, but I know the route.

I walk in the door and Kathy doesn't say a word to me. In fact, she completely ignores my presence.

I can't talk to Rowdy, because he's pissed because he just got some promotion at work and now Kathleen is making him throw it *all away.*

I want to tell him that if he knew what was good for him, he'd stay here.

I pack what clothes I can and whatever else fits into our beat up '67 green Maverick. I don't have a choice in the matter. All I can do is go along...and try to make new friends. See what happens. At the same time, I know that *every time* I start to build a life she throws it in the trash. On a whim. And she throws me in the trash with it.

We leave early next morning. I'm exhausted. I was too angry to sleep, so I'm numb when I get in the car and slam the door.

We start our four-day drive to California.

When we hit the highway I turn to Kathy, my malicious and unhinged mother, and tell her how much I fucking hate her.

Made in the USA
Columbia, SC
16 March 2025

55215246R00195